Resilience Builder Program for Children and Adolescents

Enhancing Social Competence and Self-Regulation

A COGNITIVE-BEHAVIORAL GROUP APPROACH

Mary Karapetian Alvord
Bonnie Zucker
Judy Johnson Grados

Research Press 2612 North Mattis Avenue, Champaign, Illinois 61822 (800) 519-2707 www.researchpress.com

RESEARCH PRESS
PUBLISHERS

All forms and handouts referenced in this book are available for
download at **www.researchpress.com/downloads.**

Copies of this book may be ordered from Research Press
at the address given on the title page.

Composition by Jeff Helgesen
Cover design by Linda Brown, Positive I. D. Graphic Design, Inc.
Printed by McNaughton & Gunn

ISBN 978-0-87822-647-4
Library of Congress Control Number 2010943239

To Greg, for his love and understanding—M. A.

To my mother, my greatest teacher and source of resilience—B. Z.

To my children, Marco Sebastian and Ana Mayela, who mean so much to me, and my husband, Marco Antonio, my partner in life—J. G.

And to all the children and families with whom we have had the honor of working over the years

Contents

Unit 2

Session

Acknowledgments

Mary Karapetian Alvord:

My professional passions have evolved from the influences of important people in my life. I thank my parents, Isabella Ordjanian and Leon Karapetian, who were my early role models for resilience. They grew up in Russia during a time of turmoil, fled (in their teens) to the Middle East, and then immigrated to the United States as a young couple. Each time they encountered a new culture, they adapted, learned new languages, overcame obstacles, and ultimately thrived. I also wish to thank my long-time mentor, Dr. K. Daniel O'Leary, who provided me the opportunity to teach at the Point of Woods Lab School at Stony Brook, my first "group" experience. I also thank my dear friend, Anne McGrath McManus, who has helped me immensely as writing advisor.

Special thanks to my husband, Greg, who adheres to the highest standards of excellence and who continues to encourage and support me. Loving gratitude goes to my three sons, Bryce, Scott, and Justin, who have put up with their mother's working "a million hours" for years.

I have had the privilege of practicing with Dr. Patricia Baker for more than 30 years; our friendship, partnership, and affirmative working relationship have nurtured the foundation of the practice. She has always been supportive and encouraging. I first began running groups in 1992, when Pat and I moved our practice to a larger space. Within two years, there was more demand for group sessions; Pat stepped in and led groups for a number of years. From there, the group program (and practice) mushroomed.

Bonnie Zucker:

I am truly privileged to be part of this wonderful field of psychology, which has afforded me the opportunity to develop rich and meaningful connections, both with clients and mentors.

Thank you to my family and friends, who have provided unending support throughout this writing process. My husband, Brian, continues to overwhelm me with his unfailing support and tremendous respect for my work. My son, Isaac, has brought me more happiness and joy than I could have ever imagined.

My mother taught me the true meaning of resilience. While her life contained many blessings, she also faced many losses. She was defined by her strength, perseverance, "can-do" attitude, and incredible warmth. By her example and guidance, she taught me to not let anything stand in the way of a goal, that every problem is workable, and that you should embrace each day with gratitude and grace.

Judy Johnson Grados:

Thank you to my friends, family, and colleagues for listening and encouraging me throughout the writing process. I would like to acknowledge and thank Anne McGrath McManus for her work in editing. Most importantly, thank you to my husband, Marco, for his patience, wisdom, and support, and to my children, Marco and Ana, who are a continual source of inspiration in my life.

From the three of us:

The Alvord Baker practice has served as the base for the Resilience Builder Program. We wish to extend our gratitude to all the children and parents who have participated in the groups, whose many ideas and suggestions have been incorporated into our program.

We wish to acknowledge the group leaders whose suggestions and expertise have contributed to the development of the program over the years: Patricia Baker, Erica Berger, Betsy Carmichael, Karan Lamb, Dorothy Moore, Monica Robb, Jessica Samson, Lisa Sanchez, Sweena Seekri, Erik Scott, Ed Spector, Marquette Turner, and Tom Verratti. We thank Maria Manolatos, office manager, for assisting with the logistics of groups over the last 13 years, and for creating great forms and charts.

Thank you to Karen Steiner for her outstanding editorial guidance and enthusiasm for this project. Moreover, her willingness to travel to Maryland to witness our groups firsthand demonstrated both her dedication to excellence and a love for her work. Working with Research Press has been a pleasure, and we thank Gail Salyards especially for her support of and investment in this project.

Introduction

Resilience refers to a set of skills and characteristics that allows individuals to adjust and cope effectively with life's challenges. Children and adolescents who are resilient believe in their ability to affect their life's course and are better able to adapt to challenging situations and bounce back after experiencing difficulties and hardships. As a result, they tend to be happier and more successful, more well-liked by their peers, and more capable of coping with change. Alvord, Baker & Associates, LLC, specializes in group therapy for children and adolescents who lack resilience and, in particular, the social competencies that are a hallmark of happy, confident people. The model we employ to help youth acquire these compentencies, the Resilience Builder Program, is based on the theoretical underpinnings of cognitive-behavioral therapy (CBT).

Resilience is a skill that can be learned and strengthened through group intervention. The purpose of this book is to provide a model curriculum. The approach fosters the development of several important protective factors that allow children to adapt to and cope with life's challenges: the ability to take the initiative (being proactive); to modulate emotions and behavior (self-regulation); to connect with and maintain relationships with peers and adults (connections and attachments); to be engaged in activities that interest them (achievements and talents); to be connected with larger groups in their environment (community); and to have parents or other close caregivers who are involved in helping them grow and develop life skills (proactive parenting). All of these protective factors are important—and interdependent. For instance, a child's ability to self-regulate will impact his or her ability to connect with others and to achieve in areas of interest.

The program as described applies particularly to groups for children in third through eighth grades. However, the content is readily adaptable for both younger and older children. Some modifications to make ideas more concrete will be necessary for younger children, but the main concepts are valid regardless of age. As with all programs, adaptations should be made in consideration of participants' developmental level and background.

Because the children and teens in our groups typically experience a lack of friendships, our model emphasizes mastery of the skills necessary to form and cultivate relationships. Social competence encompasses more than just skills acquisition; it also includes mastering one's performance in daily social interactions. For example, we teach children with AD/HD the necessary self-regulation skills and provide the framework within which they and their parents can practice and reinforce these behaviors in all settings. Socially anxious children benefit from group role-play activities, which serve as in vivo exposures that help them reduce their anxiety and offer an opportunity to apply their social skills. In sum, our model—practical, skills based, and solution oriented—offers children real opportunities to grow and improve, and takes into account the systems in which children exist.

This book is intended for mental health professionals who are trained to work with children and adolescents. Ideally, group leaders will have received basic training in CBT; however, if this is not the case, leaders will benefit from referring to sources on CBT, including those in the reference list at the back of this book. The program can be used in many settings, including private practices, schools, agencies, hospitals, and residential treatment programs, among others.

Distinguishing Program Features

Therapists and school counselors leading social skills groups today have a choice of many curricula. This book offers a curriculum that is unique in that it addresses a range of diagnoses by developing competencies and effective cognitive styles that are fundamental to functioning well in the world. It is further distinguished in the following ways.

It is based on the resilience model and highly proactive. While most curricula are designed narrowly to address social skills deficits, our model is broader, teaching children other protective factors as well. Participants practice being proactive by setting goals and developing a plan to deal with challenges. They learn to recognize their emotional triggers and irrational thoughts and come up with constructive responses. This active stance fosters resilience and improved confidence.

It applies cognitive-behavioral theory and strategies. CBT is the most empirically supported approach to treating a variety of problems commonly seen in childhood, including anxiety, depression, attentional issues, social skills deficits, low self-esteem, and anger/oppositionality (O'Brien et al., 2007; Pahl & Barrett, 2010; Weisz & Kazdin, 2010). CBT is problem focused and solution oriented. It teaches skills and strategies to address a range of presenting concerns. The goal of CBT is to alter maladaptive thinking that underlies faulty action. While the acquisition of productive behavioral skills is important, long-term change is unlikely unless underlying thought distortions and beliefs are addressed. Sessions identify, challenge, and correct distorted, or "off the mark," and pessimistic thinking. New and more balanced "on the mark" ideas are continually introduced and reinforced. Disappointments and mistakes are viewed not as failures but rather as opportunities to learn and grow.

The following is a list of some of the CBT strategies and techniques implemented in this program:

- ▶ Cognitive restructuring

- ▶ Identification and replacement of cognitive distortions

- ▶ Behavior modification and contingency management

- ▶ Coping skills (including coping thoughts and coping actions)

- ▶ Positive self-talk

- ▶ Behavioral reward system

- ▶ Relaxation strategies

- ▶ Awareness of mood states

- ▶ Self-monitoring

- ▶ Behavioral rehearsal

- ▶ Role-playing

- ▶ Modeling

- ▶ Performance feedback

- ▶ Exposure therapy (for anxiety-provoking situations)

It offers a flexible structure.   One of the primary limitations of many intervention programs is that clinicians and educators are bound to a structured curriculum that often does not meet the specific needs of the group they are leading. The program described here provides easy-to-follow sessions, but session use is flexible. Although detailed procedures are included in every session, sessions and related materials can be customized by group leaders for their use, by topic and by length.

It emphasizes generalization.   Most programs stop short of making sure children take their new skills home and to the classroom. The Resilience Builder Program, by contrast, places a strong emphasis on skills generalization. We assign weekly Resilience Builder Assignments, provide a parent letter for each session to encourage skill reinforcement within the family, and include in each unit at least one field trip to a real-world setting—a bowling alley, for example—where group members can practice their skills. Research shows that this sort of generalization is key to lasting change (Goldstein & Martens, 2000).

It is field tested. Unlike many other programs that are based on theory and perhaps short-term trials, the Resilience Builder Program has been implemented since 1992 by numerous therapists in multiple offices and settings. Our clinical practice has led hundreds of competence groups for children in kindergarten through eighth grade and currently runs approximately 36 groups led by psychologists and social workers. We conducted a pilot study, directed by Dr. Judy J. Grados, of 54 children enrolled in social competence groups during 2005 and 2006 based on the model. Parent reports on children's symptoms were obtained pre- and post-group using the Behavior Assessment System for Children, Second Edition (BASC–2; Reynolds & Kamphaus, 2004). Findings revealed a clinically significant decrease in anxious and depressive symptoms in youth, as well as decreases in withdrawal from others. At the time of this writing, in collaboration with Dr. Brendan Rich from the Department of Psychology at the Catholic University of America, a larger-scale study of group members, ages 7 through 12, and their families is under way. This study will track children's progress over a period of two years and will help determine factors that are associated with short- and long-term treatment gains. The Alvord Baker research team includes Dr. Lisa M. Sanchez (Director of Research), Dr. Kelly A. O'Brien, and Dr. Mary K. Alvord.

How to Use This Book

The book includes two parts. Part I explains the Resilience Builder Program in detail, including a review of the literature on resilience and guidelines for practitioners on group formation and other considerations.

▶ Chapter 1 defines resilience and describes the building blocks of resilience and provides a rationale for the cognitive-behavioral approach underlying the model.

▶ Chapter 2 offers an overview of the Resilience Builder Program model, briefly describing session components, outlining potential program modifications for younger participants and groups with specific needs, and suggesting means for overall program evaluation.

▶ Chapter 3 summarizes information relating to group composition and formation and explains in detail how the intake process can be used to work with parents to set individual and priority goals for group participants.

▶ Chapter 4 discusses issues relating to behavior management in the group, offering group leaders effective strategies to meet the needs of a particular participant or group.

▶ Chapter 5 details program procedures and highlights competencies emphasized throughout the program.

In Part II, we provide 30 session plans, organized into two 15-session units. Sessions cover a range of topics, focusing on building resilience and social competence by teaching a variety of skills and addressing cognitive patterns that often interfere with children's successful social interaction. Each session offers step-by-step instructions on how to lead the group and foster learning of the session's skills. These instructions are specific and include suggestions on what to say and how to cultivate understanding of session content. These are only suggestions, however, and leaders are free to substitute their own language and explanations as appropriate.

A range of topics are included in the standard 30-session curriculum. Some topics, such as maintaining conversations and being a good sport, are repeated across units because these are areas with which children with social skills problems most often struggle. Many topics are related in that they expand upon one another; for example, the session on assertiveness in Unit 1 relates to the session on teasing and bullying in Unit 2. Generally, the skills build upon one another as the unit progresses.

In addition to group use, the sessions can be used on an individual basis, in individual therapy or even in family therapy. Our clinicians frequently incorporate session content into individual work with children and teens, finding it effective in teaching important skills.

PART I

Program Overview and Guidelines

CHAPTER 1

Building Blocks of Resilience and the Cognitive-Behavioral Approach

It is hard to overstate the importance of being resilient, particularly during childhood. Children who struggle with resilience often respond in rigid, inflexible, or passive ways when faced with change, social challenges, academic difficulties such as learning differences, and other types of adversity (Wiener, 2003). These youth are at a tremendous disadvantage. They are more likely to feel powerless to influence their fate, and they are less likely to set, reach, and attain their goals. As a result, they often lose confidence and tend to become isolated and alienated from peers. Lacking strong social supports, they are at higher risk of developing anxiety, depression, and low self-esteem. Research shows that children who lack strong family and peer relationships tend to grow up to be lonely and fearful adults (Burt, Obradovic, Long, & Masten, 2008). Children who struggle with resilience may be more vulnerable to a range of physical health problems, including a compromised immune system, heart disease, and cancer (Atkinson, Martin, & Rankin, 2009). Evidence also supports the notion that coping strategies and positive emotions positively affect long-term health outcomes and longevity (Denson, Spanovic, & Miller, 2009; Pressman & Cohen, 2005).

By contrast, resilient children—those who believe in their ability to influence their life's course, adapt to its challenges, and recover after misfortunes—tend to be happier and are more apt to succeed in their academic and social pursuits. Furthermore, resilient children develop a sense of resourcefulness and an ability to take action and deal with difficult situations, an orientation that in turn contributes to overall higher satisfaction in life (Cohn, Fredrickson, Brown, Mikels, & Conway, 2009). Indeed, self-efficacy—the confidence that one has the capacity to surmount the odds and achieve desired outcomes even when the circumstances are beyond one's control—is a key determinant of resilience (Luthar & Cicchetti, 2000; Werner & Smith, 2001).

In today's fast-paced, competitive world, all children can benefit from learning the skills associated with resilience. These skills can help them to act with confidence in their daily lives and rebound from disappointments, challenges, and adversity. The Resilience Builder Program is based on the principle that children facing stressors, from being rejected by peers and excluded from birthday parties to experiencing academic struggles and parental divorce, benefit greatly from focused and intentional development of the skills of resilience.

RESILIENCE DEFINED

Resilience is broadly defined as "those skills, attributes, and abilities that enable individuals to adapt to hardships, difficulties, and challenges" (Alvord & Grados, 2005, p. 238). Although a variety of conceptual differences are reflected in the way resilience is defined in the psychological literature, a resilient individual is commonly viewed as one who copes successfully despite facing adverse situations (Neeman & Masten, 2009). Resilience is a dynamic process that encompasses a balance of risk and protective influences in one's functioning. A person's resilience can change over time and under various circumstances (Cicchetti & Rogosch, 1997; Masten & Wright, 2009). Resilience is also interactional: The individual's attributes, such as temperament and genetic makeup, impact the environment, and the environment impacts the individual (Rutter, 2003). Pioneering research that has led to this understanding includes the Kauai Longitudinal Study (Werner & Smith, 1982, 1992, 2001), the Isles of Wight studies (Rutter, Tizard, Yule, Graham, & Whitmore, 1976), and Project Competence (Garmezy, Masten, & Tellegen, 1984; Masten, Best, & Garmezy, 1990; Masten & Wright, 2009). The discovery taking place only over the past few decades that resilience is a powerful component of mental health has helped shift the study of childhood adjustment from a deficit model to a strengths-based model that examines and promotes competent functioning and positive adaptation (Luthar & Cicchetti, 2000; Masten & Obradovic, 2006). Integrating more of these adaptive abilities and skills into a child's life increases the likelihood of better coping and thriving (Alvord & Grados, 2005).

Development of Assets, Skills, Resources, and Protective Factors

Why do some individuals adapt and function successfully when confronted with varying levels of challenge and adversity, while others do not? Since the 1960s, significant longitudinal research on resilience has identified a number of internal and external protective factors "that modify, ameliorate, or alter a person's response to some environmental hazard that predisposes to a maladaptive outcome" (Rutter, 1985, p. 600). More recent research examining culturally diverse and international populations has shown that the same protective factors appear to support healthy development (American Psychological Association, 2008; Grotberg, 1995).

Based on an extensive review of the literature, Alvord and Grados (2005) organized the protective factors into six broad areas, forming the basis for the Resilience Builder Program:

1. A proactive orientation toward life

2. The ability to regulate one's attention, emotions, and behavior

3. Social connections and attachments

4. Development and acknowledgment of special talents

5. A strong community

6. Proactive parenting

The program is designed to use these six categories to guide intervention and is based on the belief that children can grow in all of these areas and become more resilient by learning very concrete skills in each. The chart on the next page shows the protective factors specifically addressed in the sessions.

Because many of the skills across these categories are interdependent, the program is designed so that sessions focus on teaching a single skill but review and build upon other skills as well. For example, the ability to self-regulate affects the ability to connect and make friends. The sessions emphasize key resilience skills: proactive behavior, effort, self-regulation, self-talk, flexibility, reciprocity, and being a good sport. While the common presenting problem in children and young teens is a lack of social competence and/or self-regulation, the model does not limit intervention to social skills development and performance but incorporates all of the six protective factors, thus making the approach comprehensive.

Being Proactive

Research has shown that a person's ability to take the initiative (Wolin & Wolin, 1993), to believe in his or her effectiveness (Bandura, 1997; Rutter, 1985), and to think positively but realistically (Seligman, 1995) is a primary determinant of that person's resilience. The program works on developing several skills that contribute to a proactive orientation. Specifically, these include setting goals, planning, problem solving, thinking optimistically, and building a more positive sense of self.

Protective Factors Addressed in Sessions

	Being proactive	Self-regulation	Connections and attachments	Achievements	Community	Proactive parenting
Unit 1 Sessions						
1.1 Introduction to Group		✓	✓	✓	✓	
1.2 Resilience and Being Proactive	✓	✓				
1.3 Personal Space		✓	✓		✓	
1.4 Leadership	✓	✓	✓	✓	✓	
1.5 Reading Verbal and Nonverbal Cues		✓	✓			
1.6 Initiating and Maintaining Conversations	✓	✓	✓			
1.7 Being a Good Sport: Team Play		✓	✓	✓	✓	
1.8 Being a Good Sport: Field Trip	✓	✓	✓	✓	✓	
1.9 Optimistic Thinking	✓	✓				
1.10 Solving Friendship Problems	✓	✓	✓			
1.11 Stress Management	✓	✓				
1.12 Assertiveness	✓	✓	✓			
1.13 Empathy and Perspective Taking		✓	✓	✓		
1.14 Being a Good Sport: Game Etiquette	✓	✓	✓	✓	✓	
1.15 Review of Sessions	✓	✓	✓	✓	✓	✓
Unit 2 Sessions						
2.1 Introduction to Group		✓	✓	✓	✓	
2.2 Flexibility	✓	✓	✓			
2.3 Maintaining Conversations	✓	✓	✓		✓	
2.4 Intent Versus Impact	✓	✓	✓		✓	
2.5 On the Mark/Off The Mark Thinking: Part 1	✓	✓			✓	
2.6 On the Mark/Off The Mark Thinking: Part 2	✓	✓				
2.7 Being a Good Sport: Team Play	✓	✓	✓	✓	✓	
2.8 Being a Good Sport: Field Trip	✓	✓	✓	✓	✓	
2.9 Self-Regulation: Anxiety Management	✓	✓				
2.10 Self-Regulation: Anger Management	✓	✓	✓			
2.11 Self-Esteem	✓	✓	✓	✓		
2.12 Teasing and Bullying	✓	✓	✓			
2.13 Choices for Handling Challenges	✓	✓	✓			
2.14 Being a Good Sport: Game Etiquette at Home	✓	✓	✓	✓	✓	
2.15 Review and Showcase	✓	✓	✓	✓	✓	✓

Self-Regulation

The ability to modulate one's emotions and behavior is necessary for cultivating and sustaining rewarding relationships and for succeeding in school. Indeed, research has shown that mastery of these abilities in childhood, along with executive functioning and the ability to focus, is fundamental for later development of more sophisticated social and cognitive skills (Calkins & Marcovitch, 2010). The program teaches children strategies to calm themselves down by identifying triggers, challenging their negative thoughts, and using relaxation exercises. Children learn to identify what they are feeling and to express their emotions in more productive and appropriate ways.

Connections and Attachments

Having strong and healthy relationships with family and peers is fundamental to a child's sense of belonging and self-worth. It is a prerequisite to his or her ability to cope with stress and thus to avoid isolation and depression. Several factors contribute to a child's ability to connect with family and friends, including communication skills, tendency to act and react in emotionally and behaviorally appropriate ways, and ability to interpret and respond to social cues (Bierman, 2004). By contrast, children who lack prosocial skills are more likely to be rejected by their peers. Research has indicated that peer rejection, in turn, is a predictor of later substance abuse and involvement in antisocial activities (Substance Abuse and Mental Health Services Administration, 2007). To help foster a child's competence at forming connections, groups work on starting and maintaining conversations, reading verbal and nonverbal cues, listening and responding with empathy, sharing and taking turns (reciprocity), compromising and negotiating, and understanding another person's perspective.

Achievements

Resilient children are involved and actively engaged in the world around them. They can point to areas of enjoyment and areas of competence (Brooks, 1994). There are multiple benefits to this ability, including developing connections with others. For example, those who participate in sports or other school activities are more likely to have good friends and are less likely to skip school. They also have a stronger sense of positive self-identity. The program aims to improve self-esteem by asking children to identify what they enjoy and what they have accomplished that took effort, and to compliment one another in the sessions. Typically, in the final session, they take turns "showcasing" what skills they have learned in group and recent personal accomplishments: trophies and awards that they have received, something they have made, books they have read, and other skills they have mastered.

Community

Supportive relationships outside the family serve as buffers against stress and provide children with additional positive role models and feedback. Relationships may be with grandparents, aunts, uncles, neighbors, parents of friends, youth leaders, therapists, and members and leaders of religious organizations, among others (Werner & Smith, 2001). Teachers and school counselors play an important role; interventions in schools that address social-emotional competence and relationships between teachers and students are important in determining school success (Department of Health and Human Services, 2001; Elias & Haynes, 2008).

In addition to fostering skills that make it easier for children to form such relationships, leaders in our Resilience Builder Program encourage parents to provide opportunities for children to be a part of school and religious organizations, youth groups, and recreational clubs. Group leaders also encourage significant adults in the children's lives to reinforce the skills being taught in group.

Proactive Parenting

Supportive, loving parents who hold their children to high behavioral standards and who use consistent behavior management practices have been shown to be more likely to raise resilient children (Baumrind, 1991). While the Resilience Builder Program does not mandate separate parent-training sessions, it engages parents as key partners in the process of change. Through correspondence relating to each session and frequent participation in the group sessions, parents are given a full understanding of how the curriculum builds social competence and resilience. They are also instructed in how to practice the skills regularly and consistently at home. Modeling increases prosocial behavior (Alvord & O'Leary, 1985), and parents are encouraged to act as models for their children. Parent letters emphasize the importance of modeling healthy and effective behaviors, including those related to the session topics.

EVIDENCE-BASED GROUP COGNITIVE-BEHAVIORAL STRATEGIES

Research has shown that very few children with emotional and behavioral problems receive mental health treatment. When they do, often the therapies provided are not supported by evidence (La Greca, Silverman, & Lochman, 2009). A number of studies, however, have demonstrated the efficacy of cognitive-behavioral techniques to address anxiety, depression, and self-esteem issues in children (O'Brien et al., 2007; Pahl & Barrett, 2010; Weisz & Kazdin, 2010). Cognitive-behavioral therapy, or CBT, typically involves a time-limited number of sessions focused on examining how thoughts, emotions, and behaviors all affect one another and teaches concrete skills and strategies to effect change. Neenan (2009) states that CBT contributes to the development of resilience skills by modifying the way that one thinks about obstacles or challenges, which greatly affects how one feels about them and responds in turn. Studies of group CBT have demonstrated effectiveness in youth who experience anxiety, depression, and skill deficits (Clarke & DeBar, 2010; Silverman, Pina, & Viswesvaran, 2008).

Each session in the Resilience Builder Program helps participants identify their positive and faulty thoughts, emotions, and behaviors. Through discussion, role-playing, behavioral rehearsal, and home assignments, the program promotes healthy and long-lasting change. The program exceeds what is offered in traditional CBT-based groups because it incorporates resilience-building tasks and frames the cognitive and behavioral work in the context of improving upon a child's resilience. In other words, the CBT strategies are integrated and used in the program to support the development and strengthening of resilience skills in participants.

CHAPTER 2

Overview of the Resilience Builder Program

Justin is a bright third grader whose parents have decided to separate. He will be living with his mother and attending a new school, but his parents are worried about how well he will adapt because he struggles to make friends and is starting to feel rejected by his peers. Justin's parents feel that a primary reason for this is that he tends to be insensitive to his classmates' feelings and is so rigid that he does not understand the give-and-take necessary to succeed in a play activity. After brainstorming in a group session about how people "read" each other's reactions, Justin begins to understand that when someone does not want to play with him, it may be a sign that he needs to compromise or take turns. After completing a year of group, his parents report that he has had several successful play dates and is comfortable in his new school.

Susie, age 12, drives other kids away by being bossy and demanding. By switching roles with another child so she can see herself in action—and then switching back to practice more appropriate facial expressions, body posture, tone of voice, and comments—Susie has learned to tone down her behavior and attitude.

Evan, age 10, struggles with AD/HD and specific learning differences. He regularly annoys his classmates by his inability to sit still and let other people talk, and he feels set apart from the other children because he's pulled out of class for resource help several times a week. As a result, he feels lonely and isolated. By learning self-regulation skills—for example, by following a routine in which the only person who can talk is the one whose name pops up when a "name cube" is rolled—he has learned to wait his turn. After identifying his ability as an ice-skater during a group discussion of individual strengths, Evan had the courage to sign up for a beginner ice hockey team, where he quickly became a valued player.

Breakthroughs like the ones just described demonstrate the power of group intervention strategies to teach children who are struggling with peer relationships the core skills necessary to build friendships, take the initiative, and make good choices. Social competence groups are the treatment of choice because they allow children to practice appropriate interactions in a live social setting and get immediate feedback. Groups are intentionally formed to bring together children with similar issues but also with complementary strengths and weaknesses. Thus, the children serve as role models for one another and at the same time realize that they are not alone in their struggles; indeed, they gain support and an instant social circle. They learn to take turns and develop patience. They learn to be flexible and begin to see things from others' perspectives. These abilities are crucial to developing resilience.

In groups, leaders have the opportunity to observe what children are doing (or not doing) to negatively influence their relationships. In addition, children and parents tend to be more comfortable with what feels more like a "friendship group" than traditional therapy. Finally, in an age of managed care, group intervention is appealing for its cost-effectiveness.

THE RESILIENCE BUILDER PROGRAM

The Resilience Builder Program applies what is recognized in the field about promoting successful social interaction and resilience in young people. In addition to promoting social competence, the model guides children to think realistically instead of catastrophically or pessimistically—and to act accordingly. Because children exist within families and communities, the model assumes that treatment will be coordinated with school and community resources as appropriate.

The program is designed to progress over 12 to 15 sessions per semester, paralleling the academic year, with two consecutive semesters of attendance recommended for maximum benefit. In this book, we have broken the sessions into two units of 15 sessions each. The recommended enrollment for each group is four to six children. Our practice also offers a six-session summer module for families who want additional reinforcement or who desire an early start to the school-year sessions. However, the model is easily adapted to a shorter length or varied structure and can be tailored to address specific issues, as highlighted later in this chapter.

Although groups consist of children of the same gender, they include those with a range of diagnoses, including AD/HD and anxiety disorders (particularly social anxiety). A limited number of children with mild Asperger's disorder are often included in the groups. Some children also have learning differences and fine motor/gross skills deficits. Children with below average intellectual capability or severely aggressive behavior are not an appropriate fit for the groups. Research indicates that placing children with severe behavioral issues together results in interventions that are often ineffective and may even increase the likelihood of delinquency (Dishion, McCord, & Poulin, 1999).

The model consists of five structural components, briefly outlined here and described at greater length in chapter 5: the interactive-didactic component, free play and behavioral rehearsal, relaxation and self-regulation techniques, generalization, and parent involvement.

The interactive-didactic component. The interactive-didactic component involves presenting and demonstrating the social and resilience skills that we want to teach and enhance. The children are asked to think about the skill of the day, offer ideas about the behaviors involved in performing the skill, and, in selected cases, role-play as a way of establishing mastery of it.

Free play and behavioral rehearsal. The purpose of free play is to offer a real-life play situation in which children undergo a structured process of negotiation and compromise. The children view the play as a fun and natural activity while the group leader uses it for observation of social behavior and intervention to promote change when necessary.

Relaxation and self-regulation techniques. One of the inner strengths that resilient individuals possess is the ability to regulate their emotions and behavior. One or more self-regulation techniques, such as progressive muscle relaxation, guided imagery, and positive self-talk, are taught and practiced during each session.

Generalization. It is essential to generalize the thinking and behavioral changes learned in the group to the natural settings of home, school, and community in order to promote better social functioning. The program incorporates multiple strategies, such as weekly homework assignments, reinforcement of skills at home by parents, a field trip to practice modified behaviors in a public setting, and, when appropriate and if feasible, collaboration with the child's school.

Parent involvement. Parents receive a letter that describes the topic of each session and includes tips on how to reinforce the skills at home. Parents are also invited periodically to join the group for part of the session so the children can share what they have learned. Although the program does not require parents to participate in therapy on a regular basis, it is highly recommended that they receive some parent training. Such training is especially helpful in developing behavior management strategies for children with AD/HD, for example, and in learning how to effectively expose socially anxious children to situations they might otherwise avoid.

PROGRAM MODIFICATIONS

As mentioned in the introduction, the curriculum can be tailored to meet the needs of the particular group. Many of the concepts and skills taught in the program originate in the adult literature. We have adapted them to be more or less concrete depending on the age and developmental level of the group participants. Our high school groups follow most of the session topics and have added a few others, such as initiating and maintaining contact through texting and social media, dating, and changes and transitions. In addition, teens often spend more time in discussions and role-play instead of "free time" for games. The level of discussion matches group developmental abilities.

Some specific alterations to make language, concepts, and activities of group sessions developmentally appropriate for younger children are helpful, however.

Modifications for Younger Children

During the intake process discussed in chapter 3, it is important to ensure that the younger child knows what a goal is so goal setting is possible. For children who are unfamiliar with the concept, a useful analogy is the concept of making a goal while playing sports: players identify what they are aiming for, come up with a plan, and then take steps to follow the plan. To help children understand the goal of attending group, they may be asked about their friendships and whether they believe that they could get better at making or keeping friends.

Session Accommodations

When working with younger children, it is important to use simple language. For example, instead of referring to cognitive distortions, we discuss "silly thinking." Likewise, empathy toward others becomes "understanding how others feel." Also, we make sure that the examples offered are ones that children can relate to in their daily lives. For example, when we discuss what provokes feelings of anger, we might mention another child's stealing your toy or cutting in front of you in line. When we discuss sadness, we might talk about what it feels like if a pet passes away or a friend moves to another town.

Sessions and examples must be made more concrete for younger children. The props suggested in sessions are especially helpful with younger children in explaining more abstract concepts. For example, we use a television and remote control, offering the concept of *changing the channel* as an analogy to explain how to redirect maladaptive thinking (see Session 1.9, on optimistic thinking). Leaders might show children a shoe to help one imagine walking in someone else's shoes (see Session 1.13, on empathy). Visual props also provide children with easy ways to communicate the session topic to parents and family members.

Role-playing and acting are excellent tools used with our youngest members. Children may be asked to act out situations such as how to join groups, ways to be kind to others, and how to deal with bullies. Acting also involves behavioral rehearsal, an essential component of skill acquisition, and makes the learning process more enjoyable and effective.

When teaching skills to older children, skills are broken down into several behavioral steps or components. These steps are simplified for younger children. For instance, each skill should have no more than three steps and should use clear language. When we teach greetings, for example, we ask children to look at the person, smile, and say hello.

Group Process Changes

Several modifications are made to the group structure for younger children. To ease the transition into group, we often encourage them to bring a favorite item to the first group to share with the other children. This exercise allows children to learn about one another's interests, gives them something concrete to discuss, and serves to spark connections with other children who may have the same item at home. Additionally, a favorite item can give the apprehensive or worried child something familiar to hold onto for comfort. More frequent verbal praise for appropriate behavior is also necessary for our younger group members. This fosters cooperation and aids children in understanding what is expected during group time. Earning small privileges for good behavior, such as being first in line to select a toy during free play or getting to assist the leader, is particularly valuable for younger children.

The skills instruction and discussion segments are somewhat abbreviated for younger children because they have shorter attention spans. Ideally, learning segments should be about 10 minutes in length. Activities that include physical movement are frequently used to sustain focus. For example, when children are learning about personal space, they are asked to stand, extend their arms at waist level, and proceed to move their arms slowly toward the front and back, demonstrating their personal "space bubble."

The group leader constantly gauges children's involvement and level of engagement in the group. In order to keep members focused, the leader may ask children to move from their seats to the floor or shorten the session and give children more free play. The leader may break up the teaching portion of the session with activities such as yoga or role-playing exercises. For children who have a hard time sitting still, need sensory input, or move their hands around a great deal, we offer a "fidget toy" to facilitate focus and concentration.

Parent Involvement

Parents are encouraged to be more actively involved in the groups with younger children. In contrast to groups for older children, we ask parents to attend the last 10 minutes of *every* group session to discuss the weekly skill and its implementation. This allows parents to become familiar with and gain mastery of the material and better prepares them to coach children on a daily basis. Parents are also encouraged to assist children actively with completion of homework assignments.

Modifications for Specific Types of Groups

Some group leaders may have time constraints that do not allow for the standard structure we propose. New structures can be effective, using selected sessions. Offered below are four sample modifications, customized for four different types of groups: anxiety, few friends/social isolation, hyperactivity/poor self-regulation and impulse control, and social interaction impairment associated with Asperger's syndrome.

In addition to these sample modifications, we encourage group leaders to be creative in developing their own structures, including breaking down one session into two, to meet the needs of a variety of groups, and altering sessions by duration (e.g., 30 versus 60 minutes, or extending to 90 minutes) or number (e.g., 8 versus 15 sessions).

Modification 1: Anxiety

Session

1.2   Resilience and Being Proactive

1.9   Optimistic Thinking

1.11 Stress Management

1.12 Assertiveness

2.5   On the Mark/Off the Mark Thinking: Part 1

2.6   On the Mark/Off the Mark Thinking: Part 2

2.9   Self-Regulation: Anxiety Management

2.10 Self-Regulation: Anger Management

2.11 Self-Esteem

2.13 Choices for Handling Challenges

> *For an eight-session group, we recommend doing the first eight sessions and omitting the last two.*

Modification 2: Few Friends/Social Isolation

Session

1.2   Resilience and Being Proactive

1.3   Personal Space

1.4   Leadership

1.5   Reading Verbal and Nonverbal Cues

1.6   Initiating and Maintaining Conversations

1.12 Assertiveness

1.13 Empathy and Perspective Taking

1.14 Being a Good Sport: Game Etiquette

2.4   Intent Versus Impact

2.7   Being a Good Sport: Team Play

2.11   Self-Esteem

2.12   Teasing and Bullying

> *For an eight-session group, we recommend doing all but Sessions 1.4, 1.13, 1.14, and 2.7.*

Modification 3: Hyperactivity/Poor Self-Regulation and Impulse Control

Session

1.2   Resilience and Being Proactive

1.3   Personal Space

1.5   Reading Verbal and Nonverbal Cues

1.7   Being a Good Sport: Team Play

1.13   Empathy and Perspective Taking

1.14   Being a Good Sport: Game Etiquette

2.4   Intent Versus Impact

2.9   Self-Regulation: Anxiety Management

2.10   Self-Regulation: Anger Management

2.12   Teasing and Bullying

> *For an eight-session group, we recommend omitting 1.14 and 2.12.*

Modification 4: Social Interaction Impairment Relating to Asperger's Syndrome

Session

1.2   Resilience and Being Proactive

1.3   Personal Space

1.5   Reading Verbal and Nonverbal Cues

1.6   Initiating and Maintaining Conversations

1.7   Being a Good Sport: Team Play

1.12   Assertiveness

PROGRAM EVALUATION

Program evaluation and modification is ongoing, involving group member self-reports, parent evaluations, and more formal measurement of program outcomes.

The How Am I Doing? Self-Report Scale

The How Am I Doing? scale is generally administered four times, typically during the first, fifth, tenth, and final sessions (see Appendix A). This assessment, intended to provide a snapshot of the child's state of mind that day, asks the child to rate himself or herself. The first statement, "I feel good about myself," is repeated as an eighth entry as a check of the child's focus and reliability. It is interesting to note that many children rate themselves lower as the semester progresses. When asked, parents often state their feeling that their child is becoming progressively more self-aware and realistic about how he or she is actually doing.

Parent Evaluations

When a 15-session unit comes to a close, parents are invited to assess the program on the Resilience Builder Program Parent Evaluation form (see Appendix A). Parents are asked to evaluate the therapeutic process, group structure, group topics, how well planned and well executed the sessions were, and the degree to which they feel their child has learned and is using helpful skills. Over the years, we have incorporated excellent ideas from parents for improving treatment effects. For example, many parents have requested feedback about their children's performance on a weekly basis. While it is logistically impossible to meet with each parent following each group, we have developed ways to provide feedback (e.g., a small note about what the child accomplished that day, notes on the child's Resilience Builder Assignment, certificates of praise, etc.). We also encourage parents to provide notes about the child's progress when they come in for a group session. They can also e-mail or leave phone messages to communicate their child's progress or raise any concerns to address.

Program Outcomes

As a general measure of program effectiveness, parents and older children are asked to complete the Behavior Assessment System for Children–Second Edition (BASC–2) rating scale (Reynolds & Kamphaus, 2004) before and after the series of group sessions. The BASC–2 measures maladaptive as well as adaptive behaviors, is highly reliable and valid, and is widely used among those working with youth in research and clinical settings. We find this instrument or a comparable one to be very useful because it provides comparative, objective data from a range of sources and allows us to track a child's progress.

Specifically, the BASC–2 obtains information from parents, teachers, and youth regarding symptoms of hyperactivity, aggression, conduct problems, anxiety and depression, somatization, atypicality, withdrawal, and attention problems, as well as strengths such as adaptability, social skills, leadership, and communication skills. Children who are at least eight years old complete a self-report measure, which assesses many of the same symptoms plus attitude toward school, attitude toward teachers, sensation seeking, locus of control, social stress, and sense of inadequacy. It also provides insight on adaptive behaviors such as relations with parents and peers, self-esteem, and self-reliance. Supplemental information is also produced on anger control, bullying, developmental social disorders, emotional self-control, executive functioning, negative emotionality, and resiliency.

If parents are willing, the child's primary teacher or teachers are asked to complete the BASC–2 Teacher Rating Scale. This affords a view of the child's behavior across settings, measures internalizing disorders and externalizing behaviors, and assesses adaptive skills the child exhibits, including leadership and flexibility. The TRS provides a composite score that gives a broad estimate of the child's overall level of functioning, as well as separate scores on content scales measuring anger control, bullying, and executive functioning.

In addition, we ask parents to complete the Social Skills Improvement System (SSIS; Gresham & Elliott, 2008). The system measures a variety of domains related to social functioning, including social skills (e.g., communication, empathy, engagement, self-control), problem behaviors (e.g., externalizing, hyperactivity/inattention), and academic competence. A review of social skills rating scales concluded that the SSIS is the most comprehensive.

Other rating scales that leaders might prefer to use include the Child Behavior Checklist (CBCL; Achenbach & Rescorla, 2001) and Conners Rating Scales–Revised (CRS–R) Conners, 2000).

CHAPTER 3

Group Formation and Parent Involvement

As with all types of group therapy, the success of a social competence group depends largely on how the group is formed. The main goal of the Resilience Builder Program is to teach children to develop a wide range of skills in a setting that replicates the natural peer group. As noted previously, practicing social skills and self-regulation within a group that is similar to the real world allows group members to more easily transfer the skills to their daily lives. At the same time, it is important to match children whose strengths and deficits are complementary so that they can serve as role models for one another.

The first two parts of this chapter address basic issues in group formation, including discussion of the intake process. The last part describes parent involvement once the child has been accepted and group sessions have begun.

GROUP SIZE AND CHARACTERISTICS

Ideally, a group including children in grades three through eight will have four to six members of the same gender and one group leader. Groups of younger and older children can be mixed gender because both younger children and teens tend to socialize in mixed groups, unlike third through eighth graders. In our experience, a group that is too small does not afford the necessary opportunity to practice social skills nor allow for sufficient role modeling and exchange of ideas. Similarly, when a group gets too large it can be challenging for the leader to manage behavior and give each member the appropriate attention. Individualizing therapy within the group context is critical to achieving each member's goals.

For maximum benefit, the group members need to be on equivalent developmental and intellectual levels so that they can effectively process the lessons and discussions and form positive peer relationships. Because elementary and middle school children naturally gravitate toward others who are at most one year older or younger and form social relationships within their gender, the ideal group for a child of that age will consist of others of the same gender who are no more than one to two grades apart. A fourth grader might be placed in either a third- and fourth-grade group or a fourth- and fifth-grade group, depending on his or her maturity. There may be settings where it is not possible to so neatly group children by age or gender because the numbers don't allow it—a hospital or rural clinic, for example. In that case, leaders may need to create subgroupings for some activities or discussions and provide play activities that appeal to each subgroup.

The Resilience Builder model groups children based on a description of their strengths, skills, deficits, and performance rather than by diagnosis. It is important that the members' issues are similar enough that the group can sufficiently address their needs and that each child can feel comfortable and accepted. On the other hand, the group dynamic depends on the members' strengths being different enough that they can learn from one another through the modeling of desired behaviors.

Thus, children with social anxiety are intentionally matched with children with AD/HD, who are not reluctant to join a group but whose tendency is rather to talk too much. (One models assertiveness, and one models self-control.)

When placing children and treating them in group, it is important to take cultural norms and environmental factors into account. For example, role-play vignettes could be modified to reflect the sociocultural context of the participants. Leaders should demonstrate cultural sensitivity and adapt examples when appropriate.

THE INTAKE PROCESS

The elements of successful group formation include a screening telephone interview to ensure possibility of membership, followed by an in-person intake session in which parent or parents and child are interviewed about the child's strengths and interests, difficulties, and goals. Most children can be assigned to groups following intake interviews. When more information is needed to determine group fit, we wait for the results of routine assessments administered to all children, which consist of the parent, self-report, and teacher forms of the Behavior Assessment System for Children–Second Edition (Reynolds & Kamphaus, 2004) and Socials Skills Improvement System (Gresham & Elliot, 2008).

The primary goal of the intake process is to assess whether group work is appropriate for the child. Once it is determined that group is an appropriate modality and that the child is a good fit for a specific group, individual goals are established. Some children—for example, those who are suicidal or are actively cutting or violent—have needs that cannot be met by a group approach alone and will need to be treated individually and stabilized first.

Screening Phone Call

Prior to setting up an appointment for the intake interview, the parent provides information during a screening phone conversation about the child's age, gender, presenting concerns, diagnosis, and any recommendations resulting from previous psychological testing. (See Telephone Contact, Screening, and Disposition Form, Appendix A). One goal of this conversation is to determine which type of group would likely serve the child best or whether individual therapy is a more appropriate modality.

During the phone call, parents are asked to bring to the intake session any reports or data on the child that may clarify the issues contributing to social problems (i.e., testing reports). The call also covers logistics, such as the fee structure, length and timing of the group, and expectation that the child be present at intake.

Intake Session

Assuming the group is appropriate, the group leader meets the family in an intake session, typically an hour in length. The family structure determines who will be at the intake. If parents are separated or divorced, we ask both parents to attend and sign permission for group participation. At other times, grandparents or others might be the primary caretakers. The following information is obtained from parent or parents and child.

Information Obtained from Parents

▶ Results of any previous evaluations (i.e., psychological, occupational therapy, speech/language)

▶ Past school performance, including copies of Individualized Education Program plans (IEPs) or Section 504 plans implemented by the school

▶ Developmental history, including the child's ability to regulate behaviors and emotions

▶ Child's social history (see Intake Interview: Social Interactions and Self-Regulation, Appendix A), particularly whether his or her involvement with other children has deteriorated. (A child with social skills problems may have been very involved with other children during the preschool years, when activities tend to be organized and initiated by parents, but be left out completely as a third grader once the social activity is increasingly initiated by peers.)

▶ Information about ongoing individual or family therapy, as well as any past attempts to work on the identified problem area(s)

► Style of parenting, marital relationship, and sibling interactions (because the child's difficulties are viewed within the framework of the family system)

► What parenting or intervention strategies have been tried and which have failed or been effective

► Parents' social history, both as children and as adults (because they serve as role models and may need some coaching themselves)

► A description of family strengths as well as family support systems (because emphasis is on building on the child's and family's strengths rather than focusing on deficits)

Information Obtained from the Child

After interviewing the parent or parents, the group leader then meets with the child. The leader asks the child to describe (a) strengths, interests, and friendships (e.g., what activities he or she likes to engage in outdoors and indoors, whom he or she sits with during lunch, how often he or she gets together with peers outside of school) and (b) personal goals (e.g., what he or she might like to be different as relates to peers). This discussion allows the leader to evaluate the child's ability to make eye contact, reciprocate during conversation, and express himself or herself. Depending on age, the child may select a toy or drawing materials to use during the talk. Having these materials can help establish rapport and put the child at ease.

If group participation is indicated, the leader briefly explains how the group process works. At this point the child can ask any remaining questions.

Meeting with Parents

Finally, the parents and group leader—and the child, if appropriate—discuss whether and how intervention should proceed. The recommendation may be for individual counseling instead of or before group work. It also may be advisable for the parents to get marital or parenting counseling in conjunction with the child's group experience. Sometimes no decision can be made without further information or evaluation, and referrals may be made. This might be the case if the child appears to have auditory processing problems or significant learning disabilities that make it difficult for him or her to understand information presented in a timely way.

If the group program seems appropriate, the next step is to help parents understand the components of each session. Expectations for the child as a productive member of the group, as well as what they can expect from program leaders, are discussed. We generally recommend a full 30-session course to ensure the generalization of behaviors to school and home settings, though the family is asked to commit to only a set of 15 sessions at a time.

It is important to emphasize that parents must take their role in the process seriously because this will determine how much progress the child makes. We communicate the following expectations for parents and group leaders.

Expectations for parents

▶ That they commit to bringing the child weekly for the entire semester

▶ That they read the parent letter we provide for each session

▶ That they follow through in overseeing completion of the homework assignments

▶ That they help the child practice the accumulation of skills regularly and consistently by using positive rather than negative direction. For example, instead of saying, "Don't interrupt," parents will say, "You need to wait your turn."

▶ That they practice relaxation and self-regulation exercises throughout the program and after. For example, that they refer to the Relaxation Tips for Parents and Group Members (see Appendix B) and encourage their child to practice positive self-talk.

▶ That they help the child focus on working toward his or her personal goal

▶ That they acknowledge and reward the child's efforts and progress

▶ That they meet with group leaders at least once during the semester for an individual appointment

▶ That, if beneficial, they consider getting or continuing personal counseling elsewhere

We commonly invite parents to share information about the program with school personnel and, when appropriate, have them sign releases so we may collaborate with school and outside therapists.

Expectations for leaders

▶ That we provide structure and consistency within the group and that the group environment be physically and emotionally safe

▶ That we provide parents with a weekly parent letter and homework assignment for their child

▶ That we collaborate as needed with other professionals attending to the child

▶ That we always welcome feedback from the parents (by phone, e-mail, or letter) and information about relevant events during the week

▶ That we keep parents informed about anything significant that happens during a session involving their child

Goal Setting

If the child is accepted for group participation, parents are asked during the intake session to choose and prioritize three goals for their child. The group leader also asks the family to think about the child's Resilience Builder Assignment for the first session: to identify an individual goal related to making or keeping friends or self-regulation that the child will pursue over the entire semester.

Setting appropriate goals, a key component of the program, can make the difference between a successful or an unsatisfying group experience. Goals allow the child to work toward clear targets, the parents to reinforce the child's efforts at home, and the group leader to fine-tune treatment. Having goals to work toward—for example, being able to greet others in a socially appropriate manner or use anger management techniques to calm down—puts everyone on the same page about the changes sought through group. Moreover, weekly review of progress toward meeting goals serves as a "grade card" for how the intervention is working.

Goals are defined through discussion of the child's social challenges and the quality of his or her friendships with peers. Parents share observations from teachers and other professionals who know the child well. Ideally, the end product is a set of three clear, well-defined behavioral targets for change, one of which is chosen as the child's "priority goal." The priority goal is phrased as concrete steps the child agrees to take each week at home and school—for example, "I will smile and say hello to one friend during recess each week." The children document their performance in program notebooks in their Success Journals and review their progress during each group.

General Parameters for Setting Goals

Goals should be specific and measurable, realistic, and positively stated. To know with certainty that progress is being made, it is important to have clear expectations about how behavior will change and what relationships with others will look like once goals are attained. That means avoiding global and vague goals that are difficult to measure. For example, "Ashleigh will get along with others" or "Isabella will get help when she needs it" are fuzzy goals that may confuse Ashleigh and Isabella and are not easily measured. Specific and measurable goals, such as "Ashleigh will be able to have a play date and be able to resolve disagreements with her friend by using problem-solving skills" and "Isabella will approach a teacher or other adult twice a week and ask a question about something she doesn't understand" empower both parent and child to achieve the aspired behavior change.

When you create goals that are realistic and attainable, the child can more frequently succeed in meeting them. The resulting feeling of accomplishment initiates a cycle of positive reinforcement that increases the child's self-esteem, motivation, and belief in his or her capacity to produce positive changes. Realistic goals take into account the child's current level of skill mastery. Is the behavior already present? Is it an emerging behavior, one the child demonstrates some of the time or in a partial manner? Or is the behavior not yet in the child's repertoire? The answers will indicate how high a child can aim and how quickly success can be met. Let's say Connor does not currently demonstrate the desired behavior of greeting other children. He never says hello to others and walks with his head down. Connor's first goal might be to learn the greeting skill through practice in a safe place, perhaps at home with his parents through role-play. Later, the goal can be modified to demonstrating the behavior with ease outside the home. On the other hand, consider what Connor's goal will be if he already greets others appropriately, albeit infrequently. In this situation, it is realistic to expect Connor to work on greeting others on a daily basis. An appropriate goal may be for Connor to demonstrate the skill more than, say, 75 percent of the time he sees a peer in his daily life.

It is important to tailor expectations with awareness that behavior change takes time and that small positive steps in the right direction ultimately lead to long-term enhanced day-to-day interactions with others. A common stumbling block to satisfactory goal setting stems from trying to help the child obtain the goal too quickly or setting the goal too high.

The need for a positive framing of goals is a strong underlying principle of the group model and cannot be emphasized enough. Positive goals empower professionals to engage in an encouraging way with the child to refine or add new skills, rather than putting the spotlight on negative behaviors. A teacher who encourages a child to "raise your hand before speaking" is likely to reinforce hand-raising behavior. If the same child has the goal to "stop interrupting," the teacher may attend to and inadvertently reinforce that negative behavior.

Setting Individual and Priority Goals

Two types of goals used within the group framework include individual goals and priority goals.

Individual Goals

Because parents sometimes lack experience in defining reasonable expectations for child behavior, coaching may be necessary during the goal-setting process. The professional can stimulate discussion by giving parents and children several examples of appropriate goals. A realistic aim for the child who tends to act before thinking and often interrupts others might be to wait until others finish before speaking. Likewise, for the girl who has to have things her way when playing with friends, an appropriate goal may be to let others have their way. Children should be actively engaged in identifying their goals. The more they are involved in the process, the better the "buy in" and the greater the likelihood of success. One way to choose an appropriate goal is to ask the parents to think about how their child's interaction with others would be different if the group is successful. It is also useful to ask simply what the family and child hope to get from group.

Examples of individual goals include the following:

► Appropriately join groups of two or more children to play.

► Recognize and replace negative thoughts with positive ones when _____ .

▶ Meet and greet others by looking in their eyes, smiling, and saying hello.

▶ Independently generate several ways to solve a problem when it happens and talk over ideas with a peer.

▶ Understand what is being communicated through facial expressions and body language.

▶ Calm self when angry by using anger management strategies.

▶ Be proactive by asking for help from others when needed.

Developmentally appropriate vocabulary is a must when discussing goals with children. If they do not understand what the goal is, they can hardly participate in its accomplishment! A fourth grader told that a goal is "topic maintenance" is much less likely to cooperate and succeed than if told that the aim is "to stay with the subject being discussed."

Priority Goals

Of the three individual goals identified, each family selects a priority goal, which promotes generalization of one of the individual goals. This goal is largely addressed outside of group. The purpose is to focus the child on one discrete aspect of the challenge in a very concentrated way in the real world. Progress on the priority goal is documented in the child's Success Journal, kept in the group member's program notebook, and discussed weekly in the group session. For example, if a priority goal is to start playing with another child twice a week, the group member and parent would list and date each time the child appropriately started a play interaction. Even if the interactions initially are somewhat artificial, practicing the skill outside of group is essential to successful generalization and inclusion of the skill in the child's behavioral repertoire.

Examples of priority goals include the following:

▶ Meet and greet one adult and one child each week by looking at them, smiling, and saying hello.

▶ Watch a person for five minutes and write down how the person might be feeling (by looking at his or her face and body language) once a week.

▶ Use three strategies to calm myself when I become upset each week.

▶ Each week, demonstrate being a good sport by staying calm and saying, "Good game" when I lose at a game or challenge.

▶ Think of three ways to solve a problem that at first seemed like it couldn't be solved.

▶ Start three conversations with someone at school each week.

It is vital that parents understand the importance of the weekly work toward meeting the priority goal. For one thing, frequent practice increases self-monitoring of the behavior, which alone is a powerful first step toward changing the behavior. Indeed, parents sometimes see quick early progress as children pay closer attention to their behavior. Parents will need to keep in mind that change takes time and effort and that progress may or may not continue at the initial pace of change.

PARENT INVOLVEMENT DURING GROUP

Monthly Participation in the Group Session

The first session of each unit and then approximately once a month thereafter, the free-play portion of the session is shortened or eliminated in order for parents to participate in the final 15 minutes of the session. During this time, group members take turns describing what the group has accomplished during the month. Often a relaxation exercise is demonstrated, with parents joining in. One advantage of this involvement is that the parents get a sense of the group dynamic, how their child relates to the other children, and how he or she understands what has been going on. Having this insight allows the parents to better follow up at home. Another advantage is that the parents, many of whom may be socially awkward themselves, meet other parents and become more comfortable with the process. Finally, having the opportunity to review what they have learned and to share something positive about themselves in front of the group and all of the parents reinforces the children's mastery and builds self-esteem.

Midsemester Conference

The purpose of the midsemester conference is for each child's parents and the group leader to exchange progress reports on the child. Prior to the meeting, we ask parents to complete the parent form of the Resilience and Social Competence Measure. The group leader also completes a version of this form. (See Appendix A for both versions.)

The typical structure of this meeting is as follows:

▶ Review of the results of the BASC–2, administered during the intake interview, and any teacher feedback received after group commences

▶ Review of the child's individual priority goal

▶ Discussion of specific concerns parents have, what strategies have been effective, and what further goals need to be addressed

▶ Review and comparison of parent and group leader ratings on the Resilience and Social Competence Measure (Appendix A)

▶ Discussion of whether the group member might benefit from an additional semester of group sessions. (We typically recommend but do not require a commitment for completion of two units to help generalize behavior changes.)

End-of-Group Contact

Parents are provided with a schedule for the next semester of group sessions and invited to register, with a deadline given for priority registration. After this deadline date, the group is open to new members. Parents are welcomed to further discuss their intention to have their child continue, change to another therapy modality, stop, or graduate to a booster session. Monthly booster sessions are helpful for those participants who are ready to reduce the frequency of group sessions but not quite ready to terminate contact.

CHAPTER 4

Behavior Management in Group

Effective behavior management is necessary for a successful group experience. In addition to ensuring that the group administration is smooth, it contributes to the participants' mastery of self-regulation skills. A well-trained group leader may use a host of different strategies to manage behavior, depending on the needs of a particular child or group.

A clear set of behavioral expectations for the group must be established at the onset of group. This begins during the intake session, described in chapter 3, and continues through the development of the Declaration of Group Rights in the first session. Also important is the group leader's demeanor as he or she greets the children at the beginning of each session. Adopting a firm yet gentle stance, the leader intentionally sets the tone by requiring that each group member wait patiently in line at the door and offer a formal greeting prior to entry. The procedure allows participants to demonstrate self-control, moderate their activity level, and practice appropriate greeting skills, including a pleasant demeanor and direct eye contact as they address the leader (e.g., "Good morning, Dr. Jones"). Children who arrive late are required to knock appropriately at the closed door, wait for the leader to open the door, and offer a greeting before they may enter.

When considering what kinds of strategies to adopt for a particular child, it is important to draw on information about how the child's behavior has been managed in the past. The goal is to understand what types of strategies have and have not worked so that a successful behavior management plan can be adopted. For example, if a child responds well to being a helper, the leader makes a special effort to involve the child in assisting. One child may want the opportunity to receive recognition in front of parents, while another may beam when a note outlining an accomplishment is sent home. This individualized approach promotes cooperation and boosts self-esteem.

Strategies to reinforce the group as a whole should also be given consideration. In one group, children may want to earn extra play time, while in another, an ice cream party may be a more powerful reinforcer. In any case, the reinforcers described here will need to be refreshed and varied often. As they become less novel, the power of most reinforcers decreases with time.

VERBAL PRAISE

Positive feedback is essential in group sessions, where children endure the feelings of vulnerability that go with self-examination and sharing the ways in which they need to change. Praise and encouragement allow the children to maintain a balanced view of their strengths and weaknesses, thus preserving their self-esteem.

Verbal praise and encouragement for specific behaviors and good choices are powerful agents for behavior change. For example, when a quiet child begins to participate actively, we praise the new (even if low frequency) behavior immediately. The immediacy of response is important because it links the behavior to the reinforcer and increases the likelihood of the behavior in the future. The feedback also sends a clear message to the group that everyone's participation is valued. Finally, positive feedback serves to enhance the child's self-esteem, one of the overall group goals.

The wording of positive statements to group members deserves particular attention. It is important to be aware of the difference between praise for a behavior and encouragement aimed at increasing the frequency of it. Praise is the evaluation by an authority of a behavior as a "good" or "bad" choice. Examples are "You did such a nice job in working together with Anna to clean up!" and "My, Cameron, you are doing such a nice job waiting patiently!" Encouragement, on the other hand, does not include an evaluative assumption by the adult; it simply increases the likelihood of continued effort. Examples include "You are giving a great deal of thought to your decoration of the picture" (without evaluating the picture) and "You have been very focused on the yoga relaxation exercise the entire time" (instead of evaluating how well the child is able to conduct the yoga pose). Encouragement may be useful for increasing children's effort regardless of the final product of their work.

Statements that seem to address the inherent goodness and badness of a child (versus the behavior) should be avoided. While a leader may say, "I noticed that you are participating actively today" to Ava, a leader should not say, "Ava, what a good girl you are to offer so much in group today!"

THE POINT SYSTEM: A YOUTH "PAYCHECK"

Just as their parents are rewarded for responsibly completing the tasks of their jobs, in the Resilience Builder Program, children who meet their commitments to the group earn a "paycheck" in the form of points.

The points, which add up and can be spent on prizes, offer strong encouragement to stay engaged and to participate in group. They are tabulated on a separate Points Chart for each child (see Appendix C) and are granted for putting in effort outside of group and cooperating in the sessions. Children can earn a total of five points each session: one for bringing their program notebook, one for doing the Resilience Builder Assignment, one for talking about their assignment, one for adding to their Success Journal, and one for being cooperative during the session. Typically, children can cash in their points two or three times during the unit—approximately every fifth session and at the final group session. Prizes are generally small and inexpensive, though larger prizes are available to children who save all their points until the end. Larger prizes reinforce the ability to delay gratification.

Prize selection requires careful consideration. When selecting prizes, consider group member interests. Game cards may be a strong reinforcer for members of one group, while dollar-store magic sets may motivate members of another group. Within the prize system, prizes of various points levels are offered. Smaller prizes may be worth 5 or 10 points, with larger prizes requiring up to 30 points to acquire. All prizes are kept in their original containers so that children have the thrill of opening them, and special bins labeled with point values help children determine what they have earned. Prizes should generally be inexpensive and of a good variety.

CHARTS: VISUAL REINFORCEMENT SYSTEMS

A versatile tool for reinforcing any behavior the group leader wants to increase, charts are limited only by the group facilitator's imagination and children's interests. For example, a chart might be used to reinforce cooperative play. Children can be told that when they are playing nicely with others for a period of time, the figure that represents them can be moved up on a chart (or a sticker added, depending on the type of chart). Younger children love charts that portray sports goals, that add animals to jungle or sea scenes, and that move pirate stickers closer to a treasure. Charts can also be used to reinforce completion of assignments outside group. In this case, a child can earn a sticker on a chart by bringing recorded progress on a personal goal to group each week. Charts should be colorful and personalized with the child's name. They should be openly displayed where the child can easily check his or her progress weekly. While emphasis can be placed on gaining stickers or moving to the top or finish line, it is important to refrain from commenting on slow progress because such comments may be negatively perceived by a child.

SPECIAL AWARDS

Special awards granted during the group are a great way to recognize participants as they make progress. Such recognition can be given not only in the presence of peers, but also when parents are invited into the group. For example, the Leadership Award (see Appendix C), an integral part of each unit, can be earned by one individual who demonstrates many leadership qualities. For example, perhaps it is a person who is the first to volunteer an opinion or who demonstrates flexibility or compromises with others. Initially, the recipient is determined by the group leader. Later, once the group has coalesced, the award can be determined by a vote among group members.

Likewise, a "most-improved" award may be devised for a child who has made great progress in a given session or over time. Perhaps a child is still very impulsive in group and interrupts others, but has made considerable progress since the first group session. One note of caution: The group leader should take care to assure that the child earning recognition rotates among group members to promote fairness. Other awards may be given for listening to others' ideas, participating, and maintaining good personal space. Awards could be identified each week in group with a defined privilege, such as getting to sit in a special chair. Pins that delineate a special type of reward and bracelets are two other novel ideas for reinforcing children with special types of awards.

When the group leader distributes an award, it is important to praise others for their accomplishments as well. If children do not receive this validation, they may feel disappointed and see themselves as lacking. Another powerful intervention sometimes used in older groups is allowing children to nominate and vote for peers by secret ballot. Children are not allowed to vote for themselves. This intervention is highly useful in encouraging peer validation.

TECHNIQUES FOR MANAGING NEGATIVE BEHAVIOR

Group leaders deal with negative behavior in several ways. When a group member is disruptive, the leader immediately praises appropriate role models in the group for their behavior. For example, members of the group who are paying attention are praised when one child is distracted, as are members who are sitting quietly when one child is talking in a disruptive manner. The leader attends to "how well group members are sitting with all chair legs on the floor" when a child is rocking in his or her chair. If the group member responds as hoped, the leader gives immediate praise.

Entire-group reinforcement can be very effective in encouraging positive behavior in groups in which negative behaviors dominate. In the "marble jar" strategy, for example, children are told that when they cooperate and participate actively and appropriately, they each can earn marbles to be placed in a jar. When the level of the marbles reaches a certain level, the entire group earns a reward such as extra play time.

Sometimes, negative behaviors are so prevalent that the leader may need to set up reinforcement systems that involve having parents provide incentives outside of group. Behavior contracts exemplify this approach.

Behavior contracts are most effective when they target only one or two behaviors, are clearly written and concise, include negative and positive consequences, and include the child's input. Most importantly, contracts need to be adhered to and followed consistently. The child should be given the opportunity to identify problems to address, although guidance from the group leader is usually required. At minimum, the child should be involved in the process of deciding on positive and negative consequences. A sample contract appears on the next page.

The consequences should be given during or immediately following the group session. Negative consequences administered by parents following the session generally should be limited to the day of the group session; however, positive consequences can span a longer period, especially if children are accumulating points toward earning something when the group session ends (this parallels the point system we use for earning prizes). Parents should be guided in this process. Specifically, they should be encouraged to be factual and not emotional when giving consequences, state the reason for the consequence, and refer to the content of the contract as much as possible.

Examples of positive consequences include special time with a parent, playing with a toy or video game, baking cookies or a cake, renting a movie of the child's choice, and having a special outing with a friend or sibling (e.g., sleepover, miniature golf, visiting the aquarium). Examples of negative consequences include removal of "screen" time or cell phone privileges, deductions of allowance, and doing chores (e.g., washing the car, raking the yard).

Once the child becomes engaged in the group, the reinforcers are generally no longer needed. The opportunity to socialize and the fun of free play are sufficient motivation to attend.

REINFORCING SELF-REGULATION IN INDIVIDUALS AND IN THE WHOLE GROUP

The social competence group is a forum for helping children become aware of their behavior and emotions and for reinforcing self-regulation skills. First, the leader must determine how much of a challenge self-regulation is for a given group (whole-group regulation); next, a decision can be made as to whether verbal coaching is sufficient or more elaborate props should be used. For example, sometimes the leader may simply comment to the group on regulation of voices during free play to encourage awareness. The children may attend by noting how nice it is to be with the group while they are enjoying themselves quietly. In the case of a particular child (within-individual regulation), encouragement to use a quieter voice can be followed by use of an agreed-upon signal as the group member becomes increasingly aware

---

Sample Behavior Contract for Evan

In addition to following the rules listed in the group's Declaration of Group Rights, Evan agrees to:

1. Respect others' personal space by not touching, pushing, or hitting other kids in group.

2. Stay in the room during the group meetings and not leave without permission.

Consequence A

If Evan follows Rule 1, he will earn 30 minutes of TV time that evening after group. If Evan follows Rule 2, he will earn a $1 credit for an iTunes song.

Consequence B

If Evan does not follow Rule 1, he will lose all TV privileges that evening after group. If Evan does not follow Rule 2, he will do a chore from the chore list that evening after group.

Evan	*3/10*
Signed by Evan	Date
Dr. Sanders	*3/10*
Signed by group leader	Date
Emily Smith	*3/10*
Signed by Evan's parent(s)	Date

---

of his or her voice level. The leader may also catch the child using a quiet voice and make a comment.

When regulation is a significant problem for a group as a whole, a visual prop such as a thermometer or another type of meter made of construction paper can often make a difference. The thermometer, posted where easily seen, can have a marker that can be moved to different "temperature levels." After demonstrating how the thermometer works, the group leader moves the marker up and down based on the noise level.

Leaders also may use an analog decibel meter that gives the children visual feedback on how loud their voices are based on actual sound measurement. The decibel meter captures the sound of the environment and displays the sound level through the movement of the meter's needle. The groups find this an exciting learning tool, and it gives immediate feedback when children's voices become too loud. (These meters can be purchased at local electronics stores.)

Verbal self-control (within-individual regulation) during group discussions is reinforced through the use of the Name Cube (see Appendix C). The cube is constructed from paper, and each child's name is placed on one side. Children who interrupt others are reinforced for speaking only when their name is up on the cube. This encourages and reinforces patience and appropriate verbal interchange.

TROUBLESHOOTING: COPING WITH PROBLEMS IN GROUP

This section addresses several problems that may come up during the course of running the group and provides guidelines for how to construct a behavior contract should one be warranted. The problems include the following: inappropriate fit between individual and group, incomplete homework assignments, late arrivals, absenteeism, and drop-outs.

Inappropriate Fit for Group

Occasionally, despite a thorough intake assessment, a child turns out to be an inappropriate match for the group. For example, a child may appear more mature and receptive during the one-on-one intake session; however, once in the group setting, he or she may display such extreme social and/or cognitive immaturity that other children are unable to relate to the group member. Cognitive maturity may not be adequately assessed in a 60-minute intake in which the opportunity to observe the child learning or completing lesson assignments does not occur, and it may be that the group member is unable to understand the content of the group sessions.

To address this problem, a first step is to work with the child on improving the ability to act maturely. Scheduling an individual meeting with the child may help to accomplish this, and it will be important for the child's parent or parents to be present for part of it. In this meeting, we point out a few behaviors for the child to work on (e.g., staying seated, refraining from hugging other group members, not running out of the room without permission). Making a behavior contract with the child often helps.

If a child struggles to understand session content, we recommend that the parents review the content with the child several times during the week, or if the child has a tutor, the content can be reviewed in tutoring. In addition, scheduling a 30-minute individual session with the child to teach the session content one on one may be quite useful. It is best if individual teaching takes place in advance of the group meeting, when it can serve the prelearning or preteaching function.

The idea of dismissing a child from group is challenging for us. On the one hand, these children have often experienced social and/or academic rejection, and it seems hurtful to be another source of such rejection. However, if a child is preventing other group members from having an effective group experience, it is a disservice to these other members to keep the child in the group. It can actually make things worse for the child because he or she may feel out of place or rejected by other members. If possible, the child can be referred to another group with children who are a year or two younger.

At times, the child may be taken out of the group and receive individual counseling instead. In this case, to destigmatize the referral out of group it is explained that many children require individual treatment first. It is often the case that the child will enjoy the individual attention. If individual treatment is not possible and attempts to help the child acquire the skills to be a better match for the group have failed, then having the child discontinue group may be the only option. In such a case, we may suggest trying again in a year or two and give the parents recommendations for other activities that may lead to maturation, such as martial arts.

Incomplete Homework

Many group members will miss a Resilience Builder Assignment here and there; however, sometimes a child misses all of the assignments and is losing points as a result. If this happens, setting up a brief 10-minute meeting either before or after a group session with the child and parents to discuss the problem is recommended. It is important to establish why the assignments are not getting done. Usually, involving parents cures this problem. If it does not, then the group leader could call and check in with the child between sessions to remind him or her about the assignment. While this may be time consuming, the assignments are essential for generalization of the skills.

Late Arrivals

The Resilience Builder Program involves 60-minute group sessions, and starting and ending on time is of utmost importance. Because many children with attention issues have parents with attention issues, time management may be a problem, and some children may regularly arrive late to group. If a child comes late, he or she is expected to pick up from the point of joining in. During free play, the group leader can check in with the child to ensure that the homework is complete and award points accordingly. This problem needs to be addressed with parents: Parents should be told that chronic lateness not only interferes with their child's learning experience, but also can be very disruptive to group members and overall group process.

Absenteeism

In our practice, groups range between 12 and 15 sessions; of these, we allow each child to miss two groups without being charged for those groups. If a child misses three or more groups, the parents are responsible for paying for each of those missed sessions. For schools and some clinical settings where payment is not necessary, attendance expectations should be clearly delineated.

Drop-Outs

Occasionally a child will drop out of group. It is essential to discuss why this has happened. Depending on why and when, our practice may or may not hold the parents responsible for the missed sessions. If a child's parent develops a serious illness and needs to attend medical treatments that conflict with the group meeting time and no other transportation is available, we will clearly permit the drop-out without any charges. Other times, the circumstances may be less clear. For example, if a child comes to one or two group sessions and then refuses to come back, we will meet with the child individually as a first step. If this fails, we will usually allow the child to drop out without having to pay and then may accept another child into group. If a child has attended seven or eight sessions and stops because parents find coming to be inconvenient, we will charge them for the remaining sessions. Fortunately, dropouts rarely occur in our practice, which is why we are generally flexible.

CHAPTER 5

Session Structure and Guidelines

The Resilience Builder Program sessions consist of five structural components (Alvord & Grados, 2005):

1. The interactive-didactic component

2. Free play and behavioral rehearsal

3. Relaxation and self-regulation techniques

4. Generalization

5. Parent component (i.e., proactive parenting)

The *interactive-didactic component* introduces or continues work on a specific resilience-based skill, such as staying in one's own personal space, maintaining conversations, problem solving, and managing stress.

The goal of *free play and behavioral rehearsal* is to foster flexibility and encourage the skill of compromising with others, characteristics that allow resilient children and teens to cope with disappointments. During this part of the session, group members participate in a structured process of negotiation and compromise while leaders facilitate the process.

Resilient people have the ability to modulate their emotions and behavior in response to their circumstances. Many children and teens with difficulties in interpersonal relationships lack self-control and experience emotional and behavioral dysregulation. Practicing *relaxation and self-regulation techniques* such as deep breathing, progressive muscle relaxation, guided imagery, yoga, and positive self-talk gives group members tools they can use to soothe themselves and calm down.

Generalization of change to natural settings is the end goal of the program. While the "practice makes perfect" principle steers us in the right direction, it is actually *successful* practice that is key (Goldstein & Martens, 2000). In particular, successful practice of multiple strategies in multiple settings results in successful generalization. Program strategies include Resilience Builder Assignments, free play, field trips, parent reinforcement of skills, and the consistent use of procedures such as the One-Minute Rule and Say Three and See Rule. In our practice, we also attempt to promote generalization by encouraging parents to provide opportunities for group members to be a part of school and religious organizations, youth groups, and recreational clubs.

Parents play a key role in facilitating lasting change because the behaviors learned in the group setting must be reinforced consistently at home. The *parent component* ensures that parents are collaborators in the group process. It is critical for parents to understand the goals and strategies of the program because they will need to model the social behaviors and resilience skills they hope to reinforce in their child. (This is especially important when a parent, like the child, lacks those skills.) As described in chapter 3, in addition to receiving weekly letters describing each session's content, contact with the child's parents includes monthly participation in group session, a midsemester conference with the group leader, and end-of-group discussion of next steps.

GUIDELINES FOR RUNNING GROUPS

The groups are designed to be lively and fast paced; there is a good amount of material and activities to cover, and this keeps group members interested and actively involved (and the time flies by!). With the exception of the field trip and team play sessions in each unit, sessions are structured in the same way. Repetition helps group members become accustomed to the following procedures.

Group Procedures

Individual Greeting

Sessions begin with a formal individual greeting upon entering the room. The point is to rehearse the components needed to make a good first impression—a smile, a courteous hello, and sustained eye contact—until the behavior becomes automatic.

Individual Goal/Success Journal and Resilience Builder

Each session after the first continues with a review of a Resilience Builder Assignment given as homework during the previous session to reinforce the skill or concept taught that day. The first assignment asks members to decide on a goal to work toward until it is met—for example, to control anger or to invite a friend over. At each succeeding session, group members take turns reminding the group of their goal and describing progress made during the week and recorded on a Success Journal (see sample portion of this journal on the next page).

To encourage participation in group activities, including completion of the Resilience Builder Assignments, the group leader assigns points to group members for their performance, as the sample Points Chart on page 51 shows. Prizes, valued between 5 and 30 points, are redeemed approximately every four to six sessions, at the end of the sessions, as group members accrue points. Group members are encouraged to save their points (i.e., delay of gratification) for higher valued prizes and redeem points the next available time. The goal of the points system is to give children who are accustomed to frequent negative feedback the opportunity to recognize and focus on the positive aspects of themselves and their performance. The use of prizes is optional, but points should still be earned, with some celebration during the last session to acknowledge group members' efforts.

Session Topics and Competencies

Next, the group leader announces the topic of the day. Rather than present a lecture on the topic, the group leader facilitates a discussion in which participants develop their own ideas, often recorded on a chalkboard or dry erase board. Frequently, group members role-play to practice a new skill. Role-plays typically follow topic discussion and allow children to have healthy modeling, which encourages prosocial behavior (Alvord & O'Leary, 1985).

Although session topics vary, there are a few competencies that leaders should promote in every session.

Being proactive and taking initiative.   Children and teens with interpersonal challenges sometimes react without careful thought or are passive; both of these reactions contribute to conflict or a sense of helplessness. On the other hand, being proactive and taking initiative means thinking through options and coming up with a plan. This skill can be encouraged at each session during the Success Journal review by asking participants what they did to work toward their goal or what their plan might be to do next time to improve their behavior or emotion. Free play also provides real-time practice for taking initiative, making choices, and solving problems. Free play affords the opportunity for immediately evaluating whether choices are realistic and whether they are helpful or unhelpful. Sessions directly addressing this competence concern resilience and being proactive, leadership, solving friendship problems, stress management, optimistic thinking, and making choices when handling challenges.

Effort.   During review of Resilience Builder Assignments and Success Journals, participants can be praised for completing and turning work in, as well as for their efforts toward achieving their individual goal. Furthermore, individual Points Charts provide a visible and tangible

Sample Success Journal

Every week, write about one time when you worked toward your personal goal or had some positive interaction with a peer. Remember, positive attempts count, too!

Session 1: Welcome to Group!

Session 2

When I was at soccer, I missed the goal and got upset but then I took a deep breath to try and calm down.

Session 3

My brother was bugging me, but I didn't react like I usually do. I asked him to stop. He didn't but I told my mom instead of hitting him.

Session 4

I kept calm when my paper began to tear. Instead I taped it.

Session 5

I got really angry with my friend Carl and thought about saying something mean. Instead, I just thought it in my head.

Session 6

I was part of a team for a school project. Susan wasn't doing her part, and we were all upset with her. We talked with her about it, but that didn't help, so we talked to the teacher about it. He spoke with her.

Session 7

This week I got invited to hang out with Seth and Carl. We did and had fun without anyone getting too upset.

Sample Points Chart

Name Christopher   **Group** 5th-grade boys   **Leader** Dr. Sanders

Session	Participant Goal/Leader Notes	Brought notebook to group	Completed Resilience Builder Assignment (RB)	Discussed assignment	Made entry in Success Journal (SJ)	Participated in cooperative manner	Points tally
1	Think before I react and use coping skills to calm myself	✓	✓	✓	✓	✓	5
2		✓	✓	✓	✗	✓	9
3	Absent—sent parent letter and RB by mail	—	—	—	—	—	9
4	Leadership Award—last session's RB	✓	✓✓	✓✓	✓	✓	16
5	Redeemed 20 points for prize—1 point carried over	✓	✓	✓	✓	✓	21/1
6	Forgot notebook and SJ entry	✗	✓	✓	✗	✓	4
7		✓	✓	✓	✓	✓	9
8	**FIELD TRIP** Got frustrated but earned other points	✓	✓	✓	✓	✗	13
9	Two weeks of RB and SJ	✓	✓✓	✓✓	✓✓	✓	21
10	Absent—sent materials by e-mail	—	—	—	—	—	21
11	Last session's RB and SJ	✓	✓✓	✓✓	✓✓	✓	29
12	Leadership Award	✓	✓	✓	✓	✓	34
13	Did not complete RB, but did discuss	✓	✗	✓	✓	✓	38
14	Brought last week's RB / only discussed one	✓	✓✓	✓	✓	✓	44
15	Redeemed 49 plus 20 bonus points	✓	✓	✓	✓	✓	69/0

feedback system to monitor effort. Effort counts toward success. Sessions directly emphasizing effort address resilience and being proactive, leadership, self-esteem, and being a good sport.

Self-regulation.   Self-regulation is directly practiced at each group session through relaxation exercises and self-talk. Practicing relaxation strategies helps participants incorporate self-calming techniques into their behavioral repertoires. Exposure to multiple types of relaxation strategies provides group members with a "tool box" of choices for later use, and many group members develop favorites. The Relaxation Tips for Parents and Group Members handout included in Appendix B is helpful in generalizing these skills to the home and other settings. The behavior management system also provides feedback on cooperative and regulated behavior. This feedback, in turn, allows group members to become more aware of their behavior and promotes self-monitoring of efforts to improve. Sessions directly addressing this competence concern personal space, reading verbal and nonverbal cues, stress management, assertiveness, anxiety management, and anger management.

Self-talk.   Self-talk is one critical component of self-regulation that is emphasized throughout the sessions. These private conversations we have in our minds allow us to solve problems and to calm ourselves by thinking realistically and positively. For example, a group leader might encourage an impulsive group member to think first by "talking it out" in his or her head to decide what would be appropriate to do or say before taking action. Sessions specifically promoting self-talk center on the topics of resilience and being proactive, leadership, being a good sport, optimistic thinking, stress management, on the mark/off the mark thinking, anxiety and anger management, self-esteem, and choices for handling challenges.

Flexibility.   Cognitive and behavioral flexibility allows us to deal with stress, solve problems, build friendships, and be good leaders. The ability to generate multiple alternatives in a given situation and to be willing to take appropriate action sets the foundation for flexibility. Discussions during sessions gradually improve in quality as participants become more flexible and develop the capacity to listen to one another's ideas. Free play affords the opportunity to increase flexibility through compromise with other group members. In addition to discussion and free play, sessions specifically focusing on flexibility address resilience and being proactive, as well as being a good sport.

Reciprocity.   Reciprocity, the "back and forth" quality fundamental to any relationship, is emphasized throughout the program. Reciprocity is required for maintaining conversations and friendships. In order to develop reciprocity on an ongoing basis, leaders employ a Name Cube to encourage participants to take turns talking, listening to one another, and staying on topic. (In a session devoted to initiating and maintaining conversations, group members also toss a question ball.) Leaders can encourage the Say Three and See Rule (Session 2.3), which aims to help a speaker become more aware of his or her listener. For example, if the speaker continues to talk without tuning in to the listener's response, the listener may lose interest in the conversation. Specific sessions addressing reciprocity include the introductory meetings and sessions on verbal and nonverbal cues, intent versus impact, and initiating and maintaining conversations.

Being a good sport.   Free play allows for frequent and intense practice of behaviors essential to being a good sport, from taking turns and being a good loser to negotiating and compromising. Giving and receiving compliments is also practiced during sessions, especially during discussion and free play. Specific sessions devoted to being a good sport emphasize team play and game etiquette, as well as provide the opportunity to practice being a good sport during community field trips.

Although these competencies are described individually, it is important to point out that they are interrelated. For instance, to be proactive instead of reactive, one must apply self-regulation. If one is flexible, then he or she is more likely to be a good sport and a good leader. Some skills are taught across several competence areas. For example, we emphasize that we all make mistakes and want to learn from them. Learning from mistakes means making changes, which requires flexibility. Leadership is another example of a combination of many of the competencies because it includes being proactive, self-regulation, flexibility, reciprocity, and being a good sport. In addition, we continually point out the connection between social competence and friendship. For example, managing feelings of anger and knowing how to problem-solve are skills that promote friendships and can influence how others respond to us.

Because session topics relate and build upon one another, leaders are encouraged to reference skills learned in earlier lessons to tie concepts together. For example, leaders should reference what the group has learned about resilience, assertiveness, and cognitive distortions when leading the lesson on self-esteem because these earlier lessons support the development of positive self-worth.

Free Play/Behavioral Rehearsal

After the session topic has been introduced, discussed, and practiced, the period of free play allows an opportunity for behavioral rehearsal, during which group members are encouraged to negotiate and interact in a flexible, prosocial manner.

Each group member must play with at least one other member, so the first step is to reach agreement on who wants to play with which game or toy. Each participant states his or her first choice, then another participant asks to play with the first. The next participant states his or her choice of remaining toys or games, and the process of selection continues until all group members are paired. As the sessions progress, it is more likely (and encouraged) that several group members can negotiate and compromise on the same activity, thereby expanding the play group to three, four, or even the whole group.

During the free-play time, the group leader observes the interactions, addresses negative behaviors, and reinforces positive behaviors as they occur. Typically, group members have heard (again and again) what they *should not* do and do not know what they *should* do. Structured free play gives them the opportunity to see a range of positive options and practice a behavior until they achieve an approximation of the desired response (i.e., behavioral rehearsal). Behavioral rehearsal allows the group leader to stop a nonproductive action and help a group member replace it with one that will get desired results.

Relaxation/Self-Regulation

Self-regulation, critical to maintaining strong relationships with others, is a key factor in building resilience. Relaxation exercises vary from session to session. If all the sessions in a unit are not administered, then leaders should review the relaxation exercises across sessions and substitute relaxation exercises so group members are exposed to, at minimum, one example each of calm breathing, progressive muscle relaxation, guided imagery, and yoga. In later sessions, the group members may take turns actually leading the relaxation exercises because this will help them gain mastery. They may either read from one of the scripts included in Appendix B, or they may create their own relaxation exercise. If time is limited, the relaxation component of the session may be abbreviated.

Leadership Award

Early on in the sessions, the idea of leadership is introduced and the qualities of good leaders are discussed. Over the course of the semester, group members are encouraged to act like leaders, and at the end of each session, the leader identifies one member who has best exemplified leadership by providing a Leadership Award like the one provided in Appendix C.

Generalization: Resilience Builder Assignment

Generalization of change to the participant's natural environment is the end goal of the program. A key cognitive-behavioral strategy to meet this goal is the use of homework exercises to practice and apply skills in a variety of settings. Thus, we include weekly assignments to reinforce the concepts and skills that are discussed and learned in group. Repeated successful practice is the key (as noted by Goldstein & Martens, 2000).

Parent Component

Finally, parents are asked to join the first and then every fourth group or so, as it promotes proactive parenting. Proactive parenting implies that parents are also held responsible for their child's participation in the group, including completion of Resilience Builder Assignments. Parents should help facilitate the practice of the relaxation strategies that the children learn in the group, using the scripts in Appendix B as a guide. Through weekly parent letters and by joining the group, parents learn what specific topics their child is learning and are better prepared to promote generalization of the skills. When parents join the group, generally for the last 15 minutes, their participation replaces the free-play portion of the session. If it is not possible for parents to join (e.g., when groups are held during school hours), the letters will be sufficient. Parents are also given handouts about how to have a family meeting and use the Compliment Basket strategy and are encouraged to integrate these Family Resilience Builders into their family life.

Materials Required

In addition to a chalkboard, dry erase board, or flip chart, these items are needed at every session.

1. A notebook for each group member. These are distributed during the first session. We prefer 1-inch three-ring binders with clear covers in front and back. The notebook, which group members are to bring to each session, will contain the following:

    ▶ A cover sheet with the child's name and space for his or her individual goal for the semester. The cover sheet is inserted behind the front clear cover of the binder

    ▶ Four divider pages for the binder, labeled "Group Activities," "Resilience Builder Assignments," "Success Journal," and "Parent Letters and Handouts"

    ▶ The Success Journal, which sits behind the relevant divider page and on which group members record successful attempts to reach their individual goal and interact socially

    ▶ If desired, a leader-created calendar of group meetings, inserted behind the clear cover on the back of the binder

    Many of the children and teens in our groups have executive functioning difficulties, so the binder system has an added advantage: It helps them learn to organize their work and better fulfill their responsibilities. (It is helpful to predrill holes with a hole punch before distributing assignments, parent letters, and other session materials.)

2. An individual Points Chart for each group member, which the leader uses to keep track of points earned during the sessions.

3. The Name Cube, displaying one member's name per side. This leader-constructed cube is tossed to identify whose turn it is to speak.

4. Toys and games for free-play time.

5. A Leadership Award, to recognize the member who has best demonstrated leadership qualities.

6. Copies of the Resilience Builder Assignment, the weekly assignment that reinforces the skill learned during session, generalizing it to home and school environments.

7. Copies of the parent letter describing the session and offering tips and resources for practicing skills at home.

Resilience Builder Assignments and parent letters can be found within each group session. A template for the Name Cube and blank copies of the Notebook Cover Sheet, Success Journal, Points Chart, and Leadership Award are included in Appendix C. If any other materials are needed (art supplies, for example), these are indicated in the materials list accompanying each session.

Sometimes it is helpful for group leaders to create a whole-group display or poster of certain information in advance of a session—steps in problem solving or maintaining a conversation, for example. Poster content is highlighted in the sessions and provided in an 8½ × 11–inch format on the CD accompanying this book. Resilience Builder Assignments, parent letters, handouts, and other reproducible materials are also included on the CD.

Topic cards are also useful. These are leader-created cards large enough to be read by the group that serve as prompts and reminders of session topics and other important concepts. In the final sessions of each unit, participants present session topics to a group of parents. We find it helpful to provide a card with the name of each session from which participants may choose.

Finally, we find props to be invaluable in conveying program concepts, especially to younger group members. If we are discussing resilience, for example, we demonstrate the ideas with a bouncy ball and rubber band. Similarly, when we discuss cognitive distortions, we use a dartboard and magnetic darts to illustrate on the mark versus off the mark thinking.

PART II

Group Sessions

Unit 1 Sessions

Introduction to Group

PURPOSE

A key characteristic of resilient people is that they have the ability to build strong relationships with their peers. This session introduces children and teens to the important social skill of entering a group of peers in a friendly fashion and helps them learn to operate as a group member in a situation where they don't know one another well. Socially anxious children benefit by having a safe environment in which to practice these skills. Because an ongoing goal of the program is to help participants better regulate their attention, emotions, and behavior, we also introduce the relaxation strategies that will be an integral part of each session.

GOALS

To explain the group discussion and activities format

To develop, as a group, the Declaration of Group Rights

To have group members introduce themselves to one another and learn what they have in common

To practice a relaxation/self-regulation technique

MATERIALS

Chalkboard or dry erase board and marker

Program Notebooks (one per group member)

Individual Points Chart for each group member

Name Cube

A small ball or Hacky Sack

Toys and games for free play

Copies of the following:

> My Partner Activity
>
> Resilience Builder Assignment 1.1
>
> Parent Letter 1.1
>
> Relaxation Tips for Parents and Group Members (Appendix B)

Before the session, prepare the Program Notebooks, Name Cube, Points Charts, and topic cards as instructed in chapter 5.

PROCEDURE

Individual Greeting

The components of a good first impression—a smile and a courteous hello and sustained eye contact—are rehearsed at the beginning of each session, with the goal of making the behavior automatic.

1. Stand at the entrance to the room and greet each group member by name, with a friendly face and a handshake. Ask the member to return the greeting, using your name and making eye contact.

2. At each successive group meeting, require participants to demonstrate longer sustained eye contact and a more confident greeting to enter the room.

    To help younger or especially shy group members sustain eye contact, inject a note of playfulness by saying, for example, "This doorway is the moat to my castle, and we can't unlock the drawbridge unless we find the right key."

Explain Group Procedures

1. Describe the session format by paraphrasing:

   Welcome to the Resilience Builder Program. The purpose of the program is to help you make and keep friends more easily. It's also to help you figure out what will make you happier. Each session will introduce a new topic for group discussion. We will also have free time for play, during which we will negotiate and compromise to get the toys or games we want, and five minutes or so of practice using different relaxation techniques. Your parents may join us during the last few minutes of a session from time to time.

2. Distribute the notebooks group members will maintain during the program. Use the notebooks as a concrete way to demonstrate their three main responsibilities as group participants. Explain:

   As you can see, each notebook is divided into sections that correspond to your main responsibilities as a group member.

   ▶ In one section, you'll collect all the notes and other documents we create during weekly discussions. It's important that you contribute your ideas.

   ▶ The next section is for the Resilience Builder Assignments you'll complete outside this group. These assignments will help you apply the skills we learn in group to your life at home, in school, with your sports team, and wherever else you interact with people. It's important to work on each skill you learn until you get it right and then practice it repeatedly outside of group.

   ▶ The third section is your Success Journal. *(Direct the group to these pages.)* One thing you will all be doing is to work toward a personal goal like "I'll make more nice comments to my classmates" or "I'll listen to others speak without interrupting" or "I'll start one conversation." Here's where you'll write about your progress and other experiences outside of group that you're proud of. It's important to notice the things you do well or the positive attempts you've made, even if you haven't been completely successful. You can always try again.

   ▶ The fourth section is a place for you to put letters and special handouts for your parents.

3. Explain the reward system:

   You can accumulate up to five points each session for fulfilling certain responsibilities and can spend them on prizes. You can earn:

   ▶ One point for bringing in your Program Notebook

   ▶ One point for completing the Resilience Builder Assignment

► One point for discussing the assignment

► One point for adding to your Success Journal

► One point for participating in a cooperative way during the session

I will keep a Points Chart for each of you and tell you your points as you earn them. When we are ready to turn the points in for prizes, I'll count them up and let you know the total you have earned. Today only, you will receive all five points if you participate cooperatively in the session activities.

Group Icebreaker and Self-Introductions

This game gives each participant a turn introducing himself or herself to another group member. The point is to practice the skill of communicating directly with a person by establishing eye contact and calling the person by name.

1. Make eye contact with one group member. Say, "Hi, my name is _____. What's your name?" Make sure that the group member returns the eye contact. Then toss a small ball or Hacky Sack to the participant. This serves as a signal to respond with "Hi, _____. My name is _____."

2. Instruct the participant to turn to another group member, make eye contact, and toss the ball or Hacky Sack. That person responds with "Hi, _____. My name is _____."

3. Continue the process until all group members have introduced themselves.

Develop Group Rights

Working collaboratively to develop a code of conduct establishes an expectation that participants will act with self-respect and be respectful of everyone in the group. A Sample Declaration of Group Rights is provided.

1. Initiate a discussion about what rights participants would like to enjoy as part of the group and generate a list. It is important to reframe the rules and rights in the positive. For example, if group members say, "Don't hit," ask them to restate the idea in the form of what they *should* do—that is, "Keep your hands to yourself."

2. Record ideas as group members provide them.

   After the session, you can type up and make copies of the declaration for the participants to include in their Program Notebooks. You can also make a poster of the rights for display during the group sessions.

Sample Declaration of Group Rights

We, the people of this group, declare that all shall have the following rights:

1. To listen to and accept other people's ideas

2. To speak freely

3. To be listened to without interruption

4. To be treated with respect and include everybody

5. To have conflicts resolved and leave group feeling confident

6. To make mistakes

7. To have our personal space respected and to respect others' personal space

8. To have time to think before responding

9. To be ourselves and be accepted

10. To have privacy for personal issues

11. To compromise and negotiate during free play

12. To play fair

Find Commonalities

This sharing exercise explores common interests and allows group members to begin to bond with one another and appreciate differences.

1. Have participants form pairs and interview each other about their interests using the My Partner Activity handout. If there is an odd number, you can pair up with a group member.

2. After participants have had a chance to discuss their interests among themselves, ask for volunteers to tell the entire group what interests they and their partners or small groups share.

   With younger children, you may ask each child what his or her interests are and then identify common interests.

Free Play/Behavioral Rehearsal

The point of free play is to practice negotiating and interacting in a flexible, prosocial manner. During the first couple of sessions, the process of agreeing on an activity can be quite slow as group members learn to compromise.

1. Provide a selection of age-appropriate toys, games, or other activities to choose from that encourage joint play. Explain that now there will be free time to play, but each participant must play with at least one other member of the group, so the first step is to reach agreement on who wants to play with which game or toy.

2. Taking turns, have each person state his or her first choice of game or toy. If someone else in the group wants to play with that game or toy, that person says so.

3. After everyone has had a turn, if everyone is not matched with a partner who wants to enjoy the same activity, go around again and ask for a second choice of game or toy.

4. If group members are still not all matched up, remaining participants' third choice must be an activity someone else has already chosen. The process of selection continues until everyone is paired up with someone or in a group.

5. Allow free-play time. Observe and intervene as necessary to keep the interactions positive.

Things You Can Say to Encourage Compromise

What would you like to do with someone else?

The sooner you can agree on an activity, the more time you'll have to play.

I know it's hard to not be able to do what you want to, but if you compromise this time, maybe next time the other person will compromise with you.

By letting your partner choose, you can learn a new game or activity that you've never tried before.

Relaxation/Self-Regulation

1. Introduce the concept of self-regulation and explain that the group will practice one relaxation exercise each week. Tell the group members to get into a comfortable position in their seats, with arms and legs uncrossed. Then provide these instructions:

   ▶ We are going to practice diaphragmatic breathing, which we call *calm breathing*. The goal is to breathe in through your nose and out through your mouth, with the air going all the way down to your lower belly. Tense or anxious breathing causes your upper chest to rise and fall, and the air only goes into your upper chest. Relaxed or calm breathing, on the other hand, causes your lower stomach—around your belly button—to go up and down and the air to go into your lower abdomen.

▶ Let your shoulders, head, neck, and arms relax. Place one hand on your chest and the other on the belly button area of your stomach. This exercise takes practice because we breathe mostly through our chests. I'll ask you to slowly breathe in through your nose for a count of five: 1, 2, 3, 4, and 5 . . . then hold the breath.

▶ As you breathe in, your stomach area will extend. The air should naturally push out your stomach. Now in . . . 1, 2, 3, 4, 5. Keep your chest still. Hold it . . . 2, 3. Now tighten your stomach muscles and notice your breath as you slowly breathe out through your mouth for five: 1, 2, 3, 4, 5.

▶ Again, breathe in through your nose . . . 1, 2, 3, 4, 5, with your stomach extending out. Hold it . . . 2, 3. Pay attention to your breath as you breathe out through your mouth: 1, 2, 3, 4, 5, pulling your stomach muscles in. Remember to let the air go all the way down to your lower abdomen.

If the group members have difficulty getting the air to go down into their lower abdomen, have them lie down on the floor and put a lightweight object (maybe a light book or foam yoga block) on their upper chest. Have them use the object as a way of measuring if their breathing is in their upper chest or lower abdomen (if they are doing calm breathing, the object should not move but their lower belly should).

2. Ask, "What did you notice about your breath?" and "How did that feel in your chest and lower belly?" Listen to and acknowledge responses.

Generalization: Resilience Builder Assignment

1. Give each group member a copy of the Resilience Builder Assignment and explain:

This session's Resilience Builder Assignment is to come up with a goal that you want to reach during this program. It can be part of a plan to control yourself better like "I'm going to think before I act" or "I'm going to calm myself down better when I'm upset." Or it can be part of a plan to be a better friend, such as "I'll listen and accept other people's ideas instead of arguing" or "I'll call people up and get together at least once a month." Discuss the goal with your parents, then write it or have your parents help you write it on your Individual Goal Contract. Once you have a goal, you write any progress you make toward reaching it in your Success Journal.

2. Answer any questions about the assignment.

Parent Component

Hand out copies of the parent letter, and have group members put their Resilience Builder Assignment and parent letter in their notebooks in the appropriate sections.

The first parent letter covers an introduction to the group model and discussion of logistical procedures and the nature of resilience. Provide a copy of the Relaxation Tips for Parents and Group Members and instruct group members to put it with the parent letter in their notebooks.

> *If circumstances allow, it can be helpful to bring parents in toward the end of the first session for a brief introduction to the program and to participate in the relaxation exercise.*

My Partner Activity

My name _____ **Date** _____

Fill in each blank with information about your partner.

My partner's name _____

1. His/her favorite indoor activity is

   _____

2. His/her favorite outdoor activity is

   _____

3. His/her favorite game is

   _____

4. He/she is happiest when

   _____

5. What he/she likes most about himself/herself is

   _____

6. He/she is really good at

   _____

7. Others think that he/she is good at

   _____

8. He/she is looking forward to

   _____

9. What we have in common is

   _____

Individual Goal Contract

Name _____ Date _____

I agree to work very hard at improving my social competence and self-regulation. My goal is:

Please state your goal in a specific and positive way—for example, "I will become more aware when I get upset and use strategies to calm down."

_____

_____

_____

_____

I can work on this goal by:

1. Writing in my Success Journal and noting attempts and progress on my goal.

2. _____

3. _____

My parents and I have talked about my goal, and they will help me by:

1. Each week, pointing out when I have made efforts to work on my goal or have been successful at meeting the goal.

2. _____

3. _____

Group member _____ Date _____

Parent _____ Date _____

Parent _____ Date _____

Introduction to the Group

Dear Parents:

Welcome! We are looking forward to working with you and your child during the next few months.

The purpose of our groups is to build resilience in children and teens. *Resilience* is defined as the ability to adapt well to life and its challenges. Resilient individuals share a number of competencies that can be learned, and these serve as protective factors. The group your child will participate in will foster the development of several competencies: the ability to take the initiative, to modulate emotions and behavior, to connect with and maintain relationships with peers and adults, and to engage in activities of interest. All of the protective factors are important—and interdependent.

Our major goals include helping group members have better-quality friendships and develop solid self-regulation skills. Therefore, the program emphasizes social competence by helping children learn and practice the skills necessary to form and cultivate relationships. Social competence encompasses more than just acquiring skills; it also means performing these skills in the child's daily social interaction. For example, we teach children with AD/HD self-regulation skills, and these skills then allow them to use the other social skills they learn. In addition, many socially anxious children benefit from regular role-playing and group discussions because these activities gradually expose them to social situations and help reduce their anxiety.

The model we use provides a practical, cognitive-behavioral approach to developing resilience. If you would like to learn more about resilience, please refer to the American Psychological Association's Consumer Website at *www.apa.org/helpcenter.*

Transferring what children learn in group to home, school, and community is another critical goal of our groups. We work to accomplish this with help from parents by assigning a Resilience Builder Assignment as homework at the end of each session. To truly master and apply the skills we teach, practice is required between sessions. Each child will also set and work toward an individual goal related to his or her specific needs. We will also plan an activity outside of the group to help children generalize the behaviors we are learning in group to the community.

We start the program with introductions and an exploration of how the group members are similar to one another, emphasizing the importance of positive behavior and verbal content to make good first impressions. In addition, we develop group rules together and create a Declaration of Group Rights.

Program Topics

Topics that will be covered in group will include but are not limited to the following:

▶ The social entry skill of meeting and greeting

▶ What resilience is and how to develop it

▶ Being proactive

▶ The importance of personal space

▶ Leadership skills

▶ Self-regulation

▶ Reading verbal and nonverbal cues

▶ Initiating and maintaining conversations

▶ Being a good sport (team play and game etiquette)

▶ Optimistic thinking

▶ Problem solving (generating choices and alternative ways of behaving)

▶ Stress management

▶ Assertiveness training

▶ Empathy and perspective taking

Some Logistics and Additional Points

Periodically, parents are invited to join for the last 15 minutes of the session to discuss the skills that the children are learning.

A note on interaction outside the group: Because children often befriend each other and develop a close bond in the group, there is a desire to schedule play dates outside of group. While this may appear to be a good idea, friendships outside the group may actually disrupt the group process because they change the group's dynamics (by creating selective ties, for example). It is important that group be an accepting place for all members, so it is best not to schedule play dates with other group members. If on occasion there is a special event you would like to plan (a birthday party, for instance), you may do so as long as all group members are invited.

Your child will receive a program notebook, which he or she must bring to each session. It is divided into four parts. One section will collect all the notes and other documents we create during the sessions. One section is for the Resilience Builder Assignments your child will complete at home. The third section, the Success Journal, is where your child will record progress toward an individual goal and other successes or attempts to achieve success outside of group. A fourth section includes parent letters and special handouts.

Perhaps you could think of things to note in your child's Success Journal. It could be as simple as reporting that your child "Said something nice to_____ on Monday at home." Many children who attend group experience more than their share of negative feedback, so it's helpful and encouraging to acknowledge as many positive attempts or successful outcomes as possible.

Resilience Builder Assignments are an essential part of group. These at-home assignments help you and your child reinforce the skills the group is working on and encourage progress toward the individual goal. As is the case with music lessons, if you don't practice, progress is *much* slower. We also provide you with a handout of relaxation/self-regulation exercises that we will practice in group each week. Please practice these exercises with your child as often as possible.

Please feel free to provide me with any updates on your child. It is often difficult for children to recall a specific incident that may have occurred outside of group. We like to use real-life incidents or interactions for role-plays and discussion, without necessarily identifying the child. One of the most challenging tasks that we face is to get the children to generalize and transfer their improved understanding of their behavior and new skills to home, school, and other environments. The Resilience Builder Assignments are helpful; also useful are activities outside group. We may go bowling or miniature golfing, for example. Any suggestions for other structured activities outside the group are welcome.

Resilience Builder Assignment: Individual Goal Contract

Please assist your child in choosing an individual goal to work on during the sessions. Discuss what steps are needed to attain this goal. If writing is an issue, please have your child dictate a goal to you. We also encourage you to practice self-regulation/relaxation exercises together.

Please feel free to contact me with any questions.

Sincerely,

Program Leader

1.2

Resilience and Being Proactive

PURPOSE

Research has shown that a person's ability to believe in his or her effectiveness and to take the initiative contributes significantly to his or her ability to be flexible and rebound from life's hardships. This session provides a concrete demonstration of the concept of resilience, illustrating why it is important, then focuses on how being proactive rather than reactive or passive is an integral part of being resilient.

GOALS

To explain and discuss the concept of resilience

To introduce the concept of self-talk

To introduce the protective factor of being proactive rather than reactive or passive

To help group members understand that their actions can influence what happens to them

To practice a relaxation/self-regulation technique

MATERIALS

Chalkboard or dry erase board and marker

Program Notebooks (brought by group members)

Individual Points Charts

Name Cube

One rubber band per member (extra for those that might snap!)

One bouncy ball, preferably one that also stretches (a "Hi-Bounce Stretch Ball" may purchased through a novelty catalog)

A small object that when dropped will not break or bounce

Toys and games for free play

Copies of the following:

> Resilience Builder Assignment 1.2
>
> Parent Letter 1.2

Before the session, create a **Steps in Being Proactive** *poster.*

PROCEDURE

Individual Greeting

Conduct the individual greetings as described in Session 1.1.

Review Success Journal and Resilience Builder Assignment

> *The Resilience Builder Assignment from the last session identifies the group member's individual goal for the sessions in this unit.*

1. Throw the Name Cube to identify the first speaker, who states his or her goal. Ask: "How could reaching your goal help you with making friends and getting along better with others?"

2. Listen for negatively stated goals ("I won't scream when I'm upset") and help the participant restate as a positive goal ("When I'm upset, I'll use my relaxation strategies to calm down.") Ask, "Who can help you with your efforts to reach your goal? What can they do?"

3. Ask, "Please read to the group the efforts you made toward your goal, or another success you had, from your Success Journal." Be sure to offer genuine praise for attempts as well as successes. If a group member has not written in the Success Journal, encourage him

or her to tell the group about a positive interaction or attempt to work on the goal, and then have the member record it in the journal.

The goal is for the group members to begin to think about what goes right instead of what all too often occurs: focusing on the problems or failures. Be sure to remark how difficult it is to remember some of the positives since we often focus on the negatives.

4. When each group member finishes speaking, ask him or her to throw the Name Cube to determine the next speaker.

5. Continue until each participant has had a chance to describe homework efforts and progress toward success.

Record each group member's goal on his or her Points Chart and assign one point for bringing in the notebook, one point for identifying a goal, one point for discussing it, and one point for the first Success Journal entry. At the end of the session, you can award a point for cooperating during the session.

Discuss Resilience

1. Write "Resilience" on the board. Take a rubber band and slowly stretch it to the max, saying, "This is what happens when we are stretched, stressed, or challenged." Then slowly return the rubber band to the normal position and say, "This is how we get ourselves back to a calmer state. It's not an instant process; it might take some time. See how flexible the rubber band is when it's back to its normal state. This is called resilience."

2. Hand out rubber bands, one per group member, and let them stretch and return the bands to the normal state. Ask, "What is something that stresses you and makes you stretch out of shape? What has to happen for you to come back to normal? *(Encourage and acknowledge responses.)* Show me with the rubber band how you get stressed and how you come back to normal."

3. Collect the rubber bands. Next demonstrate the concept of bouncing back. Drop the small object that does not bounce. Then bounce the ball. Explain:

Imagine that feeling upset or stressed is like dropping the ball. What you want to happen next is that you bounce back to normal. *(If you are using a stretchy ball)* But the ball stretches and moves, and we have to work it to get it back to its round shape so that it can bounce well. So it takes effort and flexibility. *(Referring to the hard object)* This other object just stays there and doesn't move. One is active, like the rubber band. The other is passive—it just sits there.

As time permits, you can have the group members demonstrate this as well, but we suggest giving a ball to just one member at a time.

Discuss Being Proactive and Self-Talk

1. Ask the group whether they are aware that while they are awake, they are always thinking. Let the group know that *self-talk* refers to the things that we say to ourselves, usually in our own minds—the private conversation we have with ourselves. Sometimes the talk can be negative, and sometimes it can be positive.

2. On the board, write the headings "Proactive Responses," "Reactive Responses," and "Passive Responses" in three columns. Say:

   > Suppose you find out that you failed a math test. It may be tempting to ignore the problem or pretend it isn't a problem. That would be a *passive response*. Or you might immediately throw the test out and blame the teacher, or say to yourself, "I'm stupid!" or "I can't do math!" That kind of negative self-talk and behavior would be a *reactive response*. Bouncing back, on the other hand, means *being proactive*. That means you plan actions to make the situation better and stick with the specific problem—one bad math test—rather than blowing the single bad grade way out of proportion and telling yourself, "I can't do school." For example, you might use positive self-talk and tell yourself, "I didn't do well on *this* math test. So before the next test, I'll study more and ask my teacher or Mom and Dad for help with what I don't understand." This kind of positive behavior is a *proactive response*.

3. Refer the group to the Steps in Being Proactive poster. Explain that these are steps you can take when faced with a challenge or problem.

Steps in Being Proactive

1. Acknowledge the problem.

2. Keep perspective that you're having a specific problem.

3. Keep in mind that the problem won't last forever.

4. Come up with a plan to make the situation better.

5. Act on your plan.

---

4. Next encourage the group to generate the different types of statements or behaviors one might make in response to two or three problem scenarios (proactive, passive, reactive).

   Three problem scenarios and sample responses are provided on the Proactive, Reactive, and Passive Statements or Behaviors chart on page 81. You may use these or any other situations the group finds challenging (for example, your mom asks you to turn off your video game or you keep missing baskets during practice).

5. Explain:

How might you respond proactively, reactively, or passively? For instance, you can be passive and do and say nothing. You can react in a negative way by telling yourself, "I can't do it" or by getting physical. Or you can tell yourself, "I can do something proactive," then come up with a plan.

If you wish, after obtaining responses, you can have the group members write their names on the board to enhance their involvement and ownership of the proactive solutions they have generated.

6. Summarize the following idea:

Even when you're not faced with a problem, getting good results depends on initiating or taking action. For example, you might want to get together with friends, so you take action—you call them or ask them at school if they would like to come over. It might also mean that you take action and help someone. For example, if you are good at math, you might offer to help a classmate, or you could volunteer to help a teacher when you notice that something needs to be done.

Free Play/Behavioral Rehearsal

Provide the group with a selection of age-appropriate toys, games, or other activities to choose from that encourage joint play and follow the procedure described in Session 1.1 for choosing play partners and facilitating free play.

Relaxation/Self-Regulation

1. This session's relaxation component introduces progressive muscle relaxation, focusing on only a few muscle groups. Tell participants to get into a comfortable position in their seats and close their eyes. Read the following script slowly:

▶ Take a deep breath in through your nose and hold it until the count of five: 1, 2, 3, 4, and 5. Slowly, very slowly breathe out through your mouth.

▶ We are going to tense different muscle groups. I want you to pay attention to the difference in how the muscles feel when they are tight and tense versus when they are loose and relaxed.

▶ Start by making a tight fist with your right hand. Hold it until it almost hurts. Tighter, tighter, hold it, hold it. Now slowly relax. Notice how it feels. You might feel tingling or coolness or warmth, or something else.

▶ Now we are going to tighten the left fist. Pretend you are squeezing something really, really hard. Hold it, hold it, hold it. Now slowly let the fist go back to its normal position. Notice the way it feels when it's tense and when it's relaxed.

▶ Bring your shoulders up and hold them tight. Slowly relax.

▶ Now move down to your stomach. Pretend someone just punched you in the stomach. That hurts. Tighten as much as you can. Slowly let go. Notice how it feels to relax those stomach muscles.

▶ Now we will blow up your stomach as if someone is pumping air into it. Hold it, then slowly relax and let go.

▶ Now shake your head a little *(pause)*, wiggle your fingers *(pause)*, and slowly open your eyes.

2. Ask, "How did that feel? What part of your body was the most tense? What were the sensations you had when you relaxed the muscles?"

Generalization: Resilience Builder Assignment

Distribute copies of the Resilience Builder Assignment. Ask if there are any questions and discuss as needed.

Parent Component

Give each group member a copy of the parent letter for the session. Have participants place it and the Resilience Builder Assignment in the appropriate sections of their notebooks.

Proactive, Reactive, and Passive Statements or Behaviors

Scenario 1: I had to write an essay and got a poor grade on it.

Proactive Responses	*Reactive Responses*	*Passive Responses*
I can ask for help.	Rip up the paper.	There's nothing I can do.
I can practice writing.	Get angry and take it out on someone else by being mean.	No action.
I have good ideas.	Tell the teacher it's not fair.	Go to sleep.
I can take more time.	Say to myself, "I give up."	I can't do that.
I'll ask the teacher what part of it was a problem so I can work on that specifically.	Say to myself, "I'm just not good at this and can never be good at it."	Shrug my shoulders and leave the class.

Scenario 2: Someone talks to you in a mean way. He or she also tells you that you talk too loud, which your parents also tell you.

Proactive Responses	*Reactive Responses*	*Passive Responses*
Walk away but think about what was said.	Hit.	Don't deal with it.
Tell the person in a firm voice that you don't appreciate the mean talk.	Deny the correct part of what was said. You didn't do it.	Look down.
Say, "Sorry if I talk too loud. I'll work on it, but you are being mean about it."	Yell.	Stand firm. Hold your head up and shoulders back.

Scenario 3: You worked on a project that was hard to do and got frustrated.

Proactive Responses	*Reactive Responses*	*Passive Responses*
Calm down. Take deep breaths.	Get mad at the teacher, the other kids, or myself.	Give up and stop working on it.
Ask for help.	Complain.	
Say to yourself, "If at first you don't succeed, try and try again."	Lose control and slam down the pencil, etc.	
Say to yourself, "I'm not going to let the obstacle get in my way."	Take it out on someone else and get mean.	
Say to yourself, "It may be hard, but I'm still going to try."	Tell yourself you're not able to do this work.	

Proactive, Reactive, or Passive?

Name _____ Date _____

Describe two situations you faced during the past two weeks. For each situation, write two possible proactive, reactive, and passive statements or behaviors. Circle what you actually did, said, or thought.

Situation 1

_____

_____

Proactive Responses

1. _____

2. _____

Reactive Responses

1. _____

2. _____

Passive Responses

1. _____

2. _____

Situation 2

_____

_____

Proactive Responses

1. _____

2. _____

Reactive Responses

1. _____

2. _____

Passive Responses

1. _____

2. _____

Resilience and Being Proactive

Dear Parents:

The Resilience Builder Program is based on the notion that resilience can be fostered in children and teens facing all kinds of stress, from being rejected by a friend and left out of parties to academic struggles to parental illness and divorce. What is *resilience?* It is defined broadly as skills, attributes, and abilities that enable individuals to adapt well to hardships, difficulties, and challenges. Children seem to understand the meaning best with this analogy: Stress placed on a rubber band might stretch it to the breaking point; ideally, however, it will have the flexibility to withstand the stretching and slowly return to its original size and shape. Learning to make an active effort and be flexible is fundamental to building resilience skills.

An emerging body of research on resilience has identified a number of protective factors that change a person's response to challenges like having a learning difference, anxiety, or environmental adversity and that increase the chance of a positive outcome. This program organizes these protective factors into six categories: proactive orientation, self-regulation, connections and attachments, achievements and talents, community ties, and proactive parenting. We incorporate all these factors into activities throughout the sessions.

Today's session focuses on defining resilience and being proactive. A person's ability to take the initiative, believe in his or her effectiveness, and think realistically but positively contributes significantly to resilience. For example, children who can learn to compromise in their relationships with others are more apt to develop successful friendships. Students who are proactive—who aren't afraid to seek out a teacher and ask for extra help—are more likely to turn a failing grade into an A or a B. Being proactive means setting goals, planning and problem solving, thinking optimistically, and building a more positive sense of self.

Listening to what we say to ourselves and others provides a clue as to whether we are being proactive, being reactive, or being passive. Things we say to ourselves are called our "self-talk." For example, if we are told that our video play has been reduced to half the usual time, our thinking and self-talk would be positive and proactive if we ask ourselves, "What are my choices for how to best use the time available?" On the other hand, our self-talk would be negative and reactive if we say, "That's terrible! I'll get back at you for taking my time away!" If our self-talk is negative, we might also react passively by saying, "I can't do anything fun in that time" and then just give up. A proactive approach involves taking responsibility and ownership for our thoughts, feelings, and actions so that we can work on changing them.

From *Resilience Builder Program for Children and Adolescents,* © 2011 by M. K. Alvord, B. Zucker, & J. J. Grados, Champaign, IL: Research Press (800-519-2707, www.researchpress.com).

Resilience Builder Assignment: Proactive, Reactive, or Passive?

Group members are asked to describe two situations they faced during the past two weeks and to provide two examples each of proactive statements or behaviors, reactive statements or behaviors, and passive statements or behaviors. Please discuss this assignment with your child and help him or her generate responses if necessary. Please also practice a relaxation exercise this week with your child.

Sincerely,

Program Leader

Parent Letter 1.2 (p. 2 of 2)

SESSION

1.3

Personal Space

PURPOSE

When people invade others' space, they tend to make them feel uncomfortable and may alienate them. Understanding of personal space is a critical skill that enhances connections with others. This session begins with a concrete demonstration of physical personal space to illustrate its importance. Two types of personal space are discussed and demonstrated: physical distance between people depending on relationship and being "in sync" with other people—for example, by speaking and moving at a speed consistent with theirs.

GOALS

To help participants reach an understanding of the physical aspects of personal space

To define the concept of pace, or being "in sync" with others (speed of speech and movement)

To promote understanding that interrupting others and speaking too loud can be an invasion of space

To practice a relaxation/self-regulation technique

MATERIALS

Chalkboard or dry erase board and marker

Program Notebooks (brought by group members)

Individual Points Charts

Name Cube

Toys and games for free play

Sound level meter (optional—analog type preferable because dial is easier to view)

Copies of the following:

Personal Space Diagram

Personal Space Cards (copied and cut apart)

Resilience Builder Assignment 1.3

Parent Letter 1.3

Family Resilience Builder: Family Meetings (Appendix B)

A brief discussion of cultural differences in defining appropriate personal space may be appropriate during this session. It is important to consider the cultural context and be aware of what is appropriate given members' cultural background.

PROCEDURE

Individual Greeting

Conduct the individual greetings, as described in Session 1.1.

Review Success Journal and Resilience Builder Assignment

Have each group member discuss his or her individual goal and Success Journal entry and experiences completing the Resilience Builder Assignment. When participants describe real situations, praise them for sharing what might have been a difficult time. Also note any positive, proactive solutions they came up with, even if they did not accomplish them. If they made up situations, praise their recognition of what might be a sticky circumstance and their ability to generate proactive, reactive, and passive responses. When each group member finishes speaking, ask him or her to throw the Name Cube to determine the next speaker.

Record points on each group member's Points Chart for this portion of the session. Record the point for participation at the end of the session.

Discuss Personal Space

1. Paraphrase the following:

   We are going to talk about *personal space* today. Who can tell me what that means?

   Jot responses on the board. Some ideas include the idea of physical distance, not getting too close, not getting in someone's face, and so forth.

   There are a few different kinds of personal space. One is the physical kind of personal space that some of you mentioned, and another is a type that most people don't think of as personal space.

2. Give each group member a copy of the Personal Space Diagram and explain that each person has a "space bubble." The circle at the center is the person, and the safe and comfortable space around this circle varies depending on the relationship of the other person.

3. Draw a set of concentric circles on the board and label the center circle "Me." Ask the group for suggestions as to where to place various other people on the diagram: close family members, other relatives, friends, and strangers.

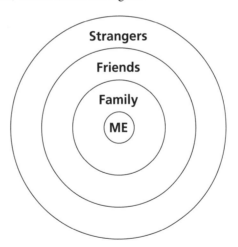

4. Have group members write the relationships in the appropriate circles on their own copy of the diagram. Encourage them to personalize the diagram with the names of real people in their lives, if they wish.

Demonstrate the Elbow-Room Rule

1. Introduce the idea of space protection. Explain that, in general, it's not a good idea to get closer to other people than you could if you had both hands on your hips, with your elbows out. Demonstrate the position.

2. Ask the group to identify some Space Busters (in other words, things that invade someone else's space bubble).

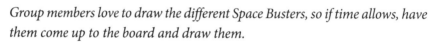

   Sample Space Busters

   Standing or sitting uncomfortably close to someone

   Pointing your finger in someone's face

   Sticking your foot out in front of someone

   Hitting someone

   Hugging or tickling someone when it's not welcome

   Group members love to draw the different Space Busters, so if time allows, have them come up to the board and draw them.

3. Point out that following the Elbow-Room Rule helps you build your own personal space. A Space Builder is when you keep the proper distance from someone and protect your own space from invasion. Ask what else you could do to protect your space.

   If you do not get sufficient answers, you could say, "Perhaps you might say something in a firm voice, move away, or just stand tall, with shoulders back and assert yourself, giving the person a message that they are in your space."

4. Have participants march randomly around the room in the hands-on-hips position, avoiding contact. Then ask a pair to demonstrate invading space. Ask another pair to demonstrate protecting one's space when another invades it.

Discuss Being "in Sync"

1. Ask, "What do you think it means to be *in sync* with others?" Point out that it means matching someone else's pace and rhythm. Demonstrate rhythm by tapping fast and hard on a table. Then tap slowly and quietly. Say:

   If you are at the ball game, and everyone is loud and active, then it's appropriate to be loud and active as well. However, when you are in a calm classroom and someone comes in with a fast pace or is loud, that's a different kind of personal space invasion. If you're loud and everyone else is quiet, you're out of sync.

2. Hand out the Personal Space Cards and explain that the group should follow the instructions written on them. Give two people the card that says, "Stare at the person" and the others the cards that say "Talk in a normal voice." The individuals in the room are to engage in quiet conversation on any topic (video games, for example).

3. Have the person holding the card that says, "Come in making a lot of noise" go out and then reenter the room noisily.

4. After the group members have enacted their roles, ask:

   ▶ *(The person who reentered)* What reactions did you notice on the faces of the others? What did it feel like to be stared at?

   ▶ *(The group)* What did it feel like to have someone walk back in and be so noisy when we were talking so quietly?

   ▶ *(Everyone)* What is important about being in sync with what other people are doing?

5. Draw a picture on the board of two people talking at the same time. (Stick figures are fine.) Ask, "How is this a Space Buster?" Discuss. If necessary, point out that interruption is an invasion of space. Ask a volunteer to draw how you can stay in your own space in conversation.

   If you wish, bring out the voice meter and speak loudly, then softly, then in a moderate "indoor voice." Have group members use the meter to demonstrate different voice volumes, being sure to end with the moderate voice.

Free Play/Behavioral Rehearsal

Provide the group with a selection of age-appropriate toys, games, or other activities to choose from that encourage joint play and follow the procedure described in Session 1.1 for choosing play partners and facilitating free play.

Relaxation/Self-Regulation

1. Today's relaxation exercise, the yoga tree pose, requires group members to respect one another's personal space. Have group members pick a spot to stand and be mindful of their personal space and that of the others in the group. Read the following aloud:

   ▶ Take a deep breath. Hold it in.

▶ As you breathe out, bend your right leg and bring your right foot to your left knee. If you feel that you might lose your balance, then bring the leg as low to the ground as you need or stand against the wall for support.

▶ As you breathe in, stretch your arms out to make a "T" or put your hands on your hips.

▶ Hold this position for a count of five or as long as you can: 1, 2, 3, 4, and 5.

▶ If you need to, bring your legs together but keep your arms outstretched. Notice the tension in your muscles as you hold the position.

▶ Bring your hands together so that the palms touch.

▶ Slowly bring your arms to your side.

▶ Slowly bring your right leg down.

Repeat the preceding steps with the left leg, then continue.

▶ Take a deep breath in: 5, 4, 3, 2, and 1.

▶ Slowly breathe out. Let your muscles loosen and your body relax.

▶ Now take a seat.

2. Ask, "How did your body feel? What does it feel like when you hold the position and tense your muscles? What were the sensations you had when you relaxed the muscles? What did you do to stay in your personal space?" Let the group know that they can practice the tree pose at home.

Generalization: Resilience Builder Assignment

Give each participant a copy of the Resilience Builder Assignment. Go over the assignment and answer any questions.

Parent Component

Give each participant a copy of the parent letter for the session. In addition, provide a copy of the Family Meetings handout. You can briefly explain the family meeting to the group if you wish.

> *Have group members place the parent letter, the Personal Space Diagram, the Resilience Builder Assignment, and the Family Meetings handout in the appropriate sections of their notebooks.*

Personal Space Diagram

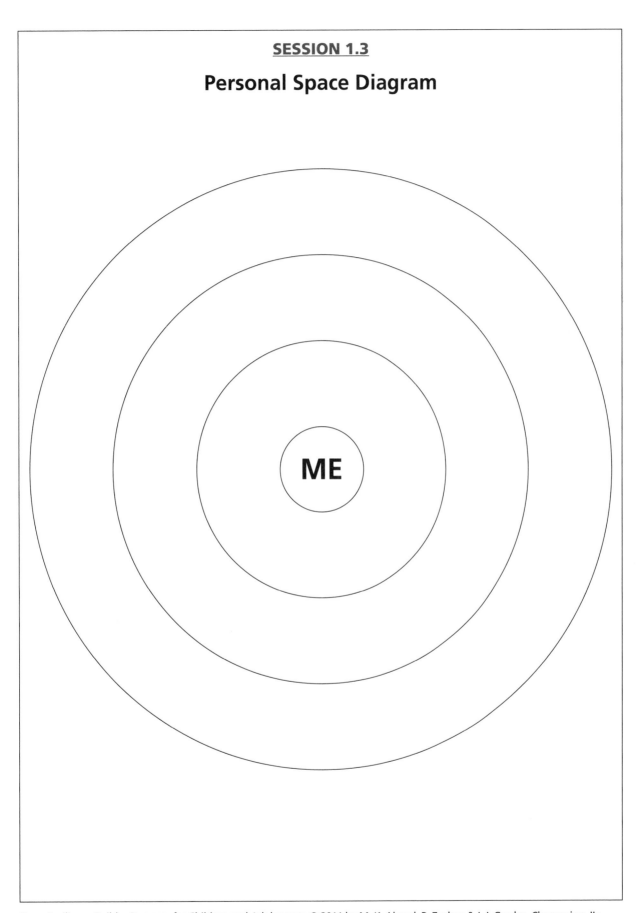

Personal Space Cards

1. **Come in making a lot of noise.**

2. **Stare at the person coming in the room.**

3. **Stare at the person coming in the room.**

4. **Talk in a normal voice with the rest of group members.**

5. **Talk in a normal voice with the rest of group members.**

6. **Talk in a normal voice with the rest of group members.**

Space Builders and Space Busters

Name _____ **Date** _____

Remember the Elbow-Room Rule. Try to be at least elbow distance from a person you are next to or talking with. Be aware of your pace and try to stay "in sync." Watch how others stay in their space.

Tell about two times when you respected someone's personal space and/or protected your own space bubble.

1. _____

 _____

2. _____

 _____

Now tell about two times you got too close to someone (busted their space bubble) and/or two times you were not able to protect your own space.

1. _____

 _____

2. _____

 _____

How did you do this week? (Check one.)

☐ I wasn't aware of my behavior.

☐ I tried to stay in my space but had a hard time.

☐ I tried and did a good job of staying in my space at least one time this week.

☐ I tried and did a good job of staying in my space most of the time.

Personal Space

Dear Parents:

This session focuses on awareness of personal space as a nonverbal way of communicating. First, we examine the concrete notion of physical space. How close should we sit or stand to others? In group, we define personal physical space as one's "space bubble," and we follow the Elbow-Room Rule. That is, you should be no closer to another person than the distance of your arms when they are bent at the elbow and your hands are on your hips. We refer to Space Builders (staying in your own and respecting others' space) and Space Busters (things that interfere with appropriate space).

Next, we teach the group about the concept of being "in sync" with what others are doing. This involves matching the pace and rhythm of speech and movement and includes the idea that interruption is an invasion of space. Mastering one's own pace starts by recognizing the pace of others, such as the speed at which they speak, move, and play. Pace also involves knowing what your speed of speech and behavior is and then adapting it to be more in sync with that of others. Being in sync with another's pace can make others feel more comfortable, while being out of sync may make them annoyed with you.

When you see your child invading someone's space, please help identify the situation and tell or show your child how to behave in a more positive way. If the situation does not lend itself to immediate feedback, you can discuss and role-play the situation later to practice the more socially appropriate behavior. Always praise success! If you see your child having a positive interaction, be sure to point the moment out.

Resilience Builder Assignment: Space Builders and Space Busters

This session's assignment asks your child to identify times he or she respected someone else's personal space and times he or she did not, either intentionally or unintentionally. Please invite your child to tell you about the assignment and provide assistance if needed. We also invite you to begin having Family Meetings and to continue practicing relaxation exercises with your child.

Sincerely,

Program Leader

From *Resilience Builder Program for Children and Adolescents,* © 2011 by M. K. Alvord, B. Zucker, & J. J. Grados, Champaign, IL: Research Press (800-519-2707, www.researchpress.com).

SESSION

1.4

Leadership

PURPOSE

Leadership abilities, which include solid interpersonal skills and self-confidence, are fundamental to resilience. The purpose of this session is to introduce the importance of leadership skills necessary for being effective in daily life. The session also introduces the group's Leadership Award.

GOALS

To explain and discuss six critical behaviors in a good leader

To encourage group members to provide examples for each of these six behaviors

To introduce the Compliment Basket strategy

To practice a relaxation/self-regulation technique

MATERIALS

Chalkboard or dry erase board and marker

Program Notebooks (brought by group members)

Individual Points Charts

Name Cube

Magnets or tape (to attach puzzle pieces to the board)

Basket or shoebox (to serve as the Compliment Basket) and index cards

Toys and games for free play

Copies of the following:

Leadership Jigsaw Puzzle (copied on card stock and cut out before the session)

Leadership Award (Appendix C)

Resilience Builder Assignment 1.4

Parent Letter 1.4

Family Resilience Builder: Compliment Basket (Appendix B)

*Before the session, create a **Leadership Behaviors** poster.*

PROCEDURE

Individual Greeting

Practice an appropriate initial greeting, as described in Session 1.1. At this point, the expectation is that each group member will be able to demonstrate longer eye contact and a more confident greeting to enter the room.

Review Success Journal and Resilience Builder Assignment

1. Have each group member discuss his or her individual goal and Success Journal entry and experiences completing the Resilience Builder Assignment. When each person finishes speaking, ask him or her to throw the Name Cube to determine the next speaker.

   Record points on each group member's Points Chart for this portion of the session. Record the point for participation at the end of the session.

2. Inquire about the Family Resilience Builder. Ask, "Have you and your family started having family meetings at home? How did you do it? Does your family like it?"

Discuss Leadership

1. Direct the group's attention to the Leadership Behaviors poster.

Leadership Behaviors

► Being proactive

► Communicating effectively

► Maintaining self-control

► Being a good role model

► Being a team player

► Giving compliments

---

2. Hand each group member a puzzle piece that names one leadership behavior. Say:

    Each of these puzzle pieces contributes to the whole of what makes a good leader. All of these qualities help people get along well with others and feel happy and good about themselves, even when they have no interest in being the president of the class or the captain of a sports team.

    As a variation, have each group member hold onto the puzzle piece while you lead the following discussion of what each component means. At the end of the discussion, each member may place a puzzle piece on the board and restate a characteristic of the component, until the puzzle is complete.

3. Talk about what each of the leadership behaviors means. As participants generate ideas, record them on the board.

Being Proactive

1. Paraphrase:

    We've discussed being proactive before, as opposed to being reactive or passive. Let's talk about ways that a good leader is proactive. Suppose you offer an idea of an activity to do with your friends, and one of them says, "That's stupid!" Rather than just say something mean back or stomp off, you use positive self-talk like "Maybe he or she doesn't like my idea, but it's not stupid." Before you respond, you think about the possible things you could do or say so that you can still reach your goal of having fun with the group.

2. Ask who has the "Being Proactive" puzzle piece, then invite that person to give another example of being proactive and put the puzzle piece on the board. After that person has responded, ask for additional ideas from the group.

Sample Responses

Making an action plan

Acting and thinking positively

Helping someone

"Can-do" attitude

Coming up with ideas to do something (taking initiative)

Asking for help

Communicating Effectively

1. Paraphrase:

    Good leaders know how to have a conversation so that others are willing to listen and can understand what they're saying. Suppose you're explaining the rules of a game to your brother and sister. You might say, "You have to do it this way!" in an impatient, bossy tone of voice. Or you might say, "The way I learned to play is this way," in a calm and friendly tone. Which is more effective and why? *(Encourage responses.)* What is another example of a communication skill that's important in a leader?

2. Ask who has the "Communicating" puzzle piece, then invite that person to give another example of communicating effectively and put the puzzle piece on the board. After that person has responded, ask for additional ideas from the group.

    Sample Responses

    Listening when others talk without interrupting

    Saying your ideas and staying on topic

    Contributing your ideas

    Using a nice tone of voice

    Making eye contact

    Maintaining a conversation

Maintaining Self-Control

1. Paraphrase:

    Calming yourself down when you are frustrated, angry, or worried is an important leadership skill. Can you think of a well-known athlete who handles losing or what he or she considers an unfair call by the referee in a positive way? How about famous people who are known for *not* handling themselves well? What does the public think of them? *(Point out that it takes away from the sport that they excel at.)* What does maintaining self-control mean to you?

2. Ask who has the "Self-Control" puzzle piece, then invite that person to give another example of maintaining self-control and put the puzzle piece on the board. After that person has responded, ask for additional ideas from the group.

    Sample Responses

    Staying calm

    Using an inside voice

    Waiting your turn

    Staying in your own space

    Controlling your anger

    Thinking about a positive way to handle stress

Being a Good Role Model

1. Paraphrase:

    A good role model is someone whose behavior you admire, someone you look up to. Even in group, you can be role models for each other. Can you think of someone who is a good role model for you? What makes this person a good role model?

2. Ask who has the "Role Model" puzzle piece, then invite that person to give another example of being a good role model and put the puzzle piece on the board. After that person has responded, ask for additional ideas from the group.

    Sample Responses

    Setting an example

    Following all the rules

    Doing what you are proud of

    Stepping up to the plate

    Being fair

    Acting appropriately

Being a Team Player

1. Paraphrase:

    > Being on a team doesn't always mean a sports team. When you do a group project with your classmates, you are working as part of a team. What makes a good team player on a sports team? What makes a good team player on a group project? Why does a leader need to be a good team player? How would a leader behave differently from the other members of the team?

2. Ask who has the "Team Player" puzzle piece, then invite that person to give another example of being a team player and put the puzzle piece on the board. After that person has responded, ask for additional ideas from the group.

    Sample Responses

    Listening to other people's ideas

    Compromising

    Working together

    Doing your fair share

    Cooperating with others

    Being a good sport

Giving Compliments

1. Paraphrase:

    > Noticing positive things in others helps you get along and also makes people feel good about interacting with you. How do you feel when others make negative comments about you? *(Encourage responses.)* Sometimes we need to get feedback about behaviors that aren't appropriate or might be annoying. We need to be aware of these. However, if we get negative comments often, then we tend not to feel good about ourselves or those interacting with us. It's important to accept compliments but also to be aware of what you like about what someone does or says and be able to give compliments as well. How can you give someone a compliment?

2. Ask who has the "Compliments" puzzle piece, then invite that person to give another example of giving compliments and put the puzzle piece on the board. After that person has responded, ask for additional ideas from the group.

    Sample Responses

    Noticing what people are doing well

Smiling when you like something

Saying yes

Being sincere

Saying something positive

Giving a high-five

Saying it in a good tone of voice

3. Point out that it is important to accept compliments as well and that when you get a compliment, a good way to respond is just to say, "Thank you."

Introduce the Compliment Basket

1. One by one, have each group member give a compliment to the person to his or her right, until everyone has given and received a compliment. Let the group know that it is important for it to be a genuine compliment based on something that they have observed or experienced with the person. For instance, while they might think a boy has on a nice shirt, it would be better to compliment him for something he has accomplished today, like "You had some good ideas when we were talking about leadership" or "You listened to my idea when we were playing."

2. On an index card, write each group member's name, today's date, and the compliment he or she received and put the card in the basket. Explain that you will keep these compliments in the Compliment Basket to be read during other sessions and that additional compliments may be added at future sessions.

   We encourage you to use the Compliment Basket strategy during as many subsequent sessions as possible.

Explain the Leadership Award

Let the group know that at the end of each session one of them will be selected for a Leadership Award based on participation in group that day. In addition to showing leadership qualities, the person recognized as leader must have completed the day's assignment, shown effort throughout the session, and demonstrated progress toward his or her individual goal.

Free Play/Behavioral Rehearsal

Provide the group with a selection of age-appropriate toys, games, or other activities to choose from that encourage joint play and follow the procedure described in Session 1.1 for choosing play partners and facilitating free play.

Relaxation/Self-Regulation

1. This exercise introduces participants to visualization/imagery relaxation. Tell group members to get into a comfortable position in their seats and close their eyes, then provide these instructions:

   ▶ Take a deep breath and hold it until the count of five: 1, 2, 3, 4, and 5. Slowly and quietly breathe out.

   ▶ Think about a place that would be safe and comfortable where no one will bother you and you can be completely relaxed. It can be a real place you love, a made-up place, or a place you'd like to go.

   ▶ Imagine the colors that you see. What colors are relaxing to you?

   ▶ Now listen to the sounds. What do you hear? If you're at the beach, you might hear the ocean waves or the wind blowing. If you're inside, you might hear some people talking or music playing. Or maybe it's silent, and that's the most peaceful to you.

   ▶ Decide the temperature of the air around you that makes you feel good. How does the air feel on your skin? What makes you feel cozy?

   ▶ Become aware of the smells around you. Maybe you smell the salty air or flowers or trees. Or maybe food cooking in the kitchen. What are the smells that comfort you?

   ▶ And now focus on taste. Can you taste anything with your tongue? Salt in the air? Food that you'd want to eat?

   ▶ Now decide if you want to be in this place by yourself or with one or more other people. Think about who they would be and what you would be doing there.

   ▶ Now take a deep breath again and hold it in for the count of five: 5, 4, 3, 2, and 1. Slowly breathe out, shake your head gently, and slowly open your eyes.

2. Individually, ask children to describe where they went, with whom, and some of what they saw or sensed. Let them know they can call up these images any time they like.

Leadership Award

Select a group member to receive the Leadership Award and provide praise for what the person did well.

Generalization: Resilience Builder Assignment

Give each group member a copy of the Resilience Builder Assignment. Go over the assignment and answer any questions.

Parent Component

Give each participant a copy of the parent letter for the session. In addition, provide a copy of the Compliment Basket handout for parents.

Have participants place the parent letter, Resilience Builder Assignment, and Compliment Basket handout in the appropriate sections of their notebooks.

OPTIONAL ACTIVITY: LEADERSHIP ACROSTIC

If time permits, have the group make an acrostic using the word *leadership*. Participants identify qualities or actions defining leadership that begin with each letter. For example:

L listen, leader, lend a hand

E enthusiastic, expertise, excellence

A attention, alert, attitude, accepting, authentic

D decisive, disciplined, do your part

E energetic, eye contact, everyone's friend

R resilient, reliable, respectful, right thing to do

S stay in your space, sharing, silence when needed, sincere

H help or ask for help, honest

I interact, intermingle, initiate

P plan, proactive, patient, positive, praise

Leadership Jigsaw Puzzle

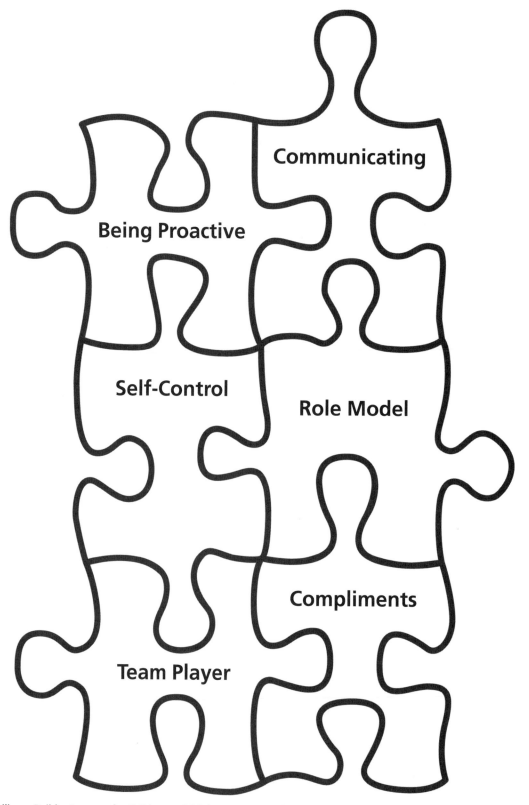

Leadership Behaviors

Name _____ Date _____

Please give one example of each of the six leadership behaviors we discussed in group.

1. **Being proactive**

   _____

   _____

   _____

2. **Communicating effectively**

   _____

   _____

   _____

3. **Maintaining self-control**

   _____

   _____

   _____

4. **Being a good role model**

   _____

   _____

   _____

5. **Being a team player**

   _____

   _____

   _____

6. **Giving compliments**

   _____

   _____

   _____

From *Resilience Builder Program for Children and Adolescents,* © 2011 by M. K. Alvord, B. Zucker, & J. J. Grados, Champaign, IL: Research Press (800-519-2707, www.researchpress.com).

Leadership

Dear Parents:

Good leadership behaviors help us be more effective in daily life. Our emphasis is on developing solid interpersonal skills and healthy self-esteem, fundamental to resilience. The goal is not necessarily to become leaders in the traditional sense of being class president or captain of a team. Rather, we teach six specific leadership behaviors:

1. Being proactive

2. Communicating effectively

3. Maintaining self-control

4. Being a good role model

5. Being a team player

6. Giving compliments

In this session, we talk about the leadership behaviors and exchange compliments using the Compliment Basket technique. We also discuss the Leadership Award: At this and following sessions, one member of the group will earn a Leadership Award. (Sometimes we may have co-leaders.) In addition to showing leadership qualities, the person recognized as leader must have completed the day's assignment, shown effort throughout the session, and demonstrated individual progress toward his or her goal.

Resilience Builder 1.4: Leadership Behaviors

The assignment for this session is for your child to describe one leadership behavior for each of the six components. Please encourage your child to think like a leader. Let your child know you will be watching for the six leadership behaviors and recognize times you observe any of them, no matter how small the attempt. We also encourage you to take the time to use the Compliment Basket technique at home and continue practicing relaxation exercises with your child.

Sincerely,

Program Leader

SESSION

1.5

Reading Verbal and Nonverbal Cues

PURPOSE

The ability to read verbal and nonverbal cues enables one to interact effectively with others by responding appropriately. This in turn allows for the development of friendships and relationships in general, enhancing one's chances of developing a support group. This session focuses on the accurate interpretation of verbal and nonverbal cues.

GOALS

To encourage identification of various verbal cues, including voice tone, volume, and pace

To promote understanding of nonverbal cues that convey attitudes and send messages

To demonstrate and interpret verbal and nonverbal cues through role-play and discussion

To practice a relaxation/self-regulation technique

MATERIALS

Chalkboard or dry erase board and marker

Program Notebooks (brought by group members)

Individual Points Charts

Name Cube

Toys and games for free play

Sound level meter; video camera and monitor for playback (optional)

Copies of the following:

> Verbal and Nonverbal Communication Role-Plays (copied and cut into strips)

> Leadership Award (Appendix C)

> Resilience Builder Assignment 1.5

> Parent Letter 1.5

One of the best ways to become aware of your own body language and interpret that of others is to view videotaped interactions. If you can, videotape the role-plays in this session. Group members can then watch and discuss their performances in place of free play for the session.

PROCEDURE

Individual Greeting

Conduct the individual greetings, as described in Session 1.1, with longer sustained eye contact and a more confident greeting.

Review Success Journal and Resilience Builder Assignment

1. Inquire about the Family Resilience Builders. Ask:

> ▶ Have you and your family started using the Compliment Basket at home? How did you do it? Does your family like it?

> ▶ Did anyone have a family meeting? If so, how did that go?

> *Ask periodically in subsequent sessions about family meetings and the Compliment Basket strategy.*

2. Have each group member discuss his or her individual goal and Success Journal entry and experiences completing the Resilience Builder Assignment. When each group member finishes speaking, ask him or her to throw the Name Cube to determine the next speaker.

   Record points on each group member's Points Chart for this portion of the session. Record the point for participation at the end of the session.

Discuss Verbal Cues

1. Ask participants to look around the room and pick an object to identify to the group in turn ("I see a _____"). In sequence, ask one group member to whisper, the next to speak in a normal indoor tone, the next to yell, and so on.

   If you have a sound meter, have the group note the differences on the meter. If not, simply help the group identify how loud each particular verbal communication is.

2. Ask:

   ▶ What do you think it means when someone whispers? How would you feel if someone whispered while you were at the movies?

   ▶ What if you were standing with two other kids, and then they whispered to each other? What might that mean?

   ▶ What about a person who yells? Is it OK to yell at a ball game? Inside the house?

   Point out that a good way of talking sometimes depends on where you are—in other words, the context.

3. Say:

   We have already learned about personal space and how the volume of your voice can be in one's own space bubble or invade another's. This week we are going to talk about how we communicate in different ways and with different meanings by what we say, how we say it, and what our faces and bodies do.

4. Explain that we communicate not just with the words we use, but with the way we say them. Give each group member a slip with an instruction from Part 1 of the Verbal and Nonverbal Communication Role-Plays handout.

5. Have the two group members who have drawn the same statement take turns making the statements, using different verbal cues. Discuss the difference in meaning, even though the words are the same.

Discuss Nonverbal Communication

1. Demonstrate an "indoor scream." Open your mouth, grimace, and scream without any sound. Have everyone try it, then ask what group members think you are communicating. *(Anger, frustration)* How do they know? Point out that you are communicating, but you didn't make any sound. Say:

   > There is a kind of communication that doesn't use words. When we use just our faces and our bodies, it's called *nonverbal communication*. We need to be able to recognize and figure out what this kind of communication means because a lot of the content of a message depends on it.

2. Say, "Let's list some ways we communicate with our faces and bodies and what we think they mean." On the board, write down what nonverbal cues the group has observed and what they think these cues mean.

Nonverbal Communication

1. Slightly leaning forward	Interested **or** wanting to hear better **or** wanting to be part of the conversation
2. Eyebrows lowered	Deep in thought **or** confused **or** upset
3. Shoulders back, head up	Self-confident **or** listening
4. Leaning away from another person	Lack of interest **or** uncomfortable
5. Head resting in hand, eyes downcast	Bored **or** tired **or** sad

---

3. Say, "Let's demonstrate some ways we move our bodies and what they communicate. Show us before you tell us what it is." Hand out the slips of paper from Part 2 of the role-play handout. Ask for a volunteer to demonstrate the nonverbal behavior listed. Ask the group members: "What do you think he or she was communicating? How can we figure this out?"

4. Again, record the cues observed and what group members think the cues mean.

   If necessary, point out that we often use several cues to figure out what someone's body is saying: how the person leans, tilts the head, raises or lowers eyebrows, makes eye contact, winks, or uses hand gestures.

Free Play/Behavioral Rehearsal

Provide the group with a selection of age-appropriate toys, games, or other activities to choose from that encourage joint play and follow the procedure described in Session 1.1 for choosing play partners and facilitating free play.

If you have videotaped role-plays, substitute viewing them for free play. Instruct the group to observe one another's tone of voice and body language, then discuss.

Relaxation/Self-Regulation

1. This session's relaxation exercise continues teaching progressive muscle relaxation and focuses on a few more muscle groups. Ask group members to get into a comfortable position in their seats and close their eyes. Read the following:

    ▶ Take a deep breath and hold it until the count of five: 1, 2, 3, 4, and 5. Slowly and quietly breathe out.

    ▶ We are going to tense a few muscle groups. I want you to pay attention to the difference in how the muscles feel when they are tight and tense versus when they are loose and relaxed.

    ▶ As your body gets more relaxed I want you to notice how it feels when all your muscles are relaxed and you feel calm. How does calm feel to you?

    ▶ Start by bringing your shoulders back. Hold the position until it almost hurts. Tighter, tighter, hold it, hold it. Now slowly relax. Notice how it feels—what the muscles feel like when they are tensed and then relaxed.

    ▶ Bring the shoulders forward. Pretend you are hugging someone with your shoulders, squeezing really hard.

    ▶ Hold it, hold it, hold it. Now slowly bring your shoulders back to their normal position. Always notice the way it feels when it's tense and when it's relaxed.

    ▶ Let's move down your body to your legs. Straighten your right leg, pointing your toes out and squeezing as hard as you can. Slowly let your leg drop to its normal position.

    ▶ Now straighten the right leg, but this time point the toes toward you. Hold it. Slowly and gently let the leg drop to the floor.

    ▶ We will do the same with the left leg. Straighten the leg with the toes pointing out. Hold that position. Now slowly and gently bring the leg to its resting position.

    ▶ Straighten the left leg again, this time pointing the toes toward you. Hold and feel the muscles tense in a different place than when the toes are pointing away from you. There are so many muscles in your body, and when your mind is tense, your body gets tense. Your mind and body are connected.

    ▶ Slowly let your leg relax. Notice how that feels. Notice the sensations when those muscles relax.

▶ Take a deep breath in again. Hold it to the count of five: 1, 2, 3, 4, and 5. Slowly, quietly breathe out.

▶ Now shake your legs *(pause)*, wiggle your toes *(pause)*, and slowly open your eyes.

2. Ask the group, "How did that feel? What part of your body was the most tense? What were the sensations you had when you relaxed the muscles?"

Leadership Award

Select a group member to receive the Leadership Award and provide praise for what the member did well.

Generalization: Resilience Builder Assignment

Give each participant a copy of the Resilience Builder Assignment. Go over the assignment and answer any questions.

Parent Component

Give each group member a copy of the parent letter for the session. Have group members place the parent letter and Resilience Builder Assignment in the appropriate sections of their notebooks.

OPTIONAL ACTIVITY: MAGAZINE OR INTERNET PICTURES

Download pictures of expressions and body language from the Internet or cut out pictures from magazines and have the group describe what nonverbal cues they see and what these cues might be communicating.

Verbal and Nonverbal Communication Role-Plays

Part 1: Verbal Communication

1. I quit! (Say this in a loud voice with a high pitch.)	1. I quit. (Say this very softly.)
2. I didn't think that was fair. What are the rules you play by? (Say this in a normal volume and calmly.)	2. I didn't think that was fair. What are the rules you play by? (Say this in a loud, angry voice.)
3. Did you like that song? (Say this in a normal volume with a friendly tone.)	3. Did you like *that* song? (Use an unfriendly tone. Put emphasis on the word *that*).
4. I like the way you did that. (Whisper.)	4. I like the way you did that. (Say this a normal, calm voice.)

Part 2: Nonverbal Communication

1. Yawn. Look away.	2. Tilt your head.
3. Look at someone and smile.	4. Raise your eyebrows and roll your eyes.
5. Lean forward and give a thumbs-up.	6. Show frustration (no words).
7. Show sadness (no words).	8. Show pride (no words).
9. Show being relaxed and calm (no words).	10. Show being confused (no words).

Reading Verbal and Nonverbal Cues

Name _____ **Date** _____

Part 1

Here are several different facial expressions, gestures, and postures. The first two have been completed with possible meanings. Please complete the rest.

1. Slightly leaning forward

   Interested or wanting to hear better or wanting to be part of the conversation

2. Eyebrows lowered

   Deep in thought or confused or upset

3. Shoulders back, head up

   _____

   _____

4. Leaning away from another person

   _____

   _____

5. Head resting in hand, eyes downcast

   _____

   _____

6. Tapping or drumming fingers

   _____

   _____

7. Eye contact for only short time

   _____

   _____

8. Hands on hips

   _____

   _____

9. Body turned away from the other person

   _____

   _____

Part 2

Observe a peer, either at school or during another activity. Watch his or her nonverbal behaviors (personal space, gestures, facial expressions, body posture) and what he or she says (verbal behaviors).

1. I observed_____ , and he or she:

_____

_____

_____

2. Did he or she get the point across to the other person? If not, why not and what could he or she do differently next time?

_____

_____

_____

Reading Verbal and Nonverbal Cues

Dear Parents:

Accurately reading cues depends on our ability to interpret both verbal and nonverbal communication in the context in which it occurs. In addition to words, verbal communication includes voice tone, volume, and pitch. Nonverbal communication involves such things as our body posture, gestures, facial expressions, eye contact, and silences. In communicating with others, what we say (the words that we choose) plays only a minor role when compared with *how* we say it (our body language and other cues) and the context or situation surrounding the communication. Accurately reading others' emotions and probable intentions leads to improved peer and other relationships.

Miscommunication or confusion frequently occurs when there is a contradiction between verbal and nonverbal messages. As communication becomes more complex, it is even more critical to understand both overt and more subtle verbal and nonverbal cues. The goal is to express verbal and nonverbal behaviors so that they are consistent, or "in sync," with people and situations.

Behavioral rehearsal is an important teaching tool. Therefore, when your child displays or "reads" a communication incorrectly, please ask him or her to replay or redo the situation. You may need to tell or show your child directly how to do it. If the situation does not lend itself to giving feedback at the time the misunderstanding or out-of-sync behavior occurs, please discuss and role-play it later to practice the more socially appropriate action or reaction.

Remember to catch your child when his or her verbal and nonverbal communication matches your child's intentions. Please point the moment out and compliment successes or positive attempts. A terrific way to reinforce this week's session would be to add "in sync" verbal and nonverbal communication to this week's Compliment Basket. Please also remember the family meetings!

Resilience Builder Assignment: Reading Verbal and Nonverbal Cues

This week's assignment asks your child to interpret some nonverbal cues and observe a peer's verbal and nonverbal cues. Please ask your child to tell you about the assignment and provide help if asked. If possible, ask your child to lead the family in a relaxation exercise.

Sincerely,

Program Leader

Initiating and Maintaining Conversations

PURPOSE

Reciprocity is the key to maintaining good relationships. This session demonstrates a central aspect of reciprocity—that starting and carrying on a conversation requires drawing the other person out and listening attentively as well as contributing appropriately on the topic under discussion.

GOALS

To explain and discuss the concept of reciprocity and how it applies to relationships and conversations

To introduce the One-Minute Rule: that you do not enter a conversation until you have listened for one minute and can offer a comment or question on the topic

To help group members understand Conversation Builders (techniques to maintain a conversation) and Conversation Busters (which are likely to offend other people and stop interaction)

To practice a relaxation/self-regulation technique

MATERIALS

Chalkboard or dry erase board and markers

Program Notebooks (brought by group members)

Individual Points Charts

Name Cube

A small beach ball with six panels, each with a word that starts a question: *who, what, when, where, why, and how* (Words can be written on the ball or written on file labels and affixed to each panel.)

Toys and games for free play

Copies of the following:

Leadership Award (Appendix C)

Resilience Builder Assignment 1.6

Parent Letter 1.6

*Before the session, create a **Steps in Good Conversation** poster.*

PROCEDURE

Individual Greeting

Conduct the individual greetings, as described in Session 1.1. Require participants to demonstrate sustained eye contact and a confident greeting to enter the room.

Review Success Journal and Resilience Builder Assignment

Have each group member discuss his or her individual goal and Success Journal entry and experiences completing the Resilience Builder Assignment. When each member finishes speaking, ask him or her to throw the Name Cube to determine the next speaker.

Record points on each group member's Points Chart for this portion of the session. Record the point for participation at the end of the session.

Discuss the One-Minute Rule

1. Describe the One-Minute Rule. Say:

> Let's pretend that you're in a group of kids talking at school, and one of you wants to enter the conversation. One mistake that many people make is to barge in, interrupting the discussion and making the other people upset. Sometimes shy people just stand next to the group, waiting to be invited in. Here's the proactive thing to do: Wait and listen for one minute before you speak so you have time to hear what the topic is, then say something that fits the subject when there is a pause.

2. Ask the group to be aware of this One-Minute Rule during the session—to point out when others are doing a good job waiting for that pause.

Discuss Reciprocity

1. Explain what *reciprocity* means and how it applies to conversations. Say:

> How does it work when one person in a conversation does all the talking? Or when someone insists on talking just about what interests him or her? *(Acknowledge responses.)* A reciprocal conversation is one that goes back and forth, that involves give and take.

> *Draw a reciprocal conversation on the board. (Stick figures are fine.)*

2. Continue:

> When a group of people are talking, everyone listens to the speaker, and everyone responds on the topic, taking turns. It can be fine to shift to a different topic if you can see a connection. For example, if the conversation is about the beach, you might talk about your vacation in the mountains. Or if the topic is dogs, you might talk about your own pets. It's also OK to change the subject completely, but only if all members of the group have had their say and the conversation has fizzled out.

Discuss Conversation Builders and Busters

1. Write the headings "Conversation Builders" and "Conversation Busters" on the board. Ask, "What do you need to do to have a good conversation?" Have the group make suggestions: listening while the other person talks, making eye contact, staying on topic. Next, ask a volunteer to come up to the board and draw a picture of a good conversation under

the "Conversation Builders" heading. As the group offers suggestions, have the volunteer add to the picture.

> *For example, they could draw big ears for listening, big eyes for eye contact, a smile, or word bubbles that show a consistent topic (e.g., soccer/soccer).*

2. Repeat the process under the "Conversation Busters" heading. Ask, "What do people do or say that interferes with conversation?" Some possible ideas include talking at the same time, interrupting, looking away from the speaker, changing the subject abruptly, and doing something else while the other person is speaking.

> *A volunteer could draw two heads, each with a talk bubble, illustrating talking at the same time or talking about different subjects, or two heads pointed in opposite directions to illustrate not listening.*

Discuss and Demonstrate the Power of Questions

1. Show the group the beach ball. Say:

> It's often easiest to enter a conversation by asking a question. There are six words on this ball: *who, what, when, where, why,* and *how.* These are the main words we use to start a question. Let's practice. What's a good topic to have a conversation about? Think of something that you all might have in common to discuss or a general enough topic that anyone could talk about. Maybe it could be a video game, somewhere you'd like to visit, or sports you like to play or watch.

2. Explain that each group member will have a turn catching the ball and asking a question on the topic, starting with the word facing the person as he or she catches the ball. Let the group know that it's important to make eye contact and get the other person's attention before asking the question.

3. Decide together on a topic and throw the ball to a participant to begin. The person holding the ball asks a question, then tosses it to another group member, who answers. That person then asks another question on the same topic. The game continues for a few rounds, with conversations on different topics, as time allows.

> *Remind group members to make and receive eye contact and ask the question BEFORE they throw the ball. If they throw the ball without first making eye contact and asking a question, have them repeat the process until it is done correctly.*

Discuss Steps in Good Conversation

Show a poster illustrating the steps needed for good communication. Say, for example, "Let's suppose two kids are starting an activity in PE class, and you would like to join in. Let's look at a poster of the steps you might take to be successful."

Steps in Good Conversation

1. Look at the person who is talking and maintain eye contact.

2. Make sure that your body language says, "I'm interested and listening."

3. Use the One-Minute Rule. Look and listen for a time when you can say something without interrupting someone. Wait for that pause!

4. Listen and note the topic being discussed.

5. Decide what you would like to say that is on topic.

6. Smile and speak in a normal volume.

7. If you are not sure what to say, ask a question on the topic. Start a good question with one of these words: *who, what, when, where, why,* and *how.*

8. Think about your personal space and the other person's. Stand at an appropriate distance. Remember the Elbow-Room Rule.

9. Be positive instead of negative (for example, say, "I like spaghetti" instead of "Soup tastes horrible!").

10. Remember to look for others' verbal and nonverbal cues.

Free Play/Behavioral Rehearsal

Provide the group with a selection of age-appropriate toys, games, or other activities to choose from that encourage joint play and follow the procedure described in Session 1.1 for choosing play partners and facilitating free play.

Relaxation/Self-Regulation

1. This week's relaxation is a visualization called "An Imagination Walk."* Ask the group to suggest places they would like to go in their imagination, then tell a story about the places they select. As the sample story illustrates, it takes a bit of creativity to think of a story intertwining the places, but the approach can be very effective.

   If participants say they want to go to a family member's home or someplace else you do not know, you can tell them that they can see that special place in their imagination and you will tell the story from your imagination.

---

*Thanks to our colleague Karan Lamb, PsyD, for this idea.

2. Tell group members to get into a comfortable position in their seats or stretch out on the floor and close their eyes. Remind them to use good control of their bodies as they listen to a story about the places they want to go in their imaginations. Read the following:

   ▶ Take a deep breath and hold it until the count of five: 1, 2, 3, 4, and 5. Slowly breathe out.

   ▶ You are going to imagine walking out of the room and down a long hallway. As you walk down the long hallway, you will pull your shoulders back and take some more deep breaths.

   ▶ As you walk, you will leave all of your worries and frustrations behind you. In your imagination, open a door at the end of the hallway and . . .

3. At this point, begin to tell the story incorporating the places the group told you about. Make the descriptors as detailed as possible, including the sensory aspects of touch, smell, taste, hearing, and vision.

4. After the story, return the group to the room:

   ▶ Go back to that door that we opened to start our imagination walk. Open it, and walk down the hallway and back in to this room.

   ▶ Slowly open your eyes. You are back here.

5. Invite comments on how it felt to go on the imagination walk as time allows.

Sample Imagination Walk

This sample imagination walk is for children up to about age 9. Replace ideas with age-appropriate interests for older group members.

Today, you have said you would like to take an imagination walk through a world made of Lego blocks, a race track, and outer space. Get your body comfortable, listen to the words of the story, and let's go on an imagination walk.

Close your eyes and pretend you are walking out the room and down a long hallway. As you walk down the long hallway, you will pull your shoulders back and take some deep breaths. You will leave all of your worries and frustrations behind. In your imagination, open a door at the end of the hallway. When you open that door, you will see a magnificent world made of Legos. Look around at all the colors. The trees are made of brown and green Legos and the road that you are walking on is made of black and gold Legos. As you walk into this Lego world, take some deep breaths, clear your mind, and think of what you would like to build. You can reach for any size and color of Legos. You may decide to start building a car. With every reach for a Lego, you feel more and more relaxed. As you put the last Lego on your car, you can hear the engine start. Open the door to the car and become the driver. Think of how fast you want the car to go. Will it speed to the race track, or will it go slow to look at the other creations in this Legos world? Remember you have control of this car.

Once you get to the race track, you will join the other cars zipping along. Look around. What colors do you see? Are there any cars just like yours? Start to go around the race track. Maybe you will also be able to smell your favorite food in the air. At this special race track, they sell ice cream. Take some deep breaths and enjoy this time on the race track with your special car. As you drive, you will go around and around. You will start to go faster and faster and leave all of your frustrations far behind you. Once your car is going fast enough, push the turbo-booster and start to fly off the ground and head toward outer space.

You will be the one in charge of piloting your vehicle toward outer space. You will go through the clouds. Remember to put on your sunglasses to deflect the sun rays. Keep going, and soon you will go past Earth's atmosphere and head into space. Whoa! You start to feel like you are floating out of your seat. Take a deep breath and fill your body with healthy oxygen that will keep you in control. You can decide if you want to see a planet up close or just continue flying. Enjoy your ride. Notice how calm and in control you feel. Now we are going to prepare to return to Earth. Buckle up your seat belt; push the important buttons on the dashboard to start the descent, and as you return, remind yourself that you can handle anything that comes your way. Use good control to slow down your vehicle and take it for a landing.

Say good-bye to this awesome car that has taken us to a race track and outer space. Walk back to the door that took you to the Legos world, open the door, walk down the hallway, and you are back in the room. Wow! We had an adventure.

Leadership Award

Select a group member to receive the Leadership Award and provide praise for what the person did well.

Generalization: Resilience Builder Assignment

Give each participant a copy of the Resilience Builder Assignment and answer any questions. Remind the group that we learn through making mistakes. What counts is that we become more self-aware and, through practice, change the behaviors that are not helpful.

Parent Component

Provide copies of the parent letter and have group members put the letter and the Resilience Builder Assignment in their notebooks.

Conversation Builders and Conversation Busters

Name _____ Date _____

Check each statement that applied to you this past week, then describe one thing you did to build and one thing you did to bust a conversation.

Things I Did to Build Conversation

☐ I smiled and looked friendly when I spoke.

☐ I used the One-Minute Rule and waited for a pause to join a conversation.

☐ I looked at people directly when they spoke and looked attentive by maintaining eye contact.

☐ I was positive when I spoke to the other person.

☐ I listened quietly when someone was talking.

☐ I asked questions starting with these words: *what, when, where, how, why,* or *who.*

☐ I stayed on the topic we were discussing.

☐ I was aware that my body showed that I was listening and interested.

☐ I was aware of the tone and volume of my voice.

☐ I changed the topic but was aware of how it connected to the topic we were talking about.

Things I Did to Bust Conversation

☐ I changed the topic when someone was talking.

☐ I didn't speak or respond.

☐ I was negative, was rude, or complained.

☐ I interrupted someone while he or she spoke.

☐ I recognized I was busting the conversation when _____.

☐ I didn't listen when someone else was talking.

☐ I barged into a conversation.

☐ I said something mean to someone to hurt his or her feelings.

☐ I realized too late that I busted the conversation.

☐ I only wanted to talk about what I was interested in.

From *Resilience Builder Program for Children and Adolescents,* © 2011 by M. K. Alvord, B. Zucker, & J. J. Grados, Champaign, IL: Research Press (800-519-2707, www.researchpress.com).

Give an example of one time when you initiated or kept a conversation going. How did you do that?

_____

_____

_____

_____

Give an example of one time that you busted a conversation. What did you do?

_____

_____

_____

_____

Initiating and Maintaining Conversations

Dear Parents:

This week's session is devoted to initiating and maintaining conversations. The group learns about the concept of *reciprocity,* or give and take, and how it applies to conversations. We will talk about conversation builders and conversation busters and learn about the One-Minute Rule, which requires listening for a minute before entering a conversation to be sure that what you say is on topic. Here are some conversation steps you can encourage at home.

Steps in Good Conversation

1. Look at the person who is talking and maintain eye contact.

2. Make sure that your body language says, "I'm interested and listening."

3. Use the One-Minute Rule. Look and listen for a time when you can say something without interrupting someone. Wait for that pause!

4. Listen and note the topic being discussed.

5. Decide what you would like to say that is on topic.

6. Smile and speak in a normal volume.

7. If you are not sure what to say, ask a question on the topic. Start a good question with one of these words: *who, what, when, where, why,* and *how.*

8. Think about your personal space and theirs. Stand at an appropriate distance. Remember the Elbow-Room Rule.

9. Be positive instead of negative (for example, say, "I like spaghetti" instead of "Soup tastes horrible!").

10. Remember to look for others' verbal and nonverbal cues.

Resilience Builder Assignment: Conversation Builders and Conversation Busters

This session's assignment asks your child to observe communications and check off the things he or she does to build and bust conversations. There are also spaces to describe a situation in which your child initiated or kept a conversation going and one in which he or she did something to interrupt it. Please ask your child about the assignment and provide help if needed. Your child might have a favorite relaxation exercise to share with you.

Please continue using the Compliment Basket and conducting family meetings as you are able. Thank you for your continued involvement!

Sincerely,

Program Leader

1.7

Being a Good Sport: Team Play

PURPOSE

Being a good sport is essential to being accepted as a teammate and as a potential friend. Whether on a sports team, participating in soccer or another activity, or playing in the neighborhood, the real winners are those who can behave positively and respectfully while maintaining good self-control. This session introduces the many skills required to be a good sport: playing fair, showing good teamwork, following rules and instructions, encouraging and complimenting others, controlling frustration and disappointment, trying your best, and being a good winner and good loser.

GOALS

To identify and discuss the elements necessary for successfully playing a sport or other team game

To discuss common frustrations and obstacles in the way of a successful and enjoyable interaction

To practice being a good sport while playing a team game

To practice a relaxation/self-regulation technique

MATERIALS

Chalkboard or dry erase board and marker

Program Notebooks (brought by group members)

Individual Points Charts

Name Cube

Watch, clock, or timer that counts seconds

Index cards (with Charades ideas written on them)

Copies of the following:

> Leadership Award (Appendix C)
>
> Resilience Builder Assignment 1.7
>
> Parent Letter 1.7

If you are conducting Session 1.8, the optional field trip, be sure you have signed permission forms from parents. Also provide a clear description of the activity and directions for getting to the site along with the usual parent letter.

PROCEDURE

Individual Greeting

Conduct the individual greetings, as described in Session 1.1. Require group members to demonstrate sustained eye contact and a confident greeting to enter the room.

Review Success Journal and Resilience Builder Assignment

Have each group member discuss his or her individual goal and Success Journal entry and experiences completing the Resilience Builder Assignment. When each participant finishes speaking, ask him or her to throw the Name Cube to determine the next speaker.

> *Record points on each group member's Points Chart for this portion of the session. Record the point for participation at the end of the session.*

Discuss Being a Good Sport

1. Write "Being a Good Sport" on the board. Ask the group to think about what this has meant to them when they've been members of a club or team and what it means to them now. Ask, "What are some examples of good sport behavior?"

Suggestions include encouraging your teammates, trying your best, listening to a coach's or teammates' ideas, and continuing to play even when you're frustrated, without giving up or losing control. Write responses on the board.

2. Summarize by saying:

   Being a good sport is important both when you're doing well or when your team wins and when you play poorly or your team loses. Even elite athletes have to deal with frequent disappointment and losses.

3. Ask, "What are some examples of being a bad sport?"

   The group may mention sports greats who have been sore losers or, worse yet, who have thrown balls, punches, rackets, and other equipment—or they may describe more personal experiences.

4. Talk about specific ways teammates can encourage each other. Say:

   What might you say or do when a player is feeling great about his or her perform-ance? *(Offer a high-five or pat on the back.)* What might you say or do when a team-mate is struggling or getting upset? *(Say, "Good try" or "Don't worry—you have more turns.")* What are some other ideas?

5. Talk about how to handle frustration when you perform poorly. Say, "Suppose you miss the ball or strike out. How can you handle it? What self-talk will make it possible to keep playing with a good attitude?"

Sample Positive Self-Talk

I could practice more and get better.

I can try that again.

I like to play this game; I just missed this time.

Everyone misses sometimes, even the pros.

I can handle this frustration.

I can take a deep breath and calm myself.

6. Emphasize that being a good sport helps to further social relationships. Say:

   When you're a good sport, it's easier to make and keep friends. Why? *(Acknowledge responses, then summarize.)* It turns people off when you get mad or lose control, and it can be annoying when you're constantly making negative statements. On the other hand, when you stay calm and act in a positive and encouraging way, other people like to play with you and be on your team. The focus should be on doing your best and having fun.

7. With the group, generate ideas for being a good sport if you do well and if you don't do as well as you expect or lose. Following are some examples.

    If You Do Well

    Smile and always pay attention to whomever you are playing with.

    Feel good inside and take pride that you are doing well, without bragging or saying something hurtful.

    Smile, make good eye contact, and thank someone who says congratulations to you.

    Say something nice to the other person.

    Shake someone's hand.

    If You Don't Do Well

    It is OK to be sad, frustrated, or mad, but it is not OK to throw a fit or act unkind.

    Be happy because your friend won. Next time, you might win.

    If you are losing, stay calm and continue to play.

    Talk to others in a quiet voice.

    Say something nice to the person who is winning.

    Encourage other players.

    Be cooperative.

Free Play/Behavioral Rehearsal

Demonstrating being a good sport in a team play situation is the specific goal of this session's free play/behavioral rehearsal.

Charades

Charades works well to practice good teamwork because it emphasizes the skills of cooperation and paying close attention to nonverbal cues. The challenge is to help participants sustain their attention and control their frustrations when they can't convey their meaning or are unable to guess the right answer.

1. Divide the group into two teams and explain that they will be playing Charades. One team will play the game while the other watches. Have the group decide which team starts first. Since time is limited, suggest two categories, one per team, depending on age and interests of the group. Feel free to create your own Charades ideas for movies, books, electronic games, songs, television shows, or other categories meaningful to your group.

2. Explain:

> In Charades, a player acts out a word or words that fit in a specific category. For example, if the category is movies, you might get a slip of paper that says "Batman." You then have to let everyone know that it is a movie and then give your team members clues so they can guess what movie it is.

3. Each team decides the order of players. (Perhaps they can do it by reverse alphabetical order.) The player chosen pantomimes the word or phrase he or she has been given, while the other team members attempt to guess. Here are some common clues:

   ▶ To indicate a book, pretend to read a book.

   ▶ To indicate a song, pretend to sing.

   ▶ To indicate a movie, pretend to crank an old movie camera.

   ▶ To indicate a video game, move your thumbs as if on a controller.

   ▶ To indicate a television show, draw a rectangle in the air to outline a TV screen.

   ▶ To indicate the number of words, hold up that many fingers. (Then hold up one finger before pantomiming the first word, two fingers before the second, and so on.)

   ▶ To pantomime a word that rhymes with the word you want players to guess, first tug on your ear to say, "Sounds like."

4. The player has two minutes to act out the idea while teammates try to guess. If it is not guessed within that time, it is the other team's turn. If it is guessed, another member on the same team goes.

5. Play continues until the available time is up.

   Keep track of the correct guesses of each team. The team with the most correct guesses is the winner.

Relaxation/Self-Regulation

1. This week's relaxation continues teaching progressive muscle relaxation and focuses on a few more muscle groups. Ask the group members to get into a comfortable position in their seats and close their eyes. Read the following:

   ▶ Take a deep breath and hold it until the count of five: 1, 2, 3, 4, and 5. Slowly and quietly breathe out.

   ▶ We are going to tense a few muscle groups. I want you to pay attention to the difference in how the muscles feel when they are tight and tense versus when they are loose and relaxed.

▶ As your body gets more relaxed, I want you to notice how it feels when all your muscles are relaxed and you feel calm. How does calm feel to you?

▶ Start by making a tight fist with your right hand. Hold it until it almost hurts. Tighter, tighter, hold it, hold it. Now slowly relax. Notice how it feels. You might feel tingling or coolness or warmth, or something else.

▶ Now we are going to tighten the left fist. Pretend you are squeezing something really, really hard. Hold it, hold it, hold it. Now slowly let the fist go back to its normal position. Notice the way if feels when it's tense and when it's relaxed.

▶ Bring your chin to touch your chest. You might feel a tension in the back of your neck. Slowly bring your head upright.

▶ Now bring your head to rest on your right shoulder. You might feel it tense or even hurt on the left side of your neck. The tighter the muscles, the more uncomfortable it is. Hold it. Hold it. Slowly bring your head up.

▶ Now bring your head to rest on your left shoulder. You might feel it tense or even hurt on the right side of your neck. The tighter the muscles, the more uncomfortable it is. Hold it. Hold it. Slowly bring your head up.

▶ Now we will move up to your face. Raise your eyebrows and tighten your forehead. Hold it. Hold it. Slowly relax the muscles and bring your eyebrows to their resting position.

▶ Now frown, squeezing your eyebrows together. You might not always notice, but you might be doing this when you are upset or angry. Hold it tight. Slowly relax. Again, notice how your body feels as it gets more relaxed.

▶ Take a deep breath in again. Hold it to the count of five: 1, 2, 3, 4, and 5. Slowly, very slowly breathe out.

▶ Now shake your head a little *(pause)*, wiggle your fingers *(pause)*, and slowly open your eyes.

2. Ask, "How did that feel? What part of your body was the most tense? What were the sensations you had when you relaxed the muscles?"

Leadership Award

Select a group member to receive the Leadership Award and provide praise for what the person did well.

Generalization: Resilience Builder Assignment

Give each group member a copy of the Resilience Builder Assignment for the next session. Go over the assignment and answer any questions.

Parent Component

Give each participant a copy of the parent letter for the session. Have participants place the letter and Resilience Builder Assignment in the appropriate sections of their notebooks.

Being a Good Sport: Team Play

Name _____ **Date** _____

Think of two games or activities you played recently. Write "video game," "board game," "soccer," "shooting baskets," or whatever you were doing on the activity line. Check the statements that were true about your behavior for that game or activity. Add any comments you might have.

Game/Activity 1 _____

☐ I took the initiative to say good things to the other players.

☐ I didn't brag.

☐ I used leadership skills, such as

_____.

☐ I shook my opponent's hand.

☐ I used only nice words.

☐ I got along with my team.

☐ I passed the ball and wasn't a ball hog.

☐ I offered to help someone else.

☐ I looked at people directly when they spoke.

☐ I said something nice to someone.

☐ I complimented someone.

☐ I said, "Good job."

☐ I said, "Good shot" or "Good move."

☐ I listened quietly when someone spoke.

☐ I followed the rules.

☐ I spoke with a normal voice tone and volume.

☐ I got frustrated and stayed calm.

☐ I stayed in control of myself.

☐ I cooperated.

☐ I handled being disappointed or losing well.

☐ I didn't quit.

☐ I used positive self-talk.

Comments:

_____

_____

_____

Game/Activity 2 _____

- ☐ I took the initiative to say good things to the other players.
- ☐ I didn't brag.
- ☐ I used leadership skills, such as

  _____.

- ☐ I shook my opponent's hand.
- ☐ I used only nice words.
- ☐ I got along with my team.
- ☐ I passed the ball and wasn't a ball hog.
- ☐ I offered to help someone else.
- ☐ I looked at people directly when they spoke.
- ☐ I said something nice to someone.
- ☐ I complimented someone.

- ☐ I said, "Good job."
- ☐ I said, "Good shot" or "Good move."
- ☐ I listened quietly when someone spoke.
- ☐ I followed the rules.
- ☐ I spoke with a normal voice tone and volume.
- ☐ I got frustrated and stayed calm.
- ☐ I stayed in control of myself.
- ☐ I cooperated.
- ☐ I handled being disappointed or losing well.
- ☐ I didn't quit.
- ☐ I used positive self-talk.

Comments:

_____

_____

_____

Being a Good Sport: Team Play

Dear Parents:

In this week's session, we focus on being a good sport. Your child may describe it in concrete terms, such as "playing fair" or "not cheating." In addition to playing fair, other parts of being a good sport include having respect for others, taking pride in accomplishments, using self-control, making good decisions, and dealing well with winning and losing.

We talk about what it means to be a good sport when you are a member of a team: listening to the coach, following the coach's instruction, working with and encouraging teammates, and sticking with the game until the end with a positive attitude. We also talk about what being a good sport means at school, at home, while playing games, and with friends.

Being a good sport is demonstrated through both words and actions. Here are some examples of verbal and nonverbal expressions of being a good sport.

If You Do Well

► Smile and always pay attention to the person you are playing with.

► Feel good inside and take pride that you are doing well, without bragging or saying something hurtful.

► Smile, make good eye contact, and thank someone who says congratulations to you.

► Say something nice to the other person.

► Shake someone's hand.

If You Don't Do Well

► It is OK to be sad, frustrated, or mad, but it is not OK to throw a fit or act unkind.

► Be happy because your friend won. Next time, you might win.

► If you are losing, stay calm and continue to play.

► Talk to others in a quiet voice.

► Say something nice to the person who is winning.

► Encourage other players.

► Be cooperative.

Children learn about being a good sport from observing the reactions of parents, teachers, and coaches. They often look for approval or disapproval. A lack of feedback from adults can be misinterpreted by a child as meaning the child must have done something wrong. At home, work on using praise for both winning and losing graciously.

Resilience Builder Assignment: Being a Good Sport—Team Play

This session's assignment involves having your child think about two recent activities or games and check off "good sport" behaviors. Please ask your child to tell you about the assignment and provide help if asked. If you are able, continue practicing relaxation, using the Compliment Basket, and conducting family meetings.

Sincerely,

Program Leader

Parent Letter 1.7 (p. 2 of 2)

1.8

Being a Good Sport: Field Trip

PURPOSE

Practicing skills correctly results in incorporating those skills into one's daily behavior and generalizing them to multiple settings. This field trip strengthens, in a community setting, the skills associated with being a good sport previously discussed: teamwork, fair play, following rules and instructions, encouraging and complimenting others, handling frustration and disappointment, trying one's best, and being a good winner and a good loser. In addition, the field trip allows practice of positive interaction with adults who work in these community settings and handling of one's behavior in a public setting.

> *The example described is for an optional bowling field trip. Other outings may be appropriate for your circumstances. Reservations at a bowling alley or another suitable recreational setting are necessary. Depending on the size and needs of the group, consider asking volunteer parents to act as scorekeepers.*

GOALS

To apply meeting and greeting skills with adults who work in the community

To discuss the rules of the game, to follow directions, and to respect the rules of the setting

To review and practice the skills of being a good sport as it applies within the community

To examine and manage the frustrations that come along with playing a game in the community

MATERIALS

Individual Points Charts

Copies of the following:

>Leadership Award (Appendix C)

>Good Sport Certificate (Appendix C)

>Resilience Builder Assignment 1.8

>Parent Letter 1.8

Group members do not generally bring their notebooks and assignments to this session. Resilience Builder Assignment and Success Journal entries are reviewed at the following session.

PROCEDURE

Individual Greeting

1. As group members arrive at the bowling alley, greet them and instruct them to wait until all members arrive. Encourage them to greet one another as each arrives. After all are present, explain the procedures of the facility: where they pick up equipment, how they pay, and where they go once they have their equipment.

   Payment is made by the group member either before or after the game, as directed by the facility.

2. Next, go to the front desk and have each group member make eye contact with the attendant and ask for shoes or other equipment, as appropriate. This provides direct practice of waiting until the attendant is available to talk and then asking politely and in a friendly tone for what is needed.

3. Throughout this process, guide and prompt group members as necessary. Compliment them in turn with specific feedback on what they did well. For example, say, "I like the way Jack waited until the attendant was finished helping the teenager."

Discuss Being a Good Sport in the Setting

1. Before choosing teams, spend a few moments reviewing what makes a good sport and a good team player. First review the elements of being a good sport in the specific community setting. Say, for example:

It's great that we can all be here today. Before we begin to play, we need to show our best manners to the staff who work here by making eye contact before we ask for something and making sure that they were not speaking with someone else or busy at the moment. During our play, we might need someone to clear a pin or help with something else, so being polite, with a smile and friendly tone, is essential. We're here to have fun and work as teams, supporting our teammates. How can we do that?

Sample responses include cheering one another on, encouraging a teammate who is frustrated by saying, "Good try," giving someone a high-five, and being sure to keep your attention focused on the person who is bowling.

2. Discuss handling frustration and disappointment. Explain:

    Remember that being a good sport applies both when you're doing well and your team wins, and when you play poorly or your team loses. You will all probably get frustrated or disappointed at some time when you play today. What are some helpful ways of handling yourself?

    Review constructive ways to handle the frustrations of not getting as many pins down as you'd like, getting a gutter ball, or having a lower score than someone else. Point out that the goal today is to do your best and have fun!

    Strategies for Dealing with Frustration

    Saying what you are frustrated about to see what, if anything, can be done about it

    Reminding yourself that you are here to have fun and can keep trying to do your best

    Telling yourself that no one can have a perfect score or do well all the time

    Taking a few deep breaths

    Practicing positive self-talk

3. Remind the group that being a good sport is not only about what we say but also what we communicate nonverbally (facial expressions, body posture). Watching and smiling will communicate interest, whereas eye rolling, walking away, yawning, and other negative behaviors communicate a lack of interest.

Review Points Earning

Explain:

Today you can earn five points on your Points Chart, but it's for slightly different behavior. You can earn one point for following the rules, one point for showing good manners with the facility staff, one point for encouraging others and maintaining a positive attitude, one point for good self-control and persistence with the activity, and one point for complimenting others throughout the game and at the end.

Free Play/Behavioral Rehearsal

1. Divide the group into two teams. Have each group decide which player will go first, next, and so forth. (They could determine this by going in reverse alphabetical order or by who arrived first.)

2. Provide the structure for the activity: Review the rules of the game and scoring. Decide where group members will wait and watch while their teammates take their turns. It is beneficial to have just one participant bowl at a time, alternating teams, so that it's easier to focus on each player, and to have the person whose turn is next sit closest to the lane. As each takes a turn, group members can shift their seats so that the one who has had his or her turn sits in the spot farthest from the lane.

3. Decide who will keep score—yourself, a parent volunteer, or one of the group members.

4. Conduct the activity. As play proceeds, the challenge is to help group members sustain their attention while watching the others play and to control their disappointment when they don't do as well as they would like. Watch for opportunities to praise appropriate behavior and correct less desirable actions.

> *There is no formal relaxation exercise for this activity. However, a reminder to the group to count and breathe if they are starting to feel frustrated might be helpful, especially if self-regulation (becoming overly excited or upset) is an obstacle.*

Leadership Award and Good Sport Certificates

Select a group member to receive the Leadership Award and provide praise for what the group member did well. In addition, before leaving the setting, give each group member a Good Sport Certificate and convey at least one thing that group member did well.

Generalization: Resilience Builder Assignment

Show group members a copy of the Resilience Builder Assignment and briefly explain and answer any questions. Explain that you will be giving a copy to their parents when they arrive.

Parent Component

Give parents a copy of the Resilience Builder Assignment and parent letter when they pick up their child. Encourage them to help their child complete the assignment if necessary.

> *You can use this opportunity to thank parents personally for supporting their child in learning the program skills.*

Being a Good Sport: Field Trip

Name _____ **Date** _____

Please state three ways in which you were a good sport during our field trip.

1. _____

2. _____

3. _____

We all get frustrated or feel disappointed sometimes. Describe any negative emotions you felt during our field trip. How did you handle them?

_____

_____

What were some thoughts you had about how you were doing during the game or about a team-mate or something else that bothered you? What was your self-talk?

_____

_____

How did you handle those negative feelings? Did your self-talk help you stay calm?

_____

_____

What behaviors for being a good sport did you show during school or during other activities in the past two weeks? What was your self-talk? Who were you with?

_____

_____

_____

Being a Good Sport: Field Trip

Dear Parents:

While on our field trip for this session, we focus on *being a good* sport and *team play.* We emphasize showing respect for others, taking pride in accomplishments, using self-control, sticking with the game until the end with a positive attitude, making good decisions, and dealing graciously with winning and losing.

Resilience Builder: Being a Good Sport—Field Trip

This session's assignment asks your child to evaluate his or her thoughts, feelings, and behavior during the field trip. Please discuss your child's experience, focusing on what your child found positive in his or her own behavior and the behavior of others. As time allows, please also practice relaxation exercises this week, perhaps with a focus on using some of the strategies when dealing with frustration or disappointment.

Sincerely,

Program Leader

Optimistic Thinking

PURPOSE

An optimistic outlook leads to greater happiness and more successful social interactions.*
This session teaches the difference between pessimistic and optimistic thinking and shows
group members ways to replace pessimistic thoughts with optimistic, yet realistic, ones. It also
defines three aspects of thinking optimistically about a problem.

GOALS

To explain and discuss the concepts of optimism versus pessimism

To help group members learn three healthy, optimistic ways to think about problems

To explain that group members can change their negative thoughts to positive, realistic
thoughts through self-talk

To reinforce the concept that we have the power to choose how we react to a situation
and act in a proactive way, thus influencing outcomes

To practice a relaxation/self-regulation technique

*Procedures in this session are based generally on the work of Seligman (1995).

MATERIALS

Chalkboard or dry erase board and marker

Program Notebooks (brought by group members)

Individual Points Charts

Name Cube

A glass of water, half full

One index card and pencil for each group member

Toys and games for free play

Copies of the following:

> Leadership Award (Appendix C)
>
> Resilience Builder Assignment 1.9
>
> Parent Letter 1.9

PROCEDURE

Individual Greeting

Conduct the individual greetings, as described in Session 1.1. Require participants to demonstrate sustained eye contact and a confident greeting to enter the room.

Review Success Journal and Resilience Builder Assignment

> *If you went on the optional field trip (Session 1.8), review the Resilience Builder Assignments for it and for Session 1.7.*

Have each group member discuss his or her individual goal and Success Journal entry and experiences completing the Resilience Builder Assignment. When each participant finishes speaking, ask him or her to throw the Name Cube to determine the next speaker.

> *Record points on each participant's Points Chart for this portion of the session. Record the point for participation at the end of the session.*

Discuss Optimism Versus Pessimism

1. Facilitate a short discussion of positive thinking, or self-talk, and optimism. Review self-talk as what we say to ourselves in our minds: For example, we might have positive self-talk and say to ourselves, "This is fun," or we might have negative self-talk and say to

ourselves, "I'll never be able to do this." Ask, "What is optimism? What is our self-talk when we are optimistic?"

Write responses on the board.

2. Distinguish between optimism and pessimism:

> Let's look at an example to better understand optimism. Let's say that you and a friend have to wait in a rather lengthy line for tickets to a movie. If you are optimistic, you might think, "Oh, well, we will have time to talk together while we wait" or "These lines happen sometimes—it must be a good movie since so many people are here to see it!" Pessimistic thinking is a negative way of thinking about things. If you are pessimistic, you might think, "This line is so long we'll miss the beginning of the movie and that will spoil the whole day."

3. Discuss the idea that there are three ways of thinking about problems that determine if you are being optimistic or pessimistic.

   ▶ First, remember that the problem is *temporary* rather than permanent. That is, the problem is not going to last forever. When a classmate refuses your invitation, that doesn't mean you'll never have a friend.

   ▶ Second, look at the problem as *specific,* rather than as pervasive or global. If you miss one goal in a soccer game, that means that you missed this one goal, not that you're terrible at all sports.

   ▶ Third, be realistic about who is *responsible* for the problem. You should take responsibility if you made a mistake, but not every problem will be your fault. If you do make a mistake, it's important to think of it as limited to a specific situation or action. Your self-talk could be "I did poorly because I didn't do the homework" instead of "I'm stupid."

4. Discuss how it feels when one thinks in a positive and negative manner. Say:

> When your self-talk is negative, a problem seems huge and permanent, which can make you feel anxious and down. When you think positively, you see the problem in a realistic way—that it's a temporary and specific situation. That gives you a feeling of hopefulness because you realize that there are ways you can fix the problem or put it in perspective (by remembering what you're grateful for, for example).

5. Point out that after you have accurately and realistically explained the cause of a problem, it's critical that you think optimistically, know that you can have some control over what happens next, and act in a proactive way. If you change how you react or what you do, you can influence what happens to you. In other words, you are not passive, and therefore you are not helpless.

Discuss Catching Negative Self-Talk

1. Point out that we can be aware of and change our thinking patterns. Explain:

   > Did you know that if you choose to think in a positive way, you can actually "catch" negative thinking and replace it with thoughts that are better for you? This kind of commitment to thinking in a positive way is called the "glass is half-full" way of thinking.

2. Demonstrate, using the glass of water. Say:

   > Raise your hand if you think this glass is half-full. How many people think this glass is half-empty? *(Acknowledge both responses.)* Guess what—you are all correct! The glass is either half-full *or* half-empty, depending on how you choose to look at it. So, when something happens, you can actually think about it in different ways.

   > The great thing about *choosing* to think in a positive but realistic way is that you can actually make yourself feel better. When negative self-talk sets in, you can catch it and replace it. When you think more positively and feel better, you are also more likely to make better choices about how to behave at those times.

3. Discuss an example of catching a negative thought. Say:

   > Suppose you have saved $25 for a new handheld computer game you want to buy, and its price is $50. You find yourself thinking, "Oh, no! I am never going to be able to save that much. I just can't save, and everything is just too expensive!" Stop and ask yourself: What is another way to see the situation? You might tell yourself instead, "I've saved quite a bit of money and am halfway there!"

"Changing the Channel" Activity

1. Remind the group members that when you change your thinking, you also change how you feel. One easy way to practice changing your thinking is to imagine that you have a flat-screen TV in your mind and that you can change channels.

2. Instruct the group to close their eyes and think about a happy scene from their life. Have them picture themselves as part of that scene. Wait 10 to 20 seconds and have them open their eyes. Ask, "What was that like?" Encourage and acknowledge responses.

3. Tell group members to close their eyes again and this time think of a funny situation. Again, wait 10 to 20 seconds. Have the group members open their eyes and ask, "What did you think of, and how did you feel this time?" Encourage volunteers to share their thoughts and ask them how these thoughts made them feel. (If time allows, group members can also visualize scenes that make them proud or excited.)

4. Tell the group members next to close their eyes and picture a scene that makes them feel sadness or anger or frustration or another negative emotion. Ask them to change the

channel to either the happy or funny one. Say that when we learn to monitor our thinking, we can be aware of when we are being optimistic and when we are engaging in negative thinking. When our thinking is negative, we can catch our thoughts and replace them with more positive thoughts.

If time allows, have the group do the optional project described at the end of this session. The television and remote are a great visual reminder that group members can "change the channels" of their thinking when they choose.

Free Play/Behavioral Rehearsal

Provide the group with a selection of age-appropriate toys, games, or other activities to choose from that encourage joint play and follow the procedure described in Session 1.1 for choosing play partners and facilitating free play.

Relaxation/Self-Regulation

In this exercise, group members develop a mantra. Briefly, a mantra is a word or group of words thought to be capable of creating personal transformation. It has its roots in Eastern religions and traditions. In its simplest form, a mantra is a statement that we may repeat to ourselves to work toward improving ourselves.

1. Ask group members to think of something positive they can say to themselves ("I am good at art" "I am a great soccer player" "I have fun playing games even though I don't always win"). Explain that they will be asked to keep the mantra in their mind during the relaxation.

2. Tell the group to get into a comfortable position in their seats and close their eyes. Read the following script:

    ▶ Take a deep breath and hold it until the count of five: 1, 2, 3, 4, and 5.

    ▶ Now slowly breathe out. I want each of you to relax and think of your mantra. Focus on your breathing as you relax.

    ▶ Say your mantra to yourself in your mind several more times, slowly. *(Wait a minute before continuing.)*

    ▶ Now count in your mind with me from five to one, with each step feeling a little more relaxed and calm: 5, 4, 3, 2, and 1. Good. Now enjoy this relaxed state. You can take this feeling with you and use it at any time during the day that you need to feel calm, quiet, and relaxed.

    ▶ In a moment, I will count from one to five, and with each number you will feel a little more awake and alert. At the count of two, you will take a deep breath. At the count of three, you will blow it out. At the count of four, you will open your eyes. At the count of five, you will be ready for the rest of the day. *(Wait 15 to 20 seconds before continuing.)*

▶ Let's begin now. One, you are rested and relaxed. Two, you take in a breath. Three, you slowly blow it out through your mouth. Four, you open your eyes . . . and five.

3. Ask group members, "How did that feel?" If you wish, participants may share their mantras.

4. Give each member an index card and tell the group that they are now going to write down their mantra so that they will remember it throughout the week. Tell them to post their mantra where they will see it, and ask them to say it two times per day for the next week.

Leadership Award

Select a group member to receive the Leadership Award and provide praise for what the person did well.

Generalization: Resilience Builder Assignment

Give each group member a copy of the Resilience Builder Assignment for the next session. Go over the assignment and answer any questions.

Parent Component

Give participants a copy of the parent letter for the session. Have them place the letter and Resilience Builder Assignment in the appropriate sections of their notebooks.

OPTIONAL ACTIVITY: TELEVISION AND REMOTE CONTROL PROJECT

1. Before the session, prepare "televisions" for each member as follows: Open a manila folder flat and cut out a rectangular section in one side to form a screen. Save the rectangle to make a "remote." Close the folder in the typical fashion and staple it closed along two sides, leaving the tabbed edge open. Have available 8½ by 11–inch sheets of white paper to be inserted into the folder to represent the different channels.

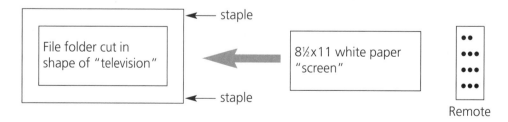

2. Tell the group, "Today we will make televisions and remote controls to remind us that we can choose to switch our thinking from negative to positive by 'changing the channel.'"

3. Give each group member three sheets of paper and markers to share. Have members draw a scene on one paper associated with a happy or calm or proud feeling. Ask them to identify the thoughts that correspond to the feeling. (They might do so using a thought bubble.) On another sheet of paper, ask them to draw a scene that reflects anger, worry, or some other strong negative feeling. Again, they are to write out a thought that corresponds to the feeling they chose. The third scene might be any feeling and corresponding thought of their choice.

4. Have group members design their remote controls and insert a scene into their pre-made television set.

5. Ask them to imagine the scene and feeling of one of their channels, then practice switching papers (channels) and imagining the new scene, with the feelings and thoughts that go along with it.

6. Give group members several other sheets of paper to take home and encourage them to work on additional drawings.

Optimistic Thinking

Name _____ **Date** _____

Describe a situation in which you were thinking in a negative way this week.

_____

_____

_____

What negative self-talk were you able to "catch"?

1. _____

2. _____

3. _____

How could you "change the channel" and replace each of these negative thoughts with positive and realistic thoughts?

Make sure the thoughts are:

► Temporary versus permanent (realize that it won't last forever)

► Specific versus global (focus on just this specific issue)

► Realistic about who is to blame (is it my responsibility to change something?)

My optimistic thoughts would be:

1. _____

2. _____

3. _____

After you have realistically explained the cause of a problem, think optimistically, know that you have some control over what happens next, and act in a proactive way.

Optimistic Thinking

Dear Parents:

Optimistic thinking contributes to a proactive stance in life and overall resilient functioning. Today's session focuses on optimistic thinking and how being optimistic and realistic allows us to live in a proactive way. We will learn that we can be optimistic (viewing the situation and seeing the glass as "half-full") or pessimistic (seeing the glass as "half-empty") and that it is up to us to choose how we will think. We also discuss imagining our thoughts as channels on a television and practice "changing the channel." Our self-talk—what we say to ourselves in our minds—influences how we feel, which in turn affects how we choose to behave.

Group members also learn three attributes of optimistic thinking in relation to problems:

1. We can realize that our problems are temporary, not permanent.

2. We can view our problems as being specific, not global and pervasive.

3. We can realistically assess what our part is and take responsibility for our actions but don't always blame ourselves or always blame others.

You can reinforce the skills of optimistic thinking and proactivity by helping your child be more realistic and gain perspective when facing a challenge. While acknowledging your child's feelings, encourage him or her to consider whether the situation is really as bad as it seems. You can also explain that, while your child may be very upset now, these feelings are temporary and will change. For example, you could say, "You have three more math problems—it won't take all night." Or you could say, "You can't control when the teacher will give you a test, but you can make sure you know the material by doing your homework and studying."

Resilience Builder Assignment: Optimistic Thinking

Group members identify negative thinking and substitute optimistic thoughts in this session's assignment. Each child is also asked to practice a mantra, or a short phrase we can say to ourselves to help us work on improving ourselves. Ask your child about the assignment and provide help if needed. And please practice a relaxation exercise together and continue using the Compliment Basket and conducting family meetings as you are able.

Sincerely,

Program Leader

Solving Friendship Problems

PURPOSE

Problem-solving skills contribute significantly to one's mental flexibility and ability to cope with life's challenges. They are also key to enhancing our relationships with others. This session focuses on being proactive in solving problems and perceiving problems as challenges to be overcome, rather than as insurmountable hurdles. By improving mental flexibility through the use of problem-solving skills, group members will be more prepared to deal with the challenges that friendships often present.

GOALS

To explain and discuss the concept of problem solving with a breakdown of the steps toward resolving interpersonal conflicts

To understand the connection between problem-solving skills and friendships

To reinforce a proactive rather than a reactive stance to addressing challenges and support the idea that one can influence what happens

To practice a relaxation/self-regulation exercise

MATERIALS

Chalkboard or dry erase board and markers

Program Notebooks (brought by group members)

Individual Points Charts

Name Cube

Toys and games for free play

Copies of the following:

Friendship Situations (copied and cut apart)

Leadership Award (Appendix C)

Resilience Builder Assignment 1.10

Parent Letter 1.10

*Before the session, create a **Problem-Solving Steps** poster.*

PROCEDURE

Individual Greeting

Conduct the individual greetings, as described in Session 1.1. Require participants to demonstrate sustained eye contact and a confident greeting to enter the room.

Review Success Journal and Resilience Builder Assignment

Have each group member discuss his or her individual goal and Success Journal entry and experiences completing the Resilience Builder Assignment. When each member finishes speaking, ask him or her to throw the Name Cube to determine the next speaker.

> *Record points on each group member's Points Chart for this portion of the session. Record the point for participation at the end of the session.*

Discuss and Demonstrate Problem Solving

1. Write "Problem Solving" on the board and ask group members, "What do you think problem solving means?" Acknowledge and record responses. Ask, "What kinds of problems can you think of that people solve? *(Math problems, problems in relationships, car problems, etc.).* Explain:

Problem solving is about finding solutions to challenges. In math, for example, it could be the process that you undertake to find the answer to a number problem. In life, there are many kinds of problems that we solve every day.

2. Next, ask group members how problem solving is related to friendships. Acknowledge responses, then paraphrase:

When we are in a relationship, there are going to be times when we don't agree with others or when we will be confronted with problems that affect our friendship. Being a good friend requires you to be responsible for solving the occasional disagreements that come up between any two people in a relationship. To do that, you have to stay calm and work things out.

3. Ask if anyone in the group has a friend with whom they can work out problems in a calm manner. Next ask, "Can anyone give an example of what happens when a friend gets upset instead of trying to solve a problem? What could you do to help work out the problem?" (Listen to and acknowledge responses in both cases.)

4. Sum up by noting that people like friends who help to solve problems and who work together with others. Reiterate that others respond negatively to those who are inflexible or reactive in response to a problem, whereas those who are flexible and proactive tend to receive a positive response.

Introduce Problem-Solving Steps

Explain that the session today is about the steps in problem solving within friendships. Present the Problem-Solving Steps poster.

Problem-Solving Steps

1. Define the problem.
2. Stay calm and remind yourself that you can work it out. Use calming strategies if you need them.
3. Think of at least three ways to solve the problem.
4. Discuss the solutions with your friend and agree on one.
5. If the solution works, you are done. If not, try another idea.

Conduct Problem-Solving Activity

1. Have participants choose from a pile of folded Friendship Situations.

2. Go around the circle and have group members read aloud the situation they received, list three possible solutions, and state what they think the best solution is and why.

   Encourage other group members to help any person who finds the task difficult. Say, "That's a hard one. Who can help out?" If time permits, members may also make up additional scenarios for discussion.

Free Play/Behavioral Rehearsal

Provide the group with a selection of age-appropriate toys, games, or other activities to choose from that encourage joint play and follow the procedure described in Session 1.1 for choosing play partners and facilitating free play.

Relaxation/Self-Regulation

1. This session's relaxation exercise combines imagery work with breathing. Tell group members to get into a comfortable position in their seats, with their arms at their sides and legs uncrossed, then close their eyes. Read the following script:

   ▶ Take a deep breath and hold it until the count of five: 1, 2, 3, 4, and 5.

   ▶ Good, now gently and slowly breathe out.

   ▶ Today we are going on a trip in our minds. We are each going to a place where we feel calm and completely relaxed. It might be at your home, in a private, comfortable spot, or it might be in a special place you like, such as the woods or by a stream. It could also be at the beach on a warm summer day.

   ▶ Picture yourself there now—any place you feel safe and relaxed.

   ▶ Now, I want you to notice in your imagination all of the sights and sounds you might experience at that place. Notice the smells that bring you comfort and peace.

   ▶ Notice what you see and hear. What colors and objects do you see? What sounds do you hear?

   ▶ Do you feel anything against your skin? Perhaps you feel sunlight on your face if you are outside.

   ▶ Now, count in your mind with me from five to one. When you hear each number, you will feel a little more relaxed and calm: 5, 4, 3, 2, 1.

   ▶ Good. Now enjoy this relaxed state, knowing that you can take this feeling with you and remember it any time during the day. *(Wait 20 to 30 seconds before continuing.)*

   ▶ Now, I will slowly count from one to five, and with each number you will feel a little more awake and alert. At two, you will take a deep breath, and on the count of three, you will blow it out and open your eyes. You will hear me say four, and when I say five, you will be ready for the rest of the day. *(Wait 15 to 20 seconds before proceeding.)*

▶ Let's begin now. One, rested and relaxed. Two, take in a breath. Three, slowly and gently, blow it out through your mouth and open your eyes. Four . . . and five.

2. Ask group members, "How did that feel? Where did you go? What did you see, hear, smell, or feel?"

Leadership Award

Select a group member to receive the Leadership Award and provide praise for what the person did well.

Generalization: Resilience Builder Assignment

Give each group member a copy of the Resilience Builder Assignment for the next session. Go over the assignment and answer any questions.

Parent Component

Give participants a copy of the parent letter for the session. Have them place the letter and Resilience Builder Assignment in the appropriate sections of their notebooks.

Friendship Situations

1. You are hanging out with a friend, and you and your friend want to do different things. What do you do?

2. You are at school talking to your friend, who asks you to get together and hang out after school. In the middle of this conversation, another student quickly approaches the two of you and starts to tell your friend that his plans have changed and that now he can get together after school. What do you do?

3. You invited a friend to your house one Saturday morning, but when you call that morning, your friend's parent informs you that she is at another friend's house. What do you do?

4. You have a really good friend who does not live near you. You want to spend time with this friend, but you have no transportation to get to each other's houses. What do you do?

5. Your friend confides in you that he is about to do something dangerous that is likely going to lead to big trouble. What do you do?

6. Your sister never leaves you alone when you have a friend over. Today, for the hundredth time, your sister is annoying you and your friend. What do you do?

7. You have a good friend you like to hang out with. The problem is that he brags all the time. What do you do?

8. Your friend recently started playing drums in a band and now seems to have no time to get together with you. What do you do?

9. Exams are coming up, and you need to put in time over the weekend and finish up a big project. Your friend asks you to go to the movies and, if you can't do that, to get together and do something else. What do you do?

10. You feel like your friend acts bossy with you. What do you do?

Solving Friendship Problems

Name _____ Date _____

Problem-Solving Steps

1. Define the problem.

2. Stay calm and remind yourself that you can work it out. Use calming strategies if you need them.

3. Think of at least three ways to solve the problem.

4. Discuss the solutions with your friend and agree on one.

5. If the solution works, you are done. If not, try another idea.

   Describe two friendship challenges that you faced in the past few weeks. Give three possible solutions for each challenge.

Challenge 1 (describe the situation)

_____

_____

Three possible solutions:

1. _____

2. _____

3. _____

Challenge 2 (describe the situation)

_____

_____

Three possible solutions:

1. _____

2. _____

3. _____

Solving Friendship Problems

Dear Parents:

Today's session addresses problem solving and responsible ways to handle challenges to making and keeping friends. A few examples of typical challenges include figuring out how to initiate a get-together with a friend, negotiating when you have different ideas about what to do, wanting to get to know a friend better but feeling uncomfortable about doing so, and dealing with concern that a friend is making a bad choice that may lead to trouble.

In this session, we break problem solving down into five steps:

1. Define the problem.

2. Stay calm and remind yourself that you can work it out. Use calming strategies if you need them.

3. Think of at least three ways to solve the problem.

4. Discuss the solutions with your friend and agree on one.

5. If the solution works, you are done. If not, try another idea.

It is important to remember and understand that when people are emotionally upset over a problem or challenge, it is often because they feel helpless and unable to generate solutions. This is a passive and powerless stance, rather than a proactive approach that empowers them.

Practice in generating solutions will help your child be able to compromise and solve problems in real-life situations. Parents can model this skill when they face a challenge by weighing the options out loud and talking through the best solutions.

Resilience Builder: Solving Friendship Problems

This session's assignment asks group members to identify two friendship challenges and three possible solutions to those challenges. Please ask your child to tell you about the assignment and provide help if asked. Please also continue to practice relaxation, conduct family meetings, and use the Compliment Basket strategy.

Sincerely,

Program Leader

From *Resilience Builder Program for Children and Adolescents,* © 2011 by M. K. Alvord, B. Zucker, & J. J. Grados, Champaign, IL: Research Press (800-519-2707, www.researchpress.com).

Stress Management

PURPOSE

Research has established that stress can cause physical ailments, among them cardiac problems and weight gain, and that it can seriously interfere with one's quality of life. Knowing how to manage stress effectively is therefore an essential life skill. By learning what is stressful and how stress affects both the mind and body, group members learn to be more aware of what is stressful to them and how to deal with stress.

GOALS

To explain the concept of stress and to facilitate awareness of how stress affects the body and mind

To help group members understand their unique individual stressors and signs of stress

To teach that there are different ways to react to stress and encourage flexibility in thinking in order to reduce stress

To encourage participants to develop a plan for coping with stress, including coping thoughts and coping actions

To practice a relaxation/self-regulation technique

MATERIALS

Chalkboard or dry erase board and marker

Program Notebooks (brought by group members)

Individual Points Charts

Name Cube

Stack of books (approximately 20)

Crayons or markers

Toys and games for free play

Copies of the following:

> My Beaker Level handout
>
> Leadership Award (Appendix C)
>
> Resilience Builder Assignment 1.11
>
> Parent Letter 1.11

PROCEDURE

Individual Greeting

Conduct the individual greetings, as described in Session 1.1. The components of a good first impression—a smile, a courteous hello, and sustained eye contact—by now should be fairly automatic.

Review Success Journal and Resilience Builder Assignment

Have each group member discuss his or her individual goal and Success Journal entry and experiences completing the Resilience Builder Assignment. When each person finishes speaking, ask him or her to throw the Name Cube to determine the next speaker.

> *Record points on each group member's Points Chart for this portion of the session. Record the point for participation at the end of the session.*

Define and Demonstrate Stress

1. Ask participants if they know what *stress* means and help them define and understand the concept. If necessary, point out that everyone feels stress from time to time. For example, it is normal to feel stress when you have too much homework or when your

parents are upset with you. Stress is another example of the mind-body connection since we also feel physically stressed in our bodies.

2. To help the group understand the concept, demonstrate the burden of stress:*

    Ask a group member to name his or her stressors. For each one, provide a book for the member to hold. As the list gets longer, the pile of books gets heavier! Then prompt the group member to come up with ideas to get rid of each book (for example, problem solving, relaxation, positive self-talk).

    It is helpful to make a list of these stressors as generated so that group members can recognize some stressors they have in common, as well as those that are stressors for some but not for others.

3. Continue until each participant has had a chance to do the exercise. To highlight the mind-body connection, you can encourage participants to put the books on their shoulders or to lie down and put the books on their chests. Say, "How does it feel? How heavy is the burden?" and "When your mind focuses on stress, your body feels it, too. How does your body feel when it is weighed down with stress? What happens to your muscles, for example?"

Discuss Stress: Beaker Analogy

If you wish, you may use a drawing of a thermometer instead, particularly for younger children, who may have trouble with the concept of a beaker.

1. Draw a picture of a glass beaker on the board. Say, "This is a beaker, like you might find in a chemistry lab, except that this beaker measures how much stress you have." Draw a line about a half-inch from the bottom and darken the space to that level with the marker. Say, "We all have *some* stress, so this is a normal level of stress."

2. Have the group give examples of things that make them stressed (for instance, too much homework, a big test, getting in trouble at home, an annoying sibling). Say, "What do you think will happen to the beaker level as the number of stressors increases?" Demonstrate how the level rises as they have more and more stressful things going on by drawing two or three additional lines, illustrating higher levels.

3. Ask what might happen if the beaker overflows. *(They may panic, get angry, yell, cry, melt down, etc.)* At the top of the beaker, write, "overflows," "freak out," and "panic."

4. Next discuss the importance of lowering your beaker level through stress management techniques. Underneath the beaker, write, "Ways to Lower Your Beaker Level." Have the

---

*Thanks to our colleague Erica Berger, LCSW-C, for this idea for illustrating the effects of stress in this very concrete way.

group generate a list of things they can do that will help them feel better and calm down. Point out that doing these things is called stress management.

Ways to Lower Your Beaker Level

Sleeping well	Spending time with friends
Eating well	Listening to music
Exercising	Playing an instrument
Relaxing	Writing in a journal
Talking about your feelings	Thinking differently about the stress ("changing the channel," for example)
Positive self-talk	
Doing yoga	Staying in the present moment
Riding your bike	Focusing on one task at a time

5. Distribute the My Beaker Level handout and crayons or markers. Say:

> Each of you now has a beaker. Sometimes it has very little liquid, or stress, in it—for example, on the last day of the school year, when all your work is done and you are on vacation. Sometimes it has a medium amount, and sometimes it can be completely full. I'd like each of you to write down things that stress you out and raise your beaker level at the side of the beaker and then color in the beaker to show how much stress you have.

6. Once group members have completed listing their stressors and coloring in the beakers, have them complete the "Ways to Lower My Beaker Level" section. Have them list different things they can do to lower their personal stress level.

> *Refer to the list you made as a group to help participants come up with their own individual ways of managing stress. Ask each member to share at least one stressor and one idea they had to lower their stress level.*

Discuss Coping Thoughts and Coping Actions

1. Explain that ways of coping with stress can be effective or ineffective. Generate a discussion of how to cope with stress. Explain that coping with stress effectively includes developing coping thoughts and coping actions.

2. Have the group come up with coping thoughts: Say, "Suppose you are stressed out when you have a lot of homework and assignments due at one time or tests coming up. What could you say to yourself or what might you think about in order to help handle this stressful situation?"

Sample coping thoughts include "I will be OK," "Everything will work out," "I can get through this," "I can handle it" and "Stay calm."

3. Also have the group generate coping actions: Say, "What can you do in response to stress when you are feeling it? What is your coping plan?"

    Sample coping actions include making a list of all the work you have to do, taking one step at a time, and taking breaks to make a task easier. Additional responses include "Get an adult," "Be assertive," "Find something else to do," and "Exercise."

4. Explain that coping well with stress requires flexibility in thinking. Say, "When we deal with stress, we have to be flexible in the way we think." Emphasize that if we don't change the way we are thinking, we will continue to feel stressed. Point out that changing the way we think can help us change the way we feel.

Free Play/Behavioral Rehearsal

Provide the group with a selection of age-appropriate toys, games, or other activities to choose from that encourage joint play and follow the procedure described in Session 1.1 for choosing play partners and facilitating free play.

Relaxation/Self-Regulation

1. This session's relaxation component focuses once more on progressive muscle relaxation, involving tightening then releasing different muscle groups. Have participants find a comfortable place to sit or lie down and close their eyes, then read the following script:

    ▶ You are now going to tighten and hold and then release and relax each different muscle group in your body, starting with your hands.

    ▶ First, I'd like you to make very tight fists—tighten up and hold the fists. Imagine that you are squeezing out a lemon. Really notice what it feels like when your muscles are tight and tense. Keep squeezing. *(Pause 7–10 seconds.)* Now let go and gently shake out your hands. Notice how it feels when the muscles in your hands are loose and relaxed.

    ▶ Now I'd like you to tighten your arms—forearms, biceps, and triceps—by squeezing your arms into your body and ribs. Be careful not to clench your fists—keep your hands relaxed while you squeeze in your arms. Now hold it. *(Pause 7–10 seconds.)* Now let go and release.

    ▶ Moving up the arms, pull your shoulders all the way up to your ears and hold them there. You will notice the back of your neck will also feel tight—that's good. Hold it *(Pause 7–10 seconds.)* Now drop your shoulders down toward your hips. Again, notice the difference—how your shoulder muscles feel when they are tight and tense versus when they are loose and relaxed.

▶ Pull your shoulders back and tighten your whole back. Hold it. Hold it. Really tighten. *(Pause 7–10 seconds.)* Now relax and bring your shoulders slightly forward. Keep breathing in through your nose and out through your mouth.

▶ Tighten your stomach muscles—your abs—squeeze them in toward your spine and hold it. Real tight. *(Pause 7–10 seconds.)* Now release.

▶ Squeeze your buttocks muscles in. Hold them tight. *(Pause 7–10 seconds.)* Then release.

▶ I'd like you to straighten out your legs and point your toes away from you. Tighten the muscles in your legs—your thighs should feel very tight. Hold it. *(Pause 7–10 seconds.)* Now, I'd like you to point your toes in toward your chest. Hold it and notice how your calves are tightening up. *(Pause 7–10 seconds.)* Now relax.

▶ Curl up your toes and your feet. Almost like you are cramping them. Hold it. *(Pause 7–10 seconds.)* Then release and let go.

▶ Now clench your jaw and tighten up all the muscles in your face, including around your eyes. Hold it tight. *(Pause 7–10 seconds.)* Then release and relax. Make a few relaxing circles with your jaw to loosen it up.

▶ Finally, I want you to tighten ALL the muscle groups in your body. Hold them all, very tight, for 10 seconds: 1, 2, 3, 4, 5, 6, 7, 8, 9, 10. Relax and let go. Go from being a robot to a rag doll. Now relax and notice how your muscles feel.

2. Ask group members, "How did doing this exercise feel?" and acknowledge responses.

Leadership Award

Select a group member to receive the Leadership Award and provide praise for what the individual did well.

Generalization: Resilience Builder Assignment

Give each group member a copy of the Resilience Builder Assignment for the next session. Go over the assignment and answer any questions.

Parent Component

Give each participant a copy of the parent letter for the session. Have participants place the letter, the My Beaker Level handout, and the Resilience Builder Assignment in the appropriate sections of their notebooks.

My Beaker Level

To the right of your beaker, write in things that make you feel stressed (make your beaker level increase).

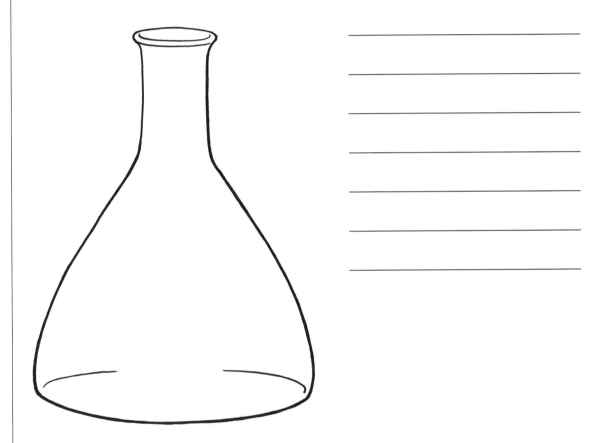

Ways to Lower My Beaker Level

1. _____   6. _____

2. _____   7. _____

3. _____   8. _____

4. _____   9. _____

5. _____   10. _____

Stress Management

Name _____ **Date** _____

What stressors did you experience?

Check the boxes by the things that got you stressed or upset.

☐ Had trouble with homework.

☐ Worried about a test.

☐ Forgot to bring something to school.

☐ Concerned about schoolwork in general.

☐ Mom or Dad got upset with me.

☐ Someone expected too much from me.

☐ Other kids teased me or were mean.

☐ Mom or Dad was in a bad mood.

☐ I expected too much from myself.

☐ Sister/brother bothered me or tried to hurt me.

☐ People told me to do too many things at the same time.

☐ Forgot to have Mom or Dad sign something.

How did you respond to your stressors?

Identify the stressor and state your reaction.

1. _____

2. _____

3. _____

What is your plan for coping? How are you going to handle your stressors?

List your coping thoughts and coping actions here.

Coping thoughts:

_____

_____

_____

Coping actions:

_____

_____

_____

Stress Management

Dear Parents:

The session today is on stress management, a self-regulation skill. The focus is on learning what stress is and how it affects the body and mind. Group members will learn how to recognize the feeling of stress and how it can increase over time, especially when nothing is done to reduce it.

Today we will learn the "beaker analogy": A beaker (like the one used in chemistry labs) measures the level of stress. It always has a little stress in it because we always have things we must do, but as more things happen, the level can get higher and higher. If stress is too high, our ability to manage is compromised and we tend to overreact or feel overwhelmed. If it gets even higher, it can overflow, and we may panic, tantrum, or "freak out."

In the session, group members list possible stressors and come up with ways that they can reduce their beaker level (reduce their stress). Examples include sleeping well, eating well, exercising, relaxing, spending time with friends, talking about their stress with an understanding listener (often parents), being in the present moment, focusing on only the task at hand, doing yoga, watching TV, writing in a journal, playing an instrument, making a schedule of what they need to do, and so on. We also discuss how to deal with stress by developing coping thoughts and coping actions. This includes being flexible in our thinking patterns.

As much as possible, we recommend that parents model healthy stress management. When this does not happen, it will be helpful for you to identify what you could have done differently and how you could have handled the stressful situation in a more appropriate way.

Resilience Builder Assignment: Stress Management

The assignment for this week asks that your child check off current stressors he or she has, then come up with a coping plan on how to handle the stressors. Please assist your child in completing the assignment, particularly the section on developing coping thoughts and actions. If you have time, please practice a relaxation exercise together and continue using the Compliment Basket and conducting family meetings.

Sincerely,

Program Leader

SESSION

1.12

Assertiveness

PURPOSE

This session focuses on assertiveness and how it differs from aggressiveness and passivity. Knowing how to be assertive is essential to establishing and maintaining healthy relationships with others. Assertive behavior also supports self-confidence; therefore, there is a strong connection between assertiveness and self-esteem. In discussing assertive behavior, it is important to consider the cultural context and be aware of what is appropriate, given your group's cultural background (for example, some Asian cultures avoid direct eye contact as part of showing respect).

GOALS

To help group members understand the concept of assertiveness and how it is different from aggressiveness and passivity

To practice the skill of responding assertively, including how to look and sound assertive

To teach the use of "I-statements" to promote effective, assertive communication

To strengthen awareness that participants can choose how to respond in any given situation

To practice a relaxation/self-regulation technique

MATERIALS

Chalkboard or dry erase board and marker

Program Notebooks (brought by group members)

Individual Points Charts

Name Cube

Markers (for role-play)

Toys and games for free play

Copies of the following:

Leadership Award (Appendix C)

Resilience Builder Assignment 1.12

Parent Letter 1.12

Before the session, create the **Assertiveness** *poster.*

PROCEDURE

Individual Greeting

Conduct the individual greetings, as described in Session 1.1. The components of a good first impression—a smile and a courteous hello, and sustained eye contact—by now should be fairly automatic.

Review Success Journal and Resilience Builder Assignment

Have each group member discuss his or her individual goal and Success Journal entry and experiences completing the Resilience Builder Assignment. When each member finishes speaking, ask him or her to throw the Name Cube to determine the next speaker.

> *Record points on each participant's Points Chart for this portion of the session. Record the point for participation at the end of the session.*

Discuss and Demonstrate Assertiveness

1. Write "Assertive" on the board. Ask the group if they know what assertiveness or being assertive means.

    Sample responses include sticking up for yourself and not letting others push you around, expressing yourself in a clear and appropriate way, and telling others when they are not treating you fairly and letting them know not to treat you this way in the future.

2. Ask why it is important to stick up for yourself; draw the connection between assertiveness and self-esteem: Say, "Being assertive is a sign of good self-esteem and shows that you are confident in yourself" and "When you feel good about yourself, you are more likely to stick up for yourself."

3. Discuss possible situations in which being assertive is an appropriate response. Situations include when you are being teased, when someone invades your personal space, or when you get marked wrong when you answered correctly on a test.

4. Explain that in addition to what you say, how you look and the way in which you say something affect how you are heard. Refer the group to the Assertiveness poster and practice each of the three components.

Assertiveness

► Posture: Body should be tall and straight, with shoulders back.

► Eye contact: Maintain eye contact when talking.

► Tone of voice: Speak in a firm but friendly way.

Posture

Say, "Can you show me what standing up tall and straight looks like? Bring your shoulders up, back, and then down to stand with good, firm posture." Model an assertive stance and encourage the group to do the same. Ask, "When you are standing tall with your shoulders back, how do you feel? How is your breathing—is it easier to breathe this way? Do you feel stronger?"

Eye contact

To illustrate, model poor eye contact first—complete avoidance or looking the other way most of the time. Then model strong eye contact—mostly maintaining eye contact while looking the other way briefly, to avoid staring.

Tone of voice

Model a soft, tentative voice, then follow with a stronger, clearer voice. Ask, "Which one sounds assertive and clear? Which one sounds weak and wimpy?" Point out that there are some situations in which using a strong voice may be inappropriate, such as when you are being reprimanded by an adult. In that case, using a strong voice might appear oppositional or rude.

5. Do several role-plays of what it looks like not to be assertive (e.g., slouching posture, looking the other way, shaky voice). You can even encourage group members to be a bit dramatic or extreme when modeling a nonassertive posture and voice, then contrast this approach with an assertive version.

> *Give feedback gently while participants are rehearsing the three parts of assertiveness. For example, if someone's voice is low or inaudible, say, "You're on the right track and doing great—just try to turn the volume up a few more notches."*

Demonstrate Assertive Communication: "I-Statements"

1. Explain the use of "I-statements" as part of talking in an assertive way. Say, "I-statements are a healthy way to express how you feel. They are another sign that you are being assertive."

2. Write the following statement form on the board, then provide some examples:

    "I feel _____when you_____."

    Examples

    I feel uncomfortable when you stand so close to me.

    I feel angry when you call me names.

    I feel annoyed when you take my markers without asking.

3. Let group members know that they also may add a request after the "I-statement," if appropriate.

    Examples

    I feel uncomfortable when you stand so close to me. Please step back a bit.

    I feel angry when you call me names. Stop doing that.

    I feel annoyed when you take my markers without asking. Please ask first.

Discuss Aggressiveness

1. Have the group come up with reasons being assertive is different from being aggressive. In brief, being aggressive often involves being disrespectful of others' rights, being physical, and using bad language, whereas being assertive involves saying what you think and feel while at the same time being respectful of others' rights and never being physical or using bad language.

2. Relate the idea that aggressiveness is a sign of poor self-regulation. Say, "When someone is aggressive, it shows that they have lost control of themselves. When someone acts assertively, they are in control of themselves."

3. Make the connection between being aggressive and not being respected by others. Ask, "What do you think of someone who is aggressive, pushes others, and speaks in a mean, harsh tone?" then encourage responses.

Discuss Passivity

1. Explain how being assertive differs from being passive. Say, "Being passive is similar to doing nothing. When others treat you badly or don't respect your rights, being passive means you don't stand up for yourself."

    Point out that sometimes "doing something" means talking to an adult and reporting a teasing or another troubling event. This is an assertive behavior, even though it is not directed at those responsible for the event.

2. Emphasize that being assertive involves expressing yourself appropriately and respectfully while setting limits on how others behave or treat you. Point out that setting these limits is a sign of healthy self-confidence. When a person does nothing in response to adversity, that person misses the chance to get what he or she wants or needs.

Conduct Role-Plays

1. Select group members act out how to respond in each of the following sample situations.

    ▶ Someone cuts in front of you in the lunch line.

    ▶ You are in art class and someone takes your markers from you.

    ▶ Your teacher marks you off for a correct answer and you end up earning a lower grade on your test.

2. Have the selected group members model aggressive, passive, and assertive responses. Say:

    ▶ Show what you would do if you responded aggressively: How would your body look, what would you say, and how would you say it? What about your eye contact?

Let the group know that they should not actually push or hurt anyone—rather, they should do it "like they do in the movies" (in other words, pretend).

▶ Show what you would do if you responded passively: How would your body look? What would you say, and how would you say it? What about your eye contact?

▶ Show what you would do if you responded assertively: How would your body look? What would you say, and how would you say it? What about your eye contact?

For assertive responses, encourage the use of "I-statements" and remind the group to apply the three parts of assertiveness: posture, eye contact, and tone of voice.

3. Have group members generate other situations (preferably from their own experiences) and encourage them to act out aggressive, passive, and assertive responses.

Free Play/Behavioral Rehearsal

Provide the group with a selection of age-appropriate toys, games, or other activities to choose from that encourage joint play and follow the procedure described in Session 1.1 for choosing play partners and facilitating free play.

Relaxation/Self-Regulation

1. Have participants stand, then read and model the following to guide them into the yoga standing mountain pose.

▶ Stand with your feet together (big toes touching) and your arms down by your sides.

▶ Stand up tall and straight with your shoulders back and your chest lifting up, as if someone has a string attached to the top of your chest and is pulling your chest up.

▶ Now slowly lift your arms straight up to the ceiling, with your palms facing together. Keep your elbows straight and lift up high.

▶ I want you to imagine that your feet are like the roots of a tree, pushing down into the earth and rooting you firmly to the ground. Push your feet into the floor and tighten your leg muscles.

▶ Now, I want you to lift the upper part of your body and arms all the way up to the sky, as much as you can lift. So your feet and legs are stretching down and your chest and arms are stretching up high. Feel the stretch and feel how strong you are.

2. Following the pose, say:

> Great job, everyone! See, when we stand strong with good posture we can breathe easily. We feel good about ourselves and our ability to handle any problems that may come up. When we do nothing in response to adversity, we miss the chance to stick up for ourselves by acting confidently.

Leadership Award

Select a group member to receive the Leadership Award and provide praise for what the person did well.

Generalization: Resilience Builder Assignment

Give each group member a copy of the Resilience Builder Assignment for the next session and answer any questions.

Parent Component

Give each participant a copy of the parent letter for the session. Have participants place the letter and Resilience Builder Assignment in the appropriate sections of their notebooks.

Assertiveness

Name _____ **Date** _____

1. What does being assertive mean?

   _____

   _____

   _____

   _____

2. How is being assertive different from being aggressive and being passive? Imagine that someone shoves in front of you and grabs the last piece of pizza at a party. Connect the different responses with the matching label.

   Assertive ▶ Shoving the person back and grabbing the pizza from his or her hands.

   Aggressive ▶ Letting the person have the pizza and deciding to wait to see if more pizza is coming out.

   Passive ▶ Looking the person in the eye and in a firm voice saying, "Excuse me, but I was in line first, and that is my piece of pizza."

3. Think of a time when you acted assertively and stuck up for yourself or your beliefs and used an "I-statement" to communicate how you felt. Write it here. If you can't think of a time, then make one up.

   I feel _____

   when you _____.

   Please _____.

   Being assertive is a sign of good self-esteem and self-confidence.

From *Resilience Builder Program for Children and Adolescents,* © 2011 by M. K. Alvord, B. Zucker, & J. J. Grados, Champaign, IL: Research Press (800-519-2707, www.researchpress.com).

Assertiveness

Dear Parents:

Today's session focuses on the skill of assertiveness. Being assertive is a way of being proactive because it involves determining an action, sticking up for oneself, and exercising self-regulation. In this session, the group learns how being assertive is different from being aggressive or passive. In particular, they learn that being assertive includes speaking in a firm, audible voice, standing up straight, and making good eye contact.

We role-play assertive and nonassertive actions, using situations group members typically encounter, then discuss the likely outcomes of each kind of action. This practice helps them see that assertive action yields a more positive result. We also discuss the use of "I-statements" as a form of assertive communication—for example, "I feel angry when you call me names. Please don't do that again."

Ideally, children learn to be assertive by observing their parents acting assertively. By demonstrating appropriate, assertive action (for example, resolving a conflict with another person), then discussing it with your child afterward, you will help your child understand the application of assertiveness in real-life situations. You can also encourage your child to respond by using an "I-statement," followed by an appropriate request, when an assertive response is warranted. Here is the formula for this kind of statement:

I feel _____

when you _____.

Please_____.

Resilience Builder Assignment: Assertiveness

Today's assignment asks your child to define assertiveness, say how being assertive differs from being aggressive or being passive, and create an "I-statement." Please provide assistance as needed and remind your child to practice a relaxation exercise. Having family meetings and using the Compliment Basket are always helpful.

Sincerely,

Program Leader

1.13

Empathy and Perspective Taking

PURPOSE

Empathy is the ability to understand another's perspective and emotional state. Showing empathy lies at the foundation of creating meaningful relationships with others. This session focuses on ways to establish and improve one's capacity for empathy and the ability to respond appropriately to another's situation.

GOALS

To explain and discuss the concepts of empathy

To guide group members in understanding and practicing the steps in an empathic response

To foster appreciation for how it feels when someone responds to you empathically

To convey the idea that empathic responses help strengthen relationships

To practice a relaxation/self-regulation exercise

MATERIALS

Chalkboard or dry erase board and marker

Program Notebooks (brought by group members)

Individual Points Charts

Name Cube

Toys and games for free play

Copies of the following:

Empathy Situations (copied and cut apart)

Leadership Award (Appendix C)

Resilience Builder Assignment 1.13

Parent Letter 1.13

*Before beginning, create the **Empathy Steps** poster.*

PROCEDURE

Individual Greeting

Practice an appropriate initial greeting, as described in Session 1.1. At this point, the expectation is for the greeting to be fairly automatic.

Review Success Journal and Resilience Builder Assignment

Have each group member discuss his or her individual goal and Success Journal entry and experiences completing the Resilience Builder Assignment. When each person finishes speaking, ask him or her to throw the Name Cube to determine the next speaker.

> *Record points on each group member's Points Chart for this portion of the session. Record the point for participation at the end of the session.*

Introduce Empathy and Perspective Taking

1. Write "Empathy" on the board and ask the group what it means. Acknowledge and record group members' responses.

   > *Sample responses include listening to and reading someone else's verbal and nonverbal cues to make sure that you understand the person, understanding other people's point of view and feelings, saying or doing something for a person to show you understand, and helping others.*

2. Discuss the expression "putting yourself in someone else's shoes" and what it means to see a situation from different perspectives. Explain that two different people will see the same situation differently and that empathy involves being able to imagine what another person might see and feel.

3. Help group members understand the reciprocal nature of relationships and how empathy impacts our friendships. Say:

> How do you feel when someone really listens and tries to understand how you feel? *(Acknowledge answers.)* It's important to know that others care about us. People who take the time to really understand others are valued and appreciated as friends. Like conversations, relationships are *reciprocal,* which means that how each person acts influences the other person in the relationship. When we feel others care how *we* feel, it often deepens our caring for others. And when we care for others, often they care even more for us. It helps us feel connected.

Discuss Steps in Responding with Empathy

1. Say, "When you respond with empathy, you show concern and understanding to others." Direct the group's attention to the Empathy Steps poster.

Empathy Steps

1. Pay attention to what the person is saying and doing.

2. Try to figure out what the person might be thinking and feeling.

3. Say or do something to show that you understand the person's perspective.

4. Ask the other person if what you did or said helped and made the person feel understood.

2. Discuss each step:

► The first step is to listen to and observe what the person is saying and how the person is acting. Look and listen to determine how the other person might feel. Use the following cues to help you: facial expressions, arm and hand movements, choice of words, and tone of voice.

► The second step is to put yourself in the other person's shoes and try to figure out what the person is thinking and feeling from his or her perspective or point of view. It might help to think about a time when you had a similar experience. If you haven't had a similar experience, then imagine what it might be like.

▶ The third step is responding to the person in an empathic way. That means showing the person that you understand. You might start by saying something like "It sounds like . . ." "I understand how you might feel that way . . ." or "Seems like you are . . ."

▶ Finally, you check in with the person to see if what you said or did was helpful and if it made the person feel understood. Remember that when sharing your understanding of the other person's thoughts and feelings, your interpretation may not be correct. Listen for the other person's reply to what you have said. If you were wrong, correct what you said or ask the person what else you could say or do to help.

When group members' empathic response is unsuccessful, they can think about what other cues they could have looked for to better understand how the person felt.

Role-Play Empathic Responses

1. Distribute the Empathy Situations and have pairs of group members take turns at role-play, with one reading the situation aloud and the other giving an empathic response.

2. After each role-play, discuss and evaluate how the role-play went and how the empathy giver could have improved his or her response. Ask group members if they have had a time in their life when something similar happened to them, or if they could imagine how such a situation would feel.

For additional practice, the group may also make up their own scenarios.

Free Play/Behavioral Rehearsal

Provide the group with a selection of age-appropriate toys, games, or other activities to choose from that encourage joint play and follow the procedure described in Session 1.1 for choosing play partners and facilitating free play.

Relaxation/Self-Regulation

1. This session's relaxation exercise includes two parts. Say, "We are doing relaxing movements today. Today, we are going to practice the 'Falling Leaves' and 'Painting Air' movements." Begin by reading the following script for the "Falling Leaves" exercise:

▶ Stand tall with your feet firmly planted shoulder's width apart.

▶ Take a deep breath in through the nose and out through the mouth. First take a breath in and hold it until the count of five: 1, 2, 3, 4, and 5. Slowly breathe out.

▶ Stand tall like a tree, with your feet planted firmly like roots. Now reach your arms up to the sky and stretch them like the branches of the tree.

▶ Good. Now with your arms straight out to your sides, bend your elbows inward so you can interlock your fingers in front of you. Your arms and elbows are up and out at chest level.

▶ Now, slowly move your elbows and wrists up and down to create a wavelike motion. Start with your arms bent and elbows straight across your body, with fingers interconnected at chest level.

▶ First lift the left elbow, then as you move it down, lift the left wrist. As you then move the left wrist down, lift the right wrist. As you then move the right wrist down, lift the right elbow.

▶ Now do this in reverse from right to left, alternating lifting and lowering elbows and wrists.

▶ Continue with these isolated steps slowly, until you are able to speed them up in a smooth, wavelike motion. As you move your arms back and forth, you will feel more and more relaxed.

▶ Now empty your mind of all thoughts, as you slowly move your arms up and down, in the falling leaf motion, from left to right. Think only about gently falling leaves and how relaxed you feel as you watch them tumble to the ground. *(Continue for 20–30 seconds.)*

2. Explain that you are now going to change positions for "Painting Air." Read the following script:

▶ Sit down quietly for a moment and close your eyes. Lift your hand and imagine that you are painting the air with slow strokes of a paintbrush.

▶ Move your arm slowly in a painting motion, picturing yourself painting the air, first with your right arm. *(Pause.)* Then switch to your left arm. Enjoy this movement and notice how your body moves in a slow and relaxing way.

▶ Good. Now, I will count from one to five, and with each number you will feel a little more awake and alert. At the count of one, you will put your arms down. At the count of two, you will take a deep and gentle breath. At the count of three, you will blow it out. At four, you will open your eyes. When you hear the count of five, you will be ready for the rest of the day. *(Wait 15–20 seconds before proceeding.)*

▶ One, two, three, four, and five. Excellent work.

3. Ask group members, "How did that feel? Could you imagine the falling leaves and painting the sky?"

Leadership Award

Select a group member to receive the Leadership Award and provide praise for what the person did well.

Generalization: Resilience Builder Assignment

Give each group member a copy of the Resilience Builder Assignment for the next session. Go over the assignment and answer any questions.

Parent Component

Give each participant a copy of the parent letter for the session. Have participants place the letter and Resilience Builder Assignment in the appropriate sections of their notebooks.

Empathy Situations

1. Your friend has just found out that he was not picked to be in the school play, something your friend very much wanted.

2. Your friend is angry because the teacher thinks she cheated on a test when she actually did not.

3. Your friend made poor behavior choices when angry at a sports practice, and the coach has informed your friend that she cannot play for the next three games.

4. A boy in your class is upset because he was teased in the cafeteria.

5. Your friend's parent has just told him that they are moving to another state.

6. Your friend has just told you that her parents are getting divorced.

Empathy and Perspective Taking

Name _____ **Date** _____

Observe someone at home or in school who is expressing strong emotions. Think about how he or she might be feeling and how you might respond to show that you understand. Record the following information.

1. Whom did you observe? _____

2. What was the situation? _____

3. What facial expression did the person have? (Examples: smile, frown, wide-open eyes)

    _____

4. How did the person move his or her body? (Examples: clenched fists, moved away, fidgety)

    _____

5. What words did the person use? (Examples: "I quit," "I'm not sure what to do," "About to explode," "Really excited," "That's stupid")

    _____

6. What tone of voice did the person use? (Examples: Trembling, calm, hesitant)

    _____

7. What do you think the person was thinking?

    _____

8. How do you think the person felt?

    _____

9. What do you think someone could do or say to this person that may make him or her feel understood or feel better?

    _____

    _____

10. How would you know the person felt understood?

    _____

    _____

Empathy and Perspective Taking

Dear Parents:

Empathy is the ability to recognize and understand another person's perspective and emotional state. It also involves accurately communicating one's understanding to another by showing concern and caring. Empathic responses include verbal and nonverbal behavior, such as listening, offering help or support, and providing feedback and suggestions to improve the situation. Showing empathy fosters strong connections with others and is a crucial factor for building resilience.

In group, we learn the following steps in making an empathic response:

1. Pay attention to what the person is saying and doing.

2. Try to figure out what the person might be thinking and feeling.

3. Say or do something to show that you understand the person's perspective.

4. Ask the other person if what you did or said helped and made the person feel understood.

Parents can promote the development of empathy and perspective taking by modeling this behavior. When you show empathy toward your child or to someone else, explain what you have done and ask your child if he or she thinks you were correct in your interpretation. Ask how your child thinks it made a difference.

Resilience Builder Assignment: Empathy and Perspective Taking

The assignment for this week asks your child to observe someone at home or in school who is expressing strong emotions; consider what that person is thinking and feeling based on body language, words, and tone; and decide how to show understanding. Please encourage your child and provide assistance as needed and practice a relaxation exercise together. As time allows, continue with the family meetings and Compliment Basket.

Sincerely,

Program Leader

SESSION

1.14

Being a Good Sport: Game Etiquette

PURPOSE

The electronic games of this generation can be played on a computer, a portable handheld device, a cell phone, an MP3 player, a PDA, or a home gaming system. Though children and teens may "game" alone, the goal is to play these games well with others in person in order to increase social opportunity. Good "game etiquette" requires many skills, including sharing, taking turns, reciprocity, compromise, negotiating rules without adult intervention, flexibility, controlling frustration and disappointment, being a good winner/loser, and having a positive attitude toward peers. The purpose of this session is to strengthen positive social interaction during game time.

GOALS

To identify and discuss the elements necessary for success playing electronic or other games with others

To discuss common frustrations and obstacles in the way of a successful and enjoyable interaction

To promote understanding that one's actions help determine the outcomes of getting together with others

To play a game while applying the skills of good game etiquette

To practice a relaxation/self-regulation technique

MATERIALS

Chalkboard or dry erase board and marker

Program Notebook (brought by group members)

Individual Points Charts

Name Cube

An electronic gaming system (if unavailable, use board games instead)

Copies of the following:

Leadership Award (Appendix C)

Game Etiquette Award (Appendix C)

Resilience Builder Assignment 1.14

Parent Letter 1.14

In addition to the usual parent letter, you will want to provide parents with an invitation to attend the last 15 minutes of Session 1.15, the final session in the series. In the invitation, you can explain that parents will have a chance to see what the group has learned and describe any special arrangements your group has decided on.

PROCEDURE

Individual Greeting

Conduct the individual greetings, as described in Session 1.1. The components of a good first impression—a smile and a courteous hello, and sustained eye contact—by now should be fairly automatic.

Review Success Journal and Resilience Builder Assignment

Have each group member discuss his or her individual goal and Success Journal entry and experiences completing the Resilience Builder Assignment. When each person finishes speaking, ask him or her to throw the Name Cube to determine the next speaker.

> *Record points on each group member's Points Chart for this portion of the session. Record the point for participation at the end of the session.*

Discuss Game Etiquette and Team Play

1. Invite group members to tell you about their computer and video game use. Ask:

   Who plays computer and video games?

   What system or games do you have or have you played at others' homes?

   Do you play them alone, with your brothers or sisters, or with friends?

   When do you play?

   How much time do you spend playing on school days? On weekends?

2. Write "Being a Good Sport" on the board. Under that heading, write "Game Etiquette," "Team Play," and "Similarities" as column headings.

3. Explain that game etiquette and team play are similar in many ways but different in other ways. While both involve self-control and complimenting others, one way that they differ is that video games are typically played by two or three players competing with one another, often at someone's home. Team play typically refers to team sports, though it may also refer to group projects.

4. Solicit the group's ideas about what being a good sport in each type of play might mean and what behaviors are most likely to end in success. Ask, "What do you think some of the differences are between game etiquette and team play?" Write these ideas down on the board.

   > *The chart on the next page lists differences and similarities in each type of play.*

5. Invite responses on the similarities and write these on the board under the third heading.

Free Play/Behavioral Rehearsal

> *The challenge at the beginning of free play is helping group members negotiate what they will play and in which group. Throughout the interaction, encourage*

Game Etiquette and Team Play

Game Etiquette	Team Play	Similarities
Electronic or board games	Sports and general behavior when competing	Play fair (play by the rules)
Typically no adult instruction or supervision	Coach or referee teaches skills and directs activities	No bragging
		Have fun
Players give each other feedback	Coach or referee gives you feedback	Must deal well with frustration, disappointment (show self-control)
One to three players	Typically three or more players	Cheer each other on
		No put-downs
Helping other player(s) learn to beat a level	All learn skills together	Stick with the activity (don't quit)
Mostly sitting	Active	Congratulate the other players
Fellow players help each other understand instructions	More formality at end of game (often shake hands)	

group members to make compromises, take turns, and sustain attention while watching those who are actively playing.

1. Provide several choices of video or computer games.

2. Let the group know how many controllers there are or how many may play at a time. Inform them that they will have to divide up into pairs or groups of three and decide which group of players goes first. (There are many opportunities for negotiation here!) You can also have group members draw straws or flip a coin to determine order of play.

3. Encourage those who are waiting their turn to play to watch and, ideally, cheer the players on.

4. Have group members observe and take turns until all groups or pairs have had a chance to play.

Relaxation/Self-Regulation

1. This week's relaxation will likely be brief due to time spent on the game exercise. Explain that the group will be doing a yoga pose called the cobra or snake pose. Read the following script:

   ▶ Lie down on the floor on your stomach with your chin on the floor. Place your arms by your sides. Take a deep breath in and slowly let the air out.

   ▶ Now bring your hands in front of you (shoulder width apart) and slowly lift your upper body so that your head is up. Keep your hips on the floor.

   ▶ Hold the position. Notice the tension and tightness in your muscles.

   ▶ Now hiss like a snake.

   ▶ Take a deep breath and hold it until the count of five: 1, 2, 3, 4, and 5.

   ▶ Slowly breathe out, and as you do, slowly bring your body so that it is again resting on the floor.

   ▶ Now slowly get up and stand up straight with your feet together and your arms by your sides.

   ▶ Hold this position for the count of five or as long as you can. Notice the tension in your muscles as you hold the position.

   ▶ Let your body muscles relax, then take a seat.

2. Ask, "How did that feel? What part of your body was the most tense? What were the sensations you had when you relaxed the muscles?"

Leadership and Game Etiquette Awards

Select a group member to receive the Leadership Award and provide praise for what the person did well. Give all members who played fairly and maintained good self-control a Game Etiquette Award.

> *To personalize the Game Etiquette Award, you may circle the words or phases that reflect behaviors individual group members displayed.*

Generalization: Resilience Builder Assignment

Give each group member a copy of the Resilience Builder Assignment for the next session. Go over the assignment and answer any questions.

Parent Component

Give each group member a copy of the parent letter for the session. Have group members place the letter, Resilience Builder Assignment, and Game Etiquette Award in the appropriate sections of their notebooks.

> *Let the group know that the next session will be the final session in the series and that they will have an opportunity to redeem final points for prizes and show parents what they have learned over the course of the group. Discuss any special arrangements. Refreshments are optional for the final session and provide another opportunity to work on manners and cooperation.*

Being a Good Sport: Game Etiquette

Name _____ **Date** _____

Keep track of how much free time (time not devoted to school-related work) you spend each day playing a game on a "screen." Note how much time you spent playing alone and how much time playing with another person. Also note whom you played with and whether you were exhibiting good game etiquette.

	Game Time (Minutes)		Good Game Etiquette
	Alone	With whom?	Circle yes or no.
Monday	_____	_____	Yes No
Tuesday	_____	_____	Yes No
Wednesday	_____	_____	Yes No
Thursday	_____	_____	Yes No
Friday	_____	_____	Yes No
Saturday	_____	_____	Yes No
Sunday	_____	_____	Yes No

Describe one time that you played a game with someone else (sibling, friend, parent, neighbor, other). Note what went well and which game etiquette skills you exhibited.

I played a game with _____ , and I showed good game etiquette when I:

1. _____

2. _____

3. _____

I knew that it was a successful game when: _____

_____

If it did not go well, what could you have done differently?

_____

_____

_____

From *Resilience Builder Program for Children and Adolescents,* © 2011 by M. K. Alvord, B. Zucker, & J. J. Grados, Champaign, IL: Research Press (800-519-2707, www.researchpress.com).

Being a Good Sport: Game Etiquette

Dear Parents:

A common activity for children and teens is playing some form of video or computer game, whether alone or with family or friends. With increasing access to electronic games, a major concern is that youth spend too much time in front of screens and are too often alone or interacting with someone online that they may not even know. Thus, direct social interaction is often sacrificed.

Though parents may choose to limit how much time children play these games, we encourage using them as a means to improve social and family contact. By addressing what it means to be a good sport in this context, we can reinforce a host of social and self-regulation skills, including negotiating, sharing, turn taking, dealing with frustration, exhibiting a positive attitude toward a competitor, being a good loser or winner, and stopping play when asked.

During today's session, the group identifies behaviors that are the ingredients of good "game etiquette." They then have the opportunity to practice, in real time, those behaviors while they play a computer or video game. Group members negotiate not only what games are played, but also decide which members will be able to play, what the onlookers will do, which group will go first, rules about stopping the game, and so on.

You can help reinforce game etiquette skills in the home by encouraging an interactive game activity. It is especially helpful to praise losing well or handling disappointment as a natural part of any game play.

Resilience Builder Assignment: Being a Good Sport—Game Etiquette

This session's assignment asks group members to keep track of the time they spend playing electronic games and, if they played with someone else, whether they showed good game etiquette. It also asks that they describe their behavior during a specific game. Please assist and encourage your child in completing the assignment and in continuing to practice relaxation exercises. We hope you are able to continue with the Compliment Basket and family meetings.

The next session will be our final session of this unit. Please plan on joining the final half of the group. Each group member will talk about his or her accomplishments and some topics we have learned about during the sessions.

Sincerely,

Program Leader

SESSION

1.15

Review of Sessions

PURPOSE

This wrap-up and review session allows group members to practice speaking to parents as each member describes two or three session topics and what the group has learned about them. The first part of the session is devoted to review of the Resilience Builder Assignment and progress on individual goals as represented by the Success Journal. Prizes for completion are chosen during this final session. While there is no free play in this session, the presentations to parents do provide an opportunity for behavioral rehearsal of speaking assertively in a public setting.

GOALS

To briefly review what has been discussed and taught during the past sessions

To have each group member present to the parent group a portion of what he or she has learned

To invite parents to provide a compliment to their child in front of the group

To review a relaxation/self-regulation technique with parents in the session

To provide each group member with a certificate of achievement and celebrate the group

MATERIALS

Chalkboard or dry erase board and marker

Program Notebooks (brought by group members)

Individual Points Charts

Name Cube

Copies of the following:

Leadership Award (Appendix C)

Certificate of Program Completion (Appendix C)

Resilience Builder Assignment 1.15

Parent Letter 1.15

Resilience Builder Program Parent Evaluation (Appendix A)

Before the session, prepare session topic cards and assemble props.

Suggested Props and Illustrations

1.1 Introduction to Group: Declaration of Rights poster	1.8 Being a Good Sport—Field Trip: Good Sport Certificate
1.2 Resilience and Being Proactive: Rubber band and bouncy ball	1.9 Optimistic Thinking: Glass and pitcher of water
1.3 Personal Space: Copy of Personal Space Diagram	1.10 Solving Friendship Problems: Problem-Solving Steps poster
1.4 Leadership: Leadership Jigsaw Puzzle pieces	1.11 Stress Management: My Beaker Level handout or books
1.5 Reading Verbal and Nonverbal Cues: Two scenarios from the session, demonstrated by group member	1.12 Assertiveness: Yoga mountain pose, demonstrated by group member
1.6 Initiating and Maintaining Conversations: Beach ball with questions on each side	1.13 Empathy and Perspective Taking: Pair of shoes or picture of shoes
1.7 Being a Good Sport—Team Play: Two Charades categories, demonstrated by group member	1.14 Being a Good Sport—Game Etiquette: Game controller or board game

PROCEDURE

Individual Greeting

Conduct the individual greetings, as described in Session 1.1. The components of a good first impression—a smile and a courteous hello, and sustained eye contact—by now should be fairly automatic.

Review Success Journal and Resilience Builder Assignment

Have each group member discuss his or her individual goal and Success Journal entry and experiences completing the Resilience Builder Assignment. When each person finishes speaking, ask him or her to throw the Name Cube to determine the next speaker.

> *Record points for this portion of the session, then add up each group member's total points. Those who have completed all Resilience Builder Assignments may receive a bonus of 20 points; those who have completed at least half may get 5 extra points. Have group members select prizes before the parents join the session.*

Review of Sessions

1. Using the topic cards as a reminder, ask for volunteers to present each of the session topics to the parent group. Hand out the corresponding props. Rotate until everyone has at least two topics to share.

2. Instruct group members that they will be asked to discuss the topics they have chosen, describe what they have improved and progress on their individual goals, and say what they liked best about the group.

Behavioral Rehearsal

1. Have one of the group members invite parents into the room, then say:

    > Today the group will review what we have learned over the course of all these sessions. Group members will discuss what improvements in individual goals they have made and what they liked best about the group. After we've finished, I'll ask each of you to give your child a compliment about improvements you've noticed. We'll end by doing a brief relaxation exercise together.

2. Ask for a volunteer to start; have each group member share one topic at a time. Have the group member stand and face the parents, making eye contact, and say, "Hello, my name is _____ , and I'll tell you what I've learned about _____ *(topic)*." The group member explains the topic, using the prop to illustrate.

3. Following the explanation, the group member says, "I've improved _____ *(behavior),* and what I like best about the group is _____ *(activity or peer interaction)."*

4. After all the topics have been covered, ask one parent to begin by giving a compliment to his or her child. Continue until all parents have had a chance to speak.

Relaxation/Self-Regulation

1. A brief relaxation exercise today emphasizes calm breathing and relaxing the neck area. Inviting parents to join you, say:

   ▶ Please get as comfortable as you can.

   ▶ Calm breathing is breathing very slowly in through your nose, holding it, and slowly letting the breath out. As we have done before, it is also breathing through your lower belly instead of your chest.

   ▶ Let's do this together. Close your eyes and breathe in very slowly to the count of five, letting your belly extend. Now hold it: 1, 2, 3, 4, and 5, and slowly breathe out.

   ▶ Now bring your chin to touch your chest. Hold it: 1, 2, 3, 4, and 5, and notice how tight the back of your neck feels.

   ▶ Slowly return your head upright and notice the difference between the tense muscles and relaxed muscles.

   ▶ Now bring your head back as far as you can. Hold it, then slowly bring your head upright. Bring your head to the right toward your shoulder. Hold it to the count of five: 1, 2, 3, 4, and 5.

   ▶ Now slowly bring your head up and then lean your head to the left. Hold it. Slowly bring your head upright.

   ▶ Now take a deep breathe in. Hold. Slowly breathe out.

   ▶ Gently shake your head and slowly open your eyes.

2. Acknowledge the group's efforts and let them know that as they continue their day, they might try the tension-hold technique.

Leadership Award and Certificate of Program Completion

Give everyone a Leadership Award for being brave and speaking in front of all the parents. Have each group member come up and state one behavior that has improved as he or she receives a Certificate of Program Completion.

Generalization: Resilience Builder Assignment

Ask group members and parents to review the program notebooks at home and continue to reinforce the skills learned in group. Also encourage them to continue practicing relaxation exercises, using the Compliment Basket, and participating in family meetings.

Parent Component

1. Have group members place their Certificates of Program Completion in the appropriate section of their notebooks.

2. Give parents the parent letter and Resilience Builder Assignment, along with a copy of the Resilience Builder Program Parent Evaluation. If time allows, have parents complete the evaluation and return it to you before leaving. (The review of key topics will be helpful for parent reference as parents fill out the evaluations.)

   If you are unable to have parents fill out their evaluations at the end of the session, arrange another time to do so.

Unit 1 Review of Key Concepts

Keep up the good work with everything we learned in group! Remember to continue to use positive self-talk and relaxation techniques whenever you need them.

Session 1.1—Introduction to Group

Resilience Builder Assignments, individual goals, and Success Journal

Declaration of Group Rights

Discovering what we have in common

Session 1.2—Resilience and Being Proactive

Dealing with stress by stretching like a rubber band, then coming back to a relaxed, flexible state

Bouncing back like a ball—it takes effort to rebound

Being proactive instead of reactive or passive

Session 1.3—Personal Space

Elbow-Room Rule

Being "in sync" with pace, rhythm, volume of voice

Space Builders and Space Busters

Family meetings

Session 1.4—Leadership

Six components of being a good leader: Being proactive, communicating effectively, maintaining self-control, being a good role model, being a team player, giving compliments

Leadership Award

Compliment Basket

Session 1.5—Reading Verbal and Nonverbal Cues

Verbal communication: What is said and how it is said

Nonverbal communication: Things we do with our facial expressions and bodies to send a message

Session 1.6—Initiating and Maintaining Conversations

One-Minute Rule

Reciprocity: Back and forth in a conversation

Conversation Builders and Conversation Busters

Power of questions: Who, what, where, when, why, how

Session 1.7—Being a Good Sport: Team Play

Good sport behaviors: Encouraging teammates, trying your best, listening to the coach, continuing to play even when you're frustrated, and so forth

Having a positive attitude in social interactions

Collaborating to play Charades

Session 1.8—Being a Good Sport: Field Trip

Reviewing and reinforcing the elements of being a good sport and team play

Using skills in a real-life setting: Making requests, having good manners in public, tolerating frustration, and so on

Session 1.9—Optimistic Thinking

"Glass is half-full philosophy": Being realistic but positive

Three components of optimistic thinking: Seeing a situation as specific (not general), understanding it is temporary (not permanent), and having a realistic view of who is responsible

Being proactive once your have realistic view

Catching negative thoughts and replacing them by "changing channels"

Session 1.10—Solving Friendship Problems

Steps in solving a friendship problem

Role-playing friendship scenarios

Encouraging proactive versus reactive or passive responses to challenges in friendships

Session 1.11—Stress Management

Mind-body connection (demonstration with books)

My Beaker Level analogy

Coping with stress: Coping thoughts and coping actions

Session 1.12—Assertiveness

Three parts of assertiveness: Eye contact, posture, tone of voice

"I-statements" as assertive communication

Assertive versus aggressive and passive behavior

Session 1.13—Empathy and Perspective Taking

Concept of empathy and understanding others' feelings

Understanding others' perspectives

Role-playing empathic responses

Session 1.14—Being a Good Sport: Game Etiquette

Being a good sport when playing on a team versus playing video or board games

Negotiating and compromising to have a successful and fun game experience

Advantages of game etiquette

Session 1.15—Review of Sessions

Review of key concepts learned

Practice speaking in front of parent group

Parents' compliments

Certificate of Program Completion

Resilience Builder Assignment 1.15 (p. 2 of 2)

Review of Sessions

Dear Parents:

Today is our final session in this unit of the Resilience Builder Program. In today's group, we review what the group members have learned over the semester. Group members share with you information about the topics we have discussed, what they have improved on, progress on their individual goals, and what they liked best about the group.

After the session today, please engage your child in a discussion of what he or she has learned during the group and what has been most helpful. Encourage your child to continue to take small steps toward change and practice what has been learned.

If your child will not be continuing for the next unit, please do not hesitate to contact me with any questions. Thank you for this opportunity to work with you and your child.

Resilience Builder Assignment: Unit 1 Review of Key Concepts

Please use this summary to help you review and practice with your child. Continue to talk with your child about skills/areas in which to improve (for example, he or she might demonstrate great personal space skills but might find it harder to cope with stress or be flexible). I hope you will continue using the Compliment Basket and conducting family meetings. As always, I recommend that you continue to practice relaxation and positive self-talk together.

Sincerely,

Program Leader

Unit 2 Sessions

Introduction to Group

PURPOSE

This first session of Unit 2 is intended for ongoing groups that may include one or two new members. It reviews four key components to refresh the memory of continuing group members and introduces the concepts to anyone joining the group for the first time. These components include how to introduce yourself to a group, the most effective way to join others in conversation and activity, group rights, and the Leadership Award.

> *When the majority of group members are new to the program, leaders should use Session 1.1.*

GOALS

To review the group format for the new set of sessions

To reestablish the Declaration of Group Rights

To make group introductions and reestablish relationships among participants

To introduce the Leadership Award

To describe and discuss joining others who are already engaged in conversation or activity

To practice a relaxation/self-regulation technique

MATERIALS

Chalkboard or dry erase board and marker

Program Notebooks (brought by group members)

Individual Points Charts

Name Cube

Toys and games for free play

Copies of the following:

Leadership Award (Appendix C)

Resilience Builder Assignment 2.1

Parent Letter 2.1

Relaxation Tips for Parents and Group Members (Appendix B)

Prepare Program Notebooks, Name Cube, Points Charts, and topic cards as necessary (see instructions in chapter 5). All participants receive new Points Charts and notebook cover sheets to accommodate a new goal. Provide any newcomers with a Program Notebook.

PROCEDURE

Individual Greeting

The components of a good first impression—a smile and a courteous hello, and sustained eye contact—are rehearsed at the beginning of each session with the goal of making the behavior automatic.

1. Stand at the entrance to the room and greet each group member by name with a friendly face and a handshake. Ask the member to return the greeting using your name and making eye contact. To help younger or especially shy children sustain eye contact, say:

   Sometimes it's hard to look directly into other people's eyes. It's OK to look at my nose at first, if it feels more comfortable. You can't tell that you are not looking directly into my eyes when you do that.

2. At each successive group meeting, require participants to demonstrate appropriate body posture, longer sustained eye contact, and a more confident greeting to enter the room.

Review Group Procedures and Conduct Introductions

1. Describe the session format by paraphrasing:

> Welcome to the Resilience Builder Program. The purpose of the program is to help you make and keep friends more easily. It's also to help you figure out what will make you happier and what you can do to achieve it. Each session will introduce a new topic for group discussion. We will also have free time for play, during which we will negotiate and compromise to get the toys or games we want, and 5 minutes or so of practice using different relaxation techniques. Your parents may join us at the end of a session from time to time.

2. Have group members introduce themselves to one another and share something about their interests. Ask members to notice whether they have an interest in common with anyone else. Point out any commonalities that go unnoticed. If some time has elapsed since previous group sessions, have group members share some news about themselves. For example, they might discuss an event they attended, an accomplishment they have attained, or a social connection they have made.

Reestablish Group Rights

1. Discuss what rights group members would like in group. Say:

> What kinds of rights do you think group members should have here? Rights are like privileges and also can be like rules. For example, what would the right be concerning giving your opinions? What about personal space?

2. Acknowledge appropriate ideas and reframe negatively stated rules and rights with positive wording. For example, "Don't interrupt" becomes "Wait until another person has finished speaking."

3. Record ideas and make copies for members to place in their notebooks.

   See Session 1.1 for a sample Declaration of Group Rights. If you wish, you can make a new poster incorporating any changes to the declaration.

Explain Leadership Awards

Ask, "Why are leaders important?" If necessary, elicit the idea that leaders represent others and are role models to the community. Say:

> Leadership is valued and rewarded in group. Each week one of you will be selected for a Leadership Award based on your merit and your effort in participating in group that day. The person recognized as leader must have completed the day's assignment,

if there is one, shown effort throughout the session, and demonstrated individual progress. During group I will be observing members so that at the end of the group, I can determine who earned the Leadership Award for the week.

If appropriate, review the specific leadership behaviors described in Session 1.4.

Describe and Discuss Joining In

1. Introduce the topic of joining in. Say:

    Today we are going to talk about how to join others in a polite and respectful manner. When you enter a conversation it is important to time your entry appropriately. For example, hanging back and feeling shy while not being able to think of anything to say feels so uncomfortable! Likewise, jumping in out of turn and blurting out something completely unrelated (off topic) to what anyone is talking about can be rude.

2. Reintroduce the One-Minute Rule. Say:

    A proper conversation entry in an ongoing group discussion occurs just after someone stops talking. When you are joining others, a good strategy for doing this is called the One-Minute Rule. Let me describe it to you. As you approach two or three friends who are talking, you should wait about one minute and listen to what others are talking about. While you are listening, you should stand quietly, with an interested look on your face, looking at the person who is talking. When you are ready to join the conversation, wait for a break and say something about what is happening or what the other people are talking about. Asking someone in the group a question about what they are saying is always a great idea. Later, once you are part of the conversation, you can share your interests.

Joining-In Activity

1. Introduce a group activity to practice joining in both in an appropriate and an inappropriate manner. Explain that the group will practice entering a conversation using the One-Minute Rule.

2. Divide the larger group into groups of three and designate two people "talkers" and one a "joiner." Have the talkers pick a subject to discuss. Tell the third person that his or her job is to join the other two in conversation.

3. Instruct each group of three to role-play while other group members observe as the "audience."

    ▶ Have the joiner first enter the conversation inappropriately—for example, hanging back too far away and being too quiet or getting too close and intrusively talking about an unrelated topic. The joiner can choose the method.

▶ Next have the joiner enter the conversation appropriately, by using the One-Minute Rule. Allow group members to role-play appropriate joining.

4. Have the talkers share how the first and second attempts at joining came across, and what they would think if someone joined them in each of the two ways. Ask for comments from the audience. Ask, "What went well? What would have made the joining smoother or better?"

5. Continue until each group has had a chance to role-play. If time allows, each group of joiners and talkers may reverse roles and role-play a second time.

Free Play/Behavioral Rehearsal

The point of free play is to practice negotiating and interacting in a flexible, prosocial manner. During the first couple of sessions, the process of agreeing on an activity can be quite slow, but it is important for group members to learn to compromise and become more flexible.

1. Provide a selection of age-appropriate toys, games, or other activities to choose from that encourage joint play. Explain that now there will be free time to play, but each participant must play with at least one other member of the group, so the first step is to reach agreement on who wants to play with which game or toy.

2. Taking turns, have each group member state his or her first choice of game or toy. If someone else in the group wants to play with that game or toy, he or she says so.

3. After everyone has had a turn, if everyone is not matched with a partner who wants to enjoy the same activity, go around again and ask for a second choice of game or toy.

4. If group members are still not all matched up, remaining participants' third choice must be an activity someone else has already chosen. The process of selection continues until all participants are paired up with someone or in a group.

5. Allow free-play time. Observe and intervene as necessary to keep the interactions positive.

Things You Can Say to Encourage Compromise

What would you like to do with another group member today?

The sooner you can agree on an activity, the more time you'll have to play.

I know it's hard to not be able to do what you want, but if you compromise this time, maybe next time the other person will compromise with you.

By letting your partner choose, you can learn a new game or activity that you've never tried before.

Relaxation/Self-Regulation

1. Review or introduce the concept of self-regulation and the fact that while in the group, they will practice one relaxation/imagery exercise each week. Tell group members to get into a comfortable position in their seats, with arms and legs uncrossed. Then provide these instructions:

   ▶ We are going to practice diaphragmatic breathing, which we call *calm breathing*. The goal is to breathe in through your nose and out through your mouth, with the air going all the way down to your lower belly. Tense or anxious breathing causes your upper chest to rise and fall, and the air only goes into your upper chest. Relaxed or calm breathing, on the other hand, causes your lower stomach—around your belly button—to go up and down and the air to go into your lower abdomen.

   ▶ Let your shoulders, head, neck, and arms relax. Place one hand on your chest and the other on the belly button area of your stomach. This exercise takes practice, as most of us breathe mostly through our chests. I'll ask you to slowly breathe in through your nose for a count of five: 1, 2, 3, 4, and 5 . . . then hold the breath.

   ▶ As you breathe in, your stomach area will extend. The air should naturally push out your stomach. Now in . . . 1, 2, 3, 4, 5. Keep your chest still. Hold it . . . 2, 3. Now tighten your stomach muscles and notice your breath as you slowly breathe out through your mouth for five: 1, 2, 3, 4, 5.

   ▶ Again, breathe in through your nose . . . 1, 2, 3, 4, 5, with your stomach extending out. Hold it . . . 2, 3. Pay attention to your breath as you breathe out through your mouth…1, 2, 3, 4, 5, pulling your stomach muscles in. Remember to let the air go all the way down to your lower abdomen.

   If the group members have difficulty getting the air to go down into their lower abdomen, have them lie down on the floor and put a lightweight object (maybe a light book or foam yoga block) on their upper chest. Have them use the object as a way of measuring whether their breathing is in their upper chest or lower abdomen (if they are doing calm breathing, the object should not move but their lower belly should).

2. Ask, "What did you notice about your breath?" "How did that feel in your chest and lower belly?" Listen to and acknowledge responses.

Leadership Award

Announce the name of the Leadership Award recipient and present that person with the award. Repeat the criteria for recognition and tell group members that they may remain hopeful because if they did not receive the award this week, they will have a chance to again next week.

Generalization: Resilience Builder Activity

1. Give each participant a copy of the Resilience Builder Assignment and explain:

    > This session's Resilience Builder Assignment is to come up with a new goal that you want to reach during these sessions. It can be part of a plan to control yourself better like "I'm going to think before I act" or "I'm going to calm myself down better when I'm upset." Or it can be part of a plan to be a better friend, such as "I'll listen and accept other people's ideas instead of arguing" or "I'll call people up and get together at least once a month." Discuss the goal with your parents, then write it or have your parents help you write it on your Individual Goal Contract.

2. Answer any questions about the assignment.

Parent Component

Hand out copies of the parent letter, and have group members put their Resilience Builder Assignment and parent letter in their notebooks in the appropriate section.

The first parent letter reviews the program model and logistical procedures and describes the nature of resilience. Provide a copy of the Relaxation Tips for Parents and Group Members and instruct group members to put it with the parent letter in their notebooks.

> *If circumstances allow, it can be helpful to bring parents in toward the end of the first session for a brief introduction to the program and to participate in the relaxation exercise.*

OPTIONAL ACTIVITY: FINDING COMMON GROUND

1. Have participants form pairs and give each pair a sheet of paper and a pencil. Tell them they will be playing a game to get to know each other.

2. Ask one person in each pair to volunteer to interview the other person. His or her job is to find out and list as many things as possible about his or her partner in three minutes.

3. Time the groups, and after three minutes, have them stop. Now ask the pairs to switch roles so that the interviewer is now the one being interviewed. The second interviewer may use the other side of the paper to record findings.

4. Time the pairs again and have them stop after three minutes.

5. Have the pairs share information by telling the larger group what they learned about their partners (they may review their sheet for facts).

Individual Goal Contract

Name _____ Date _____

I agree to work very hard at improving my social competence and self-regulation. My goal is:

Please state your goal in a specific and positive way—for example, "I will become more aware when I get upset and use strategies to calm down."

_____

_____

_____

_____

I can work on this goal by:

1. Writing in my Success Journal and noting attempts and progress on my goal.

2. _____

3. _____

My parents and I have talked about my goal, and they will help me by:

1. Each week, pointing out when I have made efforts to work on my goal or have been successful at meeting the goal.

2. _____

3. _____

Group member _____ Date _____

Parent _____ Date _____

Parent _____ Date _____

Introduction to Group

Dear Parents:

I am looking forward to working with your child over the next few months as he or she takes part in the Resilience Builder Program. Our group is targeted toward building social competence, self-regulation, and overall resilience in youth. *Resilience* is the ability to adapt well to life and its challenges. We believe—and research shows—that when you foster resilience in children, they thrive and engage life in a healthy adaptive way. Toward this aim, our groups facilitate resilience through teaching social competence. We will be teaching your child to be proactive, to self-advocate, to improve his or her own self-regulation, and to better connect with both peers and adults in the family and community.

The Resilience Builder Program emphasizes social competence by helping children and teens learn and practice the skills necessary to form and cultivate relationships. We use modeling, role-play, and numerous multisensory activities to accomplish this goal. Social competence encompasses more than just acquiring skills; it also means performing these skills in daily social interaction. An essential aspect of our model is that children practice skills weekly in the community.

In order to assist with skill transfer to the home, school, and community, we give children a Resilience Builder Assignment for each session. Mastery of the skills requires this regular practice between group sessions. Each child will also set and work toward an individual goal related to his or her specific needs. In addition to the weekly Resilience Builder Assignment and Success Journal, we teach a variety of self-regulation and relaxation strategies. A handout describing relaxation exercises you can practice at home is included in your child's notebook.

We begin group today with introductions and describing and discussing joining others in conversations and activities. Members will take part in a role-play to practice joining skills. Today we also cover the format of group and member responsibilities and rights. We develop a Declaration of Group Rights, to which all members will adhere. We discuss the Leadership Award, an opportunity for a deserving group member to gain recognition each session.

We tailor topics to the needs of the particular group. Following is a list of topics we plan to cover this session:

▶ Joining in

▶ Resilience and flexibility

▶ Maintaining conversations

▶ Understanding intent versus impact in communication

▶ Self-regulation through anxiety and anger management

- ▶ Thinking errors (how to catch them and how to change them)
- ▶ Building self-esteem
- ▶ Making good choices
- ▶ Dealing with teasing and bullying
- ▶ Being a good sport

Some Logistics and Additional Points

Periodically, parents are invited to join for the last 15 minutes of the session to discuss the skills that the children are learning. We typically meet the last session of the month.

A note on interaction outside the group: Because children often befriend each other and develop a close bond in the group, there is a desire to schedule play dates outside of group. While this may appear to be a good idea, friendships outside the group may actually disrupt the group process because they change the group's dynamics (by creating selective ties, for example). It is important that group be an accepting place for all members, so it is best not to schedule play dates with other group members. If on occasion there is a special event you would like to plan (a birthday party, for instance), you may do so as long as all group members are invited.

Your child will receive a Program Notebook, which he or she must bring to each session. It is divided into four parts. One section will collect all the notes and other documents we create during the sessions. One section is for the Resilience Builder Assignments your child will complete at home. The third section, the Success Journal, is where your child will record progress toward an individual goal and other successes or attempts to achieve success outside of group. Perhaps you could think of things to note in the Success Journal as well. It could be as simple as reporting that your child "Said something nice to_____ on Monday at home." Many children who attend group experience more than their share of negative feedback, so it's helpful and encouraging to acknowledge as many positive attempts or successful outcomes as possible. The final section includes parent letters and special handouts.

Resilience Builder Assignments are an essential part of group. These at-home assignments help you and your child reinforce the skills that they are working on and encourage progress toward the individual goal. As is the case with music lessons, if you don't practice, progress is *much* slower.

Please feel free to provide me with any updates on your child. It is often difficult for children to recall a specific incident that may have occurred outside of group. We like to use real-life incidents or interactions for role-plays and discussion, without necessarily identifying the child.

Parent Letter 2.1 (p. 2 of 3)

One of the most challenging tasks that we face is to get the children to generalize and transfer their improved understanding of their behavior and new skills to home, school, and other environments. The Resilience Builder Assignments are helpful; also useful are activities outside group. We may go bowling or miniature golfing, for example. Any suggestions for other structured activities outside the group are welcome.

Resilience Builder Assignment: Individual Goal Contract

Please assist your child in choosing an individual goal to work on during the sessions. Discuss what steps are needed to attain this goal. If writing is an issue, please have your child dictate a goal to you. We also encourage you to practice self-regulation/relaxation exercises together.

Please feel free to contact me with any questions.

Sincerely,

Program Leader

SESSION

2.2

Flexibility

PURPOSE

Research shows that a person's cognitive flexibility is directly related to his or her ability to bounce back from life's hardships. Flexibility allows us to adapt to changes in circumstances and consider alternative solutions. This lesson discusses and demonstrates the concept of flexibility and the ways in which mental flexibility enhances our relationships.

GOALS

To discuss and demonstrate the concept of flexibility

To promote the understanding that cognitive flexibility involves creativity and the ability to adapt to change

To help group members understand the positive aspects of being flexible, including improved relationships

To practice a relaxation/self-regulation technique

MATERIALS

Chalkboard or dry erase board and marker

Program Notebooks (brought by group members)

Individual Points Charts

Name Cube

Rubber bands (one per participant and some extra, in case some snap)

A box of spaghetti

A common household object (e.g., clothes hanger, spoon) (optional)

Paper and pencils (optional)

Toys and games for free play

Copies of the following:

>   Leadership Award (Appendix C)
>
>   Resilience Builder Assignment 2.2
>
>   Parent Letter 2.2

PROCEDURE

Individual Greeting

Conduct the individual greetings, as described in Session 2.1.

Review Success Journal and Resilience Builder Assignment

Have each group member discuss his or her individual goal and Success Journal entry and experiences completing the Resilience Builder Assignment. When each member finishes speaking, ask him or her to throw the Name Cube to determine the next speaker.

> *Record each group member's goal on his or her Points Chart and assign one point for bringing in the notebook, one point for identifying a goal, one point for discussing it, and one point for the first Success Journal entry. At the end of the session, you can award a point for cooperating during the session.*

Discuss and Demonstrate Physical Flexibility

1. Start by introducing the idea of flexibility. Write the word "Flexibility" on the board and say, "Does anyone know what it means to be flexible? Or what it means to be inflexible or rigid?"

    Examples include going with the flow, adapting to change, and being able to move your body easily—or the opposite.

2. Say, "What does it mean to be physically flexible?" Summarize:

    Physical flexibility refers to the ability to move your body easily and bend into different positions. This is the opposite of being inflexible, when our bodies are stiff and tight. Can anyone show me flexibility in your body and joints?

    Call on someone to demonstrate flexibility in his or her own body and joints (e.g., movements of fingers, doing the splits, etc.). Limit this to one demonstration.

    Continue:

    Other things can be physically flexible as well. For example, when engineers design buildings, they make them flexible so that they can withstand changes in the weather or environment, such as strong winds and earthquakes. A building will adapt by swaying, but it will still remain stable.

Discuss Mental Flexibility

1. Explain that mental flexibility allows for thinking of a variety of solutions to a problem. Say:

    Being flexible in how you think allows you to come up with many different solutions or ways of thinking about a challenge or situation. When we are flexible in our thinking, we are better able to adapt to changes and also to be creative in solving problems in new ways. Without flexibility, people get upset and feel stuck and are unable to resolve difficult situations.

2. Explain ways to improve mental flexibility. Say:

    Because being open to changing how you think about something is necessary in problem solving, it's important to discuss ways to improve mental flexibility.

    ► First, be open to considering all ideas and options, even ones that don't seem typical. It is easy to get stuck on one idea about something; however, it is important to know that there are many different ways to handle a situation.

    ► Next, consider alternatives that initially may seem unlikely to work and even those that come from people you oppose (for example, don't fail to consider an option just because it comes from someone you do not like).

▶ Finally, consider which approach you would like to take to show flexibility in the situation.

3. Provide an example of mental flexibility. Say:

Let's say that you are invited to your friend's party on the same day as a family gathering that you cannot miss. If you are inflexible in your thinking, you will simply be upset that you will have to miss your friend's party and possibly be angry with your parents. However, if you are flexible in your thinking and self-talk, you will be able to come up with different solutions. What are some different solutions you could come up with if you are thinking in a flexible way?

Encourage responses and, if necessary, review the idea that self-talk refers to the things that we say to ourselves, usually in our own minds. Some flexible ideas include the following.

One idea would be asking your parents if you could split the time between the party and family gathering. You might also consider the option of making a special plan with your friend to have a one-on-one celebration. If you are upset about missing the party itself—let's say it was a paintball party or an ice skating party—you could see if your parents would take you and your friend on another day.

Summarize the idea that mental flexibility allows you to handle situations in a more creative and positive way.

4. Explain that when we are mentally flexible, we also are better able to adapt to change. Say:

It is normal to have expectations about how things will happen. For example, most of you expect that, when you arrive home from school each day, you will do your homework, have an activity or some time to relax, and eat dinner. Well, what if your parent's car breaks down on the way home from school one day? You suddenly have to change how you think about your evening and will need to adjust to this new event. Being flexible requires you to go with the flow even when challenges arise.

Demonstrate Flexibility

1. Hand out rubber bands and uncooked spaghetti pasta. Give one of each to every group member. Then, take a rubber band and slowly stretch it out. Ask, "Is this rubber band flexible?" *(Have group members stretch their rubber bands and comment.)* Then show them a piece of uncooked spaghetti. Ask, "Is this flexible?" Bend it in half to the point of breaking, commenting on the fact that it is rigid and stiff and therefore easily breaks. Have the group members try bending their own pieces. Now comment, "This spaghetti is raw. Now imagine that we cooked the spaghetti. It would no longer be inflexible—it would be very soft and easy to bend."

2. Make the connection between the demonstration and mental flexibility. Say:

When we show flexibility, we are like the rubber band or the cooked spaghetti. Rigid, or inflexible, thinking will not allow us to adapt to change, and instead results in our feeling overwhelmed. You might "snap" like the spaghetti strands and show frustration, anger, or sadness. When you are flexible, you "stretch" your mind to think in new and creative ways.

3. Explain that flexibility leads to identifying new solutions and experiences. Say:

When things change and we are required to be flexible, we often discover new and creative ways of handling different situations. For example, if you are a guest at someone's home for dinner and they are serving food you've never eaten before, you might be flexible and try the new food, and may discover that you really like it!

4. Once again, stretch the rubber band and return it to resting position. Say, "Remember, this is how your mind responds when you are flexible. Being flexible allows you to discover new solutions."

Discuss the Influence of Mental Flexibility on Relationships

1. Explain how flexibility is related to getting along with others and describe the pitfalls of being inflexible. Ask:

▶ How might flexibility in thinking impact your friendships?

▶ What happens when you work on a class project at school and one person will not go along with an idea the group has agreed upon? Does that make the project easier or more difficult to complete?

▶ What are some other challenges you have experienced with inflexible people in the classroom environment?

Pause for brief discussion and solicit responses.

2. Ask, "Has there ever been a time when you have made plans with friends, and at the last minute you can't get a ride? The plan may seem doomed; however, flexible thinking can be used to work things out. In some situations, plans may work out even better when everyone is flexible and adapts to changes in plans." Ask group members to tell about a time that things worked out well and people adapted to a change in circumstances (e.g., when the electricity goes out and you have a great time "camping out" in the living room, reading by flashlight).

3. Ask, "Has anyone ever been with a group of friends trying to agree on a plan, and one person gets upset because the plan is not what he or she wanted or expected to happen? It's really hard to deal with people when they are inflexible. Now think about your friends

who are willing to compromise or who are creative and skilled in coming up with different solutions. What's it like having that kind of friend?"

Elicit a short discussion about friends who were flexible in these ways and how that contributed to the friendship.

Free Play/Behavioral Rehearsal

Provide group members with a selection of age-appropriate toys, games, or other activities to choose from that encourage joint play and follow the procedure described in Session 2.1 for choosing play partners and facilitating free play.

Relaxation/Self-Regulation

1. Have group members find a comfortable place to sit or lie down. Introduce guided imagery as a means of relaxation by reading the following script:

    ▶ Close your eyes, then take a deep breath in and hold it until the count of five: 1, 2, 3, 4, 5. Slowly breathe out to the count of five: 1, 2, 3, 4, 5.

    ▶ I'd like you to imagine what it would be like to float in the sky. Imagine floating on a comfortable white cloud. The cloud looks like fluffy, soft cotton.

    ▶ You are feeling light as a feather—happy and content. Feel your body floating in the sky. Imagine what you are floating over.

    ▶ You could picture yourself floating over your house. Look down at it. You may see your yard, the roof of your house, and other familiar things. If you have a pet, you may even see it outside. You are enjoying the view and know that you are safe.

    ▶ Imagine all the things you might see in your neighborhood from the cloud.

    ▶ Picture yourself floating over any other place, real or imaginary, that you like. Maybe you will float over a waterfall or even a thick jungle where you can see only treetops. It can be anywhere you would enjoy seeing. Enjoy this sight a few moments. Notice how your body feels when it is this relaxed. *(Wait 60 seconds.)*

    ▶ Now, on the count of five, you will feel a little more awake and alert. At one, you will feel rested and relaxed. At two, you will take a deep breath, at three, you will gently blow it out, at four, open your eyes, and at five, you will be ready for the rest of the day. *(Wait 15–30 seconds before continuing.)*

    ▶ OK, let's begin. One . . . rested and relaxed. Two . . . take in a slow gentle breath. Three . . . slowly blow it out through your mouth. Four . . . open your eyes . . . and five, you are alert and relaxed.

2. Ask group members, "How did that feel? Could you make yourself feel very light and relaxed? What did you see in your mind?" Discuss.

Leadership Award

Select a group member to receive the Leadership Award and provide praise for what the person did well.

Generalization: Resilience Builder Assignment

Give each group member a copy of the Resilience Builder Assignment. Go over the assignment and answer any questions.

Parent Component

Give each participant a copy of the parent letter for the session. Have participants place it and the Resilience Builder Assignment in the appropriate sections of their notebook.

Flexibility—Staying Calm and Being Creative

Name _____ **Date** _____

Describe how you could be flexible in these challenging situations.

Situation 1

You have almost finished a school biography paper that you have been working on for a month. Now you just need to finish by making a poster. You have all the pictures and text ready to attach to it. The project is due tomorrow. As you turn to get the poster, you see that your little sister has been practicing cutting with her new scissors. She has cut your poster board! What are two ways you could be flexible in this situation?

1. _____

2. _____

Situation 2

It's Friday, and you are looking forward to going to the mall with your friends and buying a really great new game that just came out. You make plans to go, and at the last minute, one of your friends says that she can only go to a mall that is different from the one you usually go to. How could you be flexible in this situation?

1. _____

2. _____

Situation 3

You make plans to stay over at your friend's house on Saturday night. On Saturday morning, your mother tells you that your family is having an unexpected visit from Uncle Steve and Aunt Kelly. Your mother says that you need to stay home to visit with them. How could you be flexible in this situation?

1. _____

2. _____

Write about one time this week that you were inflexible and what you could have done differently to handle the situation better. If you cannot come up with an example, ask your parents for help.

_____

_____

_____

Flexibility

Dear Parents:

Research demonstrates that a person's cognitive, or mental, flexibility is directly related to his or her ability to generate alternative responses and solutions to disagreements and to bounce back from life's hardships.

Mental flexibility allows us to be proactive in taking on life's challenges by using creative thinking to develop novel alternatives. Being flexible allows us to experience new situations and be a better person and friend. The ability to adapt, to "change gears," and to tolerate changes in circumstances is central to the concept. The group will learn the components of showing mental flexibility, which includes considering alternative solutions to dealing with a problem.

The group will take part in a "snap and stretch" demonstration in group today, examining the properties of uncooked spaghetti (snaps because it is rigid) and a rubber band (stretches because it is flexible). We will then apply this analogy to group members' thoughts and responses to unexpected events and changes in plans. Group members will discuss rigidity versus flexibility and how the different ways of thinking and responding affect relationships.

It is important to remember and understand that when children and teens are emotionally upset, it is often because they are unable to be flexible in their thinking and generate different solutions, likely leading to feelings of helplessness. When we foster resilience in children, we encourage a proactive stance, one that empowers children to use their flexibility and creativity in problem solving.

You can model mental flexibility by stating simple problems out loud in front of your child. Talk through the creative solutions that you are considering and state what you are going to do and why. Children learn a tremendous amount from witnessing parents model this skill.

Resilience Builder Assignment: Flexibility—Staying Calm and Being Creative

The assignment for this session asks your child to come up with flexible and creative solutions to specific challenging situations and to describe a time when he or she could have been more flexible. Please provide help if needed. We also encourage you to refer to the Relaxation Tips for Parents and Group Members handout and practice relaxation exercises with your child.

Sincerely,

Program Leader

SESSION

2.3

Maintaining Conversations

PURPOSE

Proficiency in maintaining conversations is an essential social skill; friendships often result from meaningful and interesting conversations. This session focuses on helping group members identify those factors that facilitate conversations and those that tend to bring them to an end. If group members have participated in Session 1.6, "Initiating and Maintaining Conversations," some of this session's material will constitute review.

GOALS

To review the concept of Conversation Builders and Conversation Busters

To make the point that good conversations are an important building block in developing strong relationships

To teach three Conversation Builders: positive conversation flow, the Say Three and See Rule, and sharing opinions respectfully

To practice a relaxation/self-regulation technique

MATERIALS

Chalkboard or dry erase board and marker

Program Notebook (brought by group members)

Individual Points Charts

Name Cube

Ball of yarn

Toys and games for free play

Copies of the following:

> Leadership Award (Appendix C)
>
> Resilience Builder Assignment 2.3
>
> Parent Letter 2.3
>
> Family Resilience Builder: Family Meetings (Appendix B)
>
> *Before beginning the session, create a **Steps in Giving Your Opinion** poster.*

PROCEDURE

Individual Greeting

Practice an appropriate initial greeting, as described in Session 2.1.

Review Success Journal and Resilience Builder Assignment

Have each group member discuss his or her individual goal and Success Journal entry and experiences completing the Resilience Builder Assignment. When each member finishes speaking, ask him or her to throw the Name Cube to determine the next speaker.

> *Record points on each group member's Points Chart for this portion of the session. Record the point for participation at the end of the session.*

Discuss Conversation Builders and Busters

1. Discuss the importance of good conversation skills and their relationship to developing friendships with others. Say:

> Today we are going to talk about appropriate ways to maintain conversations with others. Have you ever had a conversation with someone in which the other person did all the talking and monopolized the conversation? Or have you ever had a

conversation in which no one talked, and when people did, they talked at the same time and no one listened? *(Acknowledge responses.)* That makes it hard to follow what people were saying.

2. Explain that we look for friends with whom we feel comfortable and that part of relationship "fit" comes from enjoying our time and conversation together. Say:

    > A good friend is someone you can talk to—a person who respects your opinion and with whom you can have a good conversation. When you find someone like that, you really value your relationship. The more you value a relationship with someone, the more time and energy you want to invest with that person. This investment with others then turns into good times spent together. So, we see that conversations are REALLY important beginning building blocks toward developing solid, strong relationships with others.

3. Write the headings "Conversation Builders" and "Conversation Busters" on the board. Say:

    > If we have a conversation, there are ways that we can be proactive to make the conversation a good one. These things that we can do are called Conversation Builders because they help to build on the conversation. There also are ways in which we may interfere with a good conversation. These behaviors are called Conversation Busters. They can bust or stop the conversation. Today, we are going to learn about some builders and busters. Let's start with the busters. What kinds of busters have you noticed in conversations?

    > *Write responses on the board and reinforce participation. Examples might include people who talk over others, people who say very little, and people who talk about only themselves.*

4. Next ask, "What kinds of Builders have you noticed when you have had conversations with others?"

    > *If group members have difficulty generating ideas, you can suggest examples such as selecting a topic that all participants agree on, looking at and listening to others, and giving everyone a chance to speak.*

5. Ask, "How did that affect your relationship with that person?" Summarize the idea that Builders allow a reciprocal exchange, that is a positive back and forth conversation. This helps develop friendships because the other person stays interested in talking with you. The more you talk with each other, the more you find out what you have in common.

6. Ask group members to reflect on and share (as they feel comfortable) which Builders they are good at and which Busters they may need to beware of in their own conversations. Say:

Now think about how you communicate with others. You do not need to share this out loud, but think about what conversation skills you could work on improving. We all have some Busters. What are some of these? What about Builders? *(Acknowledge responses.)*

Discuss and Demonstrate Flow, the Say Three and See Rule, and Giving Opinions

1. On the board, write "Flow," "Say Three and See Rule," and "Giving Opinions." Explain that these are three specific Conversation Builders.

2. Introduce the idea of conversation flow:

    First we will talk about the concept of "flow." It's one type of Conversation Builder. When we have a healthy, balanced dialogue with others, the conversation flows from one person to another. People talk about the same topic for about the same length of time as one another.

3. Tell group members that when they make statements that contribute to conversation flow, it is important not only to stay with the topic, but also to be mindful of the duration of their turn.

4. Introduce the Say Three and See Rule:

    So now let's talk about another Conversation Builder. It is the Say Three and See Rule. After you say about three sentences, you let others think about what you have said and respond to it. In other words, you wait and see if they look interested, what they have to say back, or how they respond to you.

    If they do not respond to you, then you might ask them a question about the topic. If they do respond, see if they understood what you were trying to say, and if so, respond to what they say. If not, you may need to clarify your point with about three more sentences or change the topic because they might not be interested.

    It can be helpful at this point to role-play the Say Three and See process.

5. Explain that the last Conversation Builder relates to sharing opinions in a respectful manner. Explain that to understand how to best give and accept an opinion, you need to be clear about the difference between a fact and an opinion. Ask, "What is a fact?"

    Call on group members and validate responses indicating that a fact is something that is true beyond a reasonable doubt and cannot be disputed—for example, "There are seven days in a week" or "It is 32 degrees Fahrenheit outside."

    Now ask, "What is an opinion?"

Call on group members, listen, and validate responses suggesting that an opinion is a statement about what we think or feel about something. It is something we believe and is not "right" or "wrong."

6. Direct the group's attention to the Steps in Giving Your Opinion poster.

Steps in Giving Your Opinion

1. Identify the discussion topic.

2. Listen to others' opinions.

3. Decide what your opinion is and wait for a break in the conversation.

4. State what your opinion is in a positive manner that will not offend others. Use the Say Three and See Rule.

5. Listen to others' responses.

6. If someone responds to you, respond back.

---

7. Give a second example, focusing on the idea that when we choose to give our opinion, it is important to do so in a tactful and positive manner.

   ▶ *(For girls only)* Your friend is asking how you like the dress she is trying on at the store. You don't think it compliments her. You might say, "I really liked the purple dress you put on before" or "Slacks really seem to show off your small waist better than this dress." This allows you to be truthful and positive, without hurting your friend's feelings.

   ▶ *(For boys or girls)* Suppose your friend brings up his or her favorite football team, which has lost every game this season, and you think it is primarily because of poor throws initiated by the quarterback. You might comment, 'Well, they do have a really good defensive line." Or you might choose to share your concerns about the quarterback's difficulty in making "connections" in a respectful way. In this way, you give your opinion, without being dishonest or disrespectful.

8. Explain that it is important to tolerate others' opinions. Say:

   When others give their opinion, it is important to respect their point of view. It is important to be positive and not to criticize or be negative. For example, it's not a good idea to say, "No, why don't you get it? That's not right!" when someone voices an opinion that is different from yours. Remember that opinions are NOT facts. They are not "wrong" or "right," and each of us has opinions that should be respected.

Conversation Web

1. Have group members select a timely and interesting topic, such as video games, vacations, and so forth. Next, have group members sit in a circle. Explain that the group will use the ball of yarn to create a conversation web to demonstrate how to stay on topic and have a positive conversation with good reciprocity, meaning give and take in the flow of conversation.

2. Provide the following instructions:

   ▶ Think of _____ *(the selected topic)* and your opinion of the topic. Catch the ball of yarn and state your opinion in one positive sentence. For example, if the topic is video games, you might say, "Playing video games helps you make friends." Then, while holding the end of the string, make eye contact with another group member and toss the yarn ball to him or her.

   ▶ This person catches the ball of yarn and validates your opinion—for example, saying, "So you think playing video games helps you make friends." Then that person should state his or her own opinion in a positive and respectful manner and ask a *who, what, when, where, why,* or *how* question to build on the conversation (for example, "What games help you make friends?").

   ▶ Finally, while holding the ball of yarn in the place where it was caught, that person tosses it back across the circle to another group member. This continues until the conversation "web" is formed.

   You may wish to review Session 1.6 for discussion of entering conversations using the words who, what, when, where, why, *and* how.

Sample Conversation Web Topics

What is the best country to visit on a trip? What makes you think that?

What is your favorite baseball team? Why?

What is your favorite kind of music? Why?

Should hunters be allowed to hunt endangered species of animals? When is it appropriate to do so?

What is the most important subject in school?

Is it better to live in the country or in the city? How do you know?

Should people who bully be expelled from school? When?

What is your favorite holiday? Why?

Should boys and girls play on coed or single-gender sports teams? Why?

Should you tell your friend that her new hairstyle does not look good on her? How would you do it?

Should you tell your friend when another friend tells you something negative about him? Why?

Free Play/Behavioral Rehearsal

Provide the group with a selection of age-appropriate toys, games, or other activities to choose from that encourage joint play and follow the procedure described in Session 2.1 for choosing play partners and facilitating free play.

Relaxation/Self-Regulation

1. Today's relaxation begins with imagery work around the idea of flow in conversation. Tell group members to get into a comfortable position in their seats, then read the following script:

   ▶ Close your eyes and sit quietly with your arms at your sides.

   ▶ Take a deep breath in through your nose, and hold it until the count of five: 1, 2, 3, 4, and 5. Now slowly breathe out through your mouth.

   ▶ Today we are going to picture ourselves floating down a smooth, flowing, river. The kind of river that we think of when we are thinking about the flow of good conversation. Picture yourself slowly floating on a warm summer day. You might be on an inner tube or lying on a raft.

   ▶ You feel safe and comfortable. The warm sun shines on your face, and you enjoy this light feeling. You dip your fingers into the water. The water feels cool on your fingertips, and you feel totally and completely . . . content.

   ▶ Picture yourself floating in any kind of environment you might enjoy. It could be in a tropical setting. It could be on a lazy river at your favorite amusement park, or at your favorite campground—anywhere you would feel safe, relaxed, and happy. Picture yourself there now.

   ▶ Now, I want you to notice all of the sights and sounds you might experience at that place. Feel the sun, or the breeze, or the spray from a nearby waterfall on your skin. Enjoy this time in your special place. Just relax for a few moments. *(Wait about 15 seconds and continue.)*

▶ Good. Now, enjoy this calm state that you have chosen, knowing that you can take this feeling with you and use it at any time during the day that you may need it to feel calm, quiet, and relaxed.

▶ Now, I will count from 1 to 5, and with each number you will feel a little more awake and alert. At 2, you will take a deep breath. At 3, you will blow it out. You will hear the count of 4 and open your eyes. At the count of 5, you will be ready for the rest of the day. *(Wait 15–20 seconds before continuing.)*

▶ Let's begin now. One, rested and relaxed *(wait 5 seconds).* Two, taking in a breath *(wait 5 seconds).* Three, slowly blowing it out through your mouth. Four, opening your eyes *(wait 1 to 2 seconds)* and 5.

2. Ask: "How did that feel? Where did you go? Could you feel yourself floating?"

Generalization: Resilience Builder Assignment

Give each participant a copy of the Resilience Builder Assignment. Go over the assignment and answer any questions.

Parent Component

Provide copies of the parent letter and have group members place it and the Resilience Builder Assignment in the appropriate sections of their notebook. In addition, provide a copy of the Family Meetings handout.

You can briefly explain the family meeting to the group if you wish.

OPTIONAL ACTIVITY: CONVERSATION PUZZLE

A conversation activity can also be completed using a small puzzle (12–24 pieces). Explain to the participants that they will be putting together a puzzle. Have members alternate putting in one piece of the puzzle after making a statement of one to three sentences in length on a given topic.

Maintaining Conversations—In My Opinion . . .

Name _____ Date _____

For each situation, describe how you could share your opinion in a positive and respectful manner.

Situation 1

Your friends get together and you are invited to join them. They want to play the same game that you have been playing daily for the last two weeks. How could you give an opinion about what you want to play today?

_____

_____

_____

_____

Situation 2

You find out from a friend that she is planning on playing a trick on one of your other friends. She asks what you think about the trick. You don't think it is a funny trick. In fact, you would not play the trick on your friend. How could you give her your opinion?

_____

_____

_____

_____

Situation 3

Two of your friends like to write poetry. They have both entered a school poetry contest and are asking what you think of their poems. One poem is much more creative and thoughtful than the other. How could you share your opinion with each person?

_____

_____

_____

_____

From *Resilience Builder Program for Children and Adolescents,* © 2011 by M. K. Alvord, B. Zucker, & J. J. Grados, Champaign, IL: Research Press (800-519-2707, www.researchpress.com).

Maintaining Conversations

Dear Parents:

This session focuses on the importance of maintaining reciprocal conversations by understanding and practicing Conversation Builders. Group members learn that conversations are the building blocks to developing deeper connections and relationships with others. We discuss and practice three Conversation Builders: positive flow in conversation, the Say Three and See Rule, and giving opinions in a positive and respectful manner.

► A good conversation has "flow," or a fluid rhythm among individuals. Each person contributes equally by sharing thoughts and ideas, with no one monopolizing the discussion.

► The Say Three and See Rule states that it's useful to say one to three sentences when speaking with others and then to stop and to listen to the other person's response to what we have said. Group members then decide if they have communicated effectively, if they should clarify their position, or if what they are saying isn't interesting to the other person.

► In giving opinions in a respectful and positive way, we concentrate not only on the content of what we say but also on how we state our opinion. The concepts of fact and opinion are discussed. We emphasize the ideas that opinions are not right or wrong and that they are unique to each individual. Group members learn how and when to give opinions—as well as how to remain positive and respectful when offering their point of view.

The steps to giving an opinion are as follows:

1. Identify the discussion topic.

2. Listen to others' opinions.

3. Decide what your opinion is and wait for a break in the conversation.

4. State your opinion in a positive, respectful way. (Use the Say Three and See Rule.)

5. Listen to others' responses. If someone responds to you, respond back.

Resilience Builder Assignment: Maintaining Conversations

This week's assignment provides three scenarios that require "opinion" responses. Please assist your child with positive and respectful replies. It would also be helpful to role-play the Say Three and See Rule and to practice a relaxation exercise with your child. If possible, conduct a family meeting, following the guidelines provided.

Sincerely,

Program Leader

From *Resilience Builder Program for Children and Adolescents,* © 2011 by M. K. Alvord, B. Zucker, & J. J. Grados, Champaign, IL: Research Press (800-519-2707, www.researchpress.com).

SESSION

2.4

Intent Versus Impact

PURPOSE

One important skill in enhancing relationships is effective communication, which depends on having one's intended message actually perceived correctly by other people. This session teaches group members how to improve communication by breaking the process into three parts: the communicator's intent, his or her words and behavior, and the impact of the words and behavior (measured by the other person's response).* Increased awareness of the elements of effective communication, such as recognizing the impact we have on others, improves our relationship with peers and family.

GOALS

To help participants understand that effective communication requires thinking about what they want to accomplish and whether what they say or do will be perceived correctly, or as intended.

---

*The paradigm of intent versus impact has been articulated in the research of Gottman, Notarius, Gonso, and Markman (1976).

To encourage recognition of the impact they actually have on the other person and, if it is unintended, to take responsibility and repair any damage

To practice a relaxation/self-regulation exercise that incorporates the skill of intent versus impact

MATERIALS

Chalkboard or dry erase board and marker

Program Notebooks (brought by group members)

Individual Points Charts

Name Cube

Toys and games for free play

Copies of the following:

Leadership Award (Appendix C)

Resilience Builder Assignment 2.4

Parent Letter 2.4

Family Resilience Builder: Compliment Basket (Appendix B)

*Before the session, create the **Intent Versus Impact** poster.*

PROCEDURE

Individual Greeting

Conduct the individual greetings, as described in Session 2.1.

Review Success Journal and Resilience Builder Assignment

Have each group member discuss his or her individual goal and Success Journal entry and experiences completing the Resilience Builder Assignment. When each participant finishes speaking, ask him or her to throw the Name Cube to determine the next speaker.

Record points on each group member's Points Chart for this portion of the session. Record the point for participation at the end of the session.

Discuss Intent, Behavior, and Impact

1. Write the words "Intent," "Behavior," and "Impact" on the board, with arrows, as shown. Ask group members what intent or having an intention means and record their

responses. Summarize that *intent* is what you mean to do or say—the message you want to get across.

Intent ⟶ Behavior ⟶ Impact

2. Say, "Good communication occurs when your message and corresponding behavior produce the intended impact. Poor communication, which happens when the message or actions are out of sync with the intent, often produces an unintended and unwelcome impact."

3. Point out that it is important to become more aware of what we say and do and how it affects others. You can take certain steps to be more aware of your intentions and the impact of your behavior. Direct group members' attention to the Intent Versus Impact poster.

Intent Versus Impact

1. Stop and think about what you want or expect to happen before you act.

2. Think about what would be the best way to convey your intentions to another person. What are the best words and tone of voice to use and actions to take?

3. Ask yourself if someone said or did the same thing to you, how would you feel?

4. Watch reactions to your behavior.

5. Respond appropriately to the person's reaction. (If your behavior had a negative impact, apologize and reword what you were trying to say.)

Role-Play Examples

1. Select pairs to act out one or both of the following sample situations to the group:

   ▶ A mom comes home from work and says, "What's that smell?" Dad has been cooking a delicious roast and gets all offended, thinking she means it stinks. What does the mom really mean to say, and how can she say it differently?

   ▶ A girl says, "Hey, I see that you really like the Yankees. You wore that Yankees team shirt yesterday, too!" The boy is insulted and hurt, even though the girl's intention wasn't to hurt him—she just didn't think it through before she said it that way. What does the girl mean to say, and how can she say it differently?

   As group members role-play, remind them that tone of voice, facial expressions, and body language are all important in how you convey your intent. Point out that when voice tone and volume match the pace of the setting, you are more likely to achieve a positive impact. Provide coaching as needed.

2. Encourage group members to suggest and role-play other situations where intent can be mistaken and needs to be clarified. Ask, "What are some examples of situations in which you want to match your intention with an impact?"

3. Ask, "What are the benefits of having your words and actions produce the results or have the impact that you want?" If necessary, summarize the ideas that when you get your message across, you let someone know what you really think and feel; in addition, you have a better chance of getting what you want or need.

Free Play/Behavioral Rehearsal

Provide the group with a selection of age-appropriate toys, games, or other activities to choose from that encourage joint play and follow the procedure described in Session 2.1 for choosing play partners and facilitating free play.

Relaxation/Self-Regulation

1. Today's relaxation is a guided imagery that helps group members make the connection between their intended outcome and their behavior in a school setting. Have the group find a comfortable place to sit or lie down, then read the following script:

   ▶ Gently close your eyes and take a deep breath in through your nose. Hold it: 1, 2, 3, 4, and 5. Slowly, very slowly, breathe out through your mouth.

   ▶ Let your body relax and let go of any tension or stress. Bring your head to rest on your right shoulder. Hold that position and feel the tension on the other side of your neck.

   ▶ Slowly bring your head upright while you notice the sensations. Now bring your head to rest on the other side. Hold it. Hold it. Slowly bring your head to its upright position. Notice the difference in how your neck feels when it is tense and resting on your shoulder, and when it is upright and relaxed.

   ▶ Take another deep breath in through your nose. Hold it. Now slowly, breathe out through your mouth.

   ▶ Clear your mind of any worries or undesirable thoughts. Imagine that you are at school. Maybe you are at lunch, in the hallway, or at recess.

   ▶ Pretend that you would like to talk with your classmate, perhaps sit with him or her during lunch or play a game during recess. You decide where you would like this to take place and with whom.

► What do you think to yourself? You need to communicate your intent. Think about what you can do or say to get the person's attention. You might make eye contact first, then smile and have a friendly face.

► What could you say? Remember, if you don't know what to say, you can ask a question starting with *who, what, when, where, why,* or *how.*

► Next decide what you would like to have happen. What would you need to say or do? Your breath and body are calm. Your mind is clear. Do or say what you think would work to have your desired outcome.

► Now imagine how that person might react. What might the person say or do? If the person didn't react to you as you intended, what else could you try? Try it out in your mind. Did it work?

► Take another deep breath and hold it. Now slowly breathe out. Shake your head and slowly open your eyes.

2. Have group members share their images. Praise them for both images of situations that were successful and those that were unsuccessful. Ask them to describe one or two things that made what they imagined successful and one or two things that did not work.

Leadership Award

Select a group member to receive the Leadership Award and provide praise for what the person did well.

Generalization: Resilience Builder Assignment

Give each group member a copy of the Resilience Builder Assignment for the next session. Go over the assignment and answer any questions.

Parent Component

Give each participant a copy of the parent letter for the session. In addition, provide a copy of the Compliment Basket handout for parents. Have group members place the parent letter, the Resilience Builder Assignment, and the Compliment Basket handout in the appropriate sections of their notebooks.

If appropriate, review the Compliment Basket procedure with the group.

RESILIENCE BUILDER ASSIGNMENT 2.4

Intent ⟶ Behavior ⟶ Impact

Name _____ **Date** _____

It is important to become more aware of what we say and do and how it affects others. The following steps will help you to be more aware of your intentions and the impact of your behavior:

1. **Stop** and think about what you want or expect to happen before you act.

2. **Think** about what would be the best way to convey your intentions to another person. What are the best words to use, tone of voice, and actions to take?

3. **Ask** yourself if someone said or did the same thing to you, how would you feel?

4. **Watch** reactions to your behavior.

5. **Respond** appropriately to the person's reaction. (If your behavior had a negative impact, apologize and reword what you were trying to say.)

   Think about a social interaction you have had recently and answer the following questions.

1. Who were you interacting with and where?

   _____

2. What were you trying to communicate?

   _____

   _____

3. How did you act, what did you say, what were your facial expressions or body language?

   _____

   _____

4. How did the other person react (was it positive, negative, neutral)?

   _____

5. If your intention didn't match the impact it had, what could you try to do or say differently next time?

   _____

   _____

Intent Versus Impact

Dear Parents:

We often hear, "But I didn't mean to . . ." from children and teens and often see them baffled by the reaction that a peer or adult might have in response to their actions. Today's session focuses on the communication skill of matching our intent with the actual impact we have. This skill is not as tangible as others, so we need your help.

Good communication entails statements or behaviors that result in an impact that matches the intention you have.

▶ **INTENT,** or what we want to happen. Every time we say or do something, we send a message. First, we must think about what we are trying to do.

▶ **BEHAVIOR,** both verbal and nonverbal. It's important to be aware of your actions, facial expressions, what you say, your tone of voice, and your body language.

▶ **IMPACT,** or how your behavior affects the person you are communicating with. What kind of a reaction does your behavior get from the other person? Sometimes we need to ask for feedback if we don't get it.

Understanding the relationship among these three components provides the opportunity for growth and behavior change. Please look for every opportunity over the course of the next few months to help your child match his or her intent to impact. This can be accomplished by encouraging and reinforcing behaviors that are likely to have a positive impact on others, such as being sensitive and showing empathy for other's feelings, actively listening (facing the person who is talking, making eye contact, nodding or giving some indication of paying attention, etc.), making positive comments (giving compliments, making supportive statements, etc.), and performing positive actions (hugging, shaking hands, helping, congratulatory remarks or actions, etc.). It is equally important to point out situations in which the intended outcome resulted in a negative impact. Please identify specific behaviors that next time might produce the desired outcome.

Resilience Builder: Intent ⟶ Behavior ⟶ Impact

This assignment asks your child to think of a social interaction and note the intended message, the behavior that was to convey the message, and the response. If the intent did not match the impact, please assist your child in generating ideas about what he or she could have said or done differently. Please also ask your child to lead a relaxation exercise for the family. If time allows, conduct a family meeting and use the Compliment Basket strategy.

Sincerely,

Program Leader

SESSION

2.5

On the Mark/Off the Mark Thinking: Part 1

PURPOSE

There is a strong relationship between how we think and how we feel about a situation. Children with social skills deficits, anxiety, depression, AD/HD, and low self-esteem commonly experience automatic thoughts that are distorted in nature. These cognitive distortions, or thinking errors, typically result in emotional distress and inappropriate handling of situations. Learning the most common thinking errors allows children to identify and challenge their distorted automatic thoughts. On doing so, children can become skilled at replacing these thoughts with more realistic, balanced ones; this process typically involves examining the evidence for our thoughts and being flexible.

If possible, have parents join the final 15 minutes of group to learn about cognitive distortions and practice a relaxation exercise with their child.

GOALS

To introduce the concepts of "off the mark" thinking (thinking errors or cognitive distortions) versus "on the mark" (realistic) thinking through self-talk

To teach three common off the mark thinking errors: all-or-nothing thinking, filtering, and catastrophizing

To promote understanding of the connection among thoughts, feelings, and actions

To teach one strategy to examine the evidence and challenge the thoughts

MATERIALS

Chalkboard or dry erase board and markers of different colors

Program Notebooks

Individual Points Charts

Name Cube

Dartboard and magnetic darts

Cup of clear water with rocks, marbles, or coins on the bottom

Strainer and small container

Two balloons for each group member

Toys and games for free play

Copies of the following:

> Leadership Award (Appendix C)
>
> Resilience Builder Activity 2.5
>
> Parent Letter 2.5

PROCEDURE

Individual Greeting

Conduct the individual greetings, as described in Session 2.1.

Review Success Journal and Resilience Builder Assignment

Have each group member discuss his or her individual goal and Success Journal entry and experiences completing the Resilience Builder Assignment. When each participant finishes speaking, ask him or her to throw the Name Cube to determine the next speaker.

Record points on each group member's Points Chart for this portion of the session. Record the point for participation at the end of the session.

Introduce On the Mark and Off the Mark Thinking

1. Illustrating these ideas with the dartboard, say:

    Sometimes we have automatic and negative thoughts that we call "off the mark" thinking. They seem to make sense to us, but they are not realistic, and they lead us to worry or be unhappy. We get into the habit of thinking in certain ways. This is negative self-talk—that is, what we say to ourselves in our mind. We are going to talk about three kinds of thoughts, or self-talk, that are problematic. We will also talk about some ways to help you examine the evidence and challenge your thoughts so that you can think more realistically. We call this "on the mark" thinking. We can have thoughts that are completely on target, be a little off the mark, or be way off the mark.

    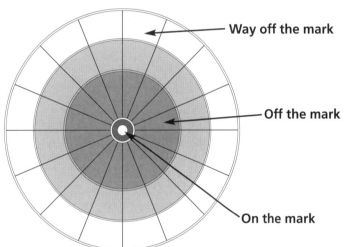

    It is important at this point to emphasize the universality of making thinking errors to avoid invalidating a child, especially when we talk in more extremes about the errors. It is helpful to show warmth and humor when discussing errors, without minimizing them.

2. Illustrate with an example that even errors can be along a continuum: small, medium or large. Say:

    Suppose you lost your school book and assume that this will negatively affect your grade. On target, on the mark thinking might be thinking, "I lost it, I will pay for it and get another copy. I can buy or borrow a copy." If you are way off the mark, you think, "What if I now fail the class because I lost the book?" A little off the mark would be that you think, "I lost the book and will pay for it. The teacher *might* be upset and it *may* affect my grade."

Discuss and Demonstrate All-or-Nothing Thinking

1. On the board, write "All-or-Nothing Thinking." Explain that when you are using all-or-nothing thinking, you are thinking in extremes, believing that something is either right or wrong, perfect or a complete failure. Say, "For example, let's say you missed a shot in the basketball game. If you feel like you've failed or are a failure, then you are using all-or-nothing thinking."

2. Demonstrate all-or-nothing thinking by drawing a horizontal line and mark one end "Perfect/All" and the other end, "Failure/None." In between, make vertical lines of various colors to demonstrate that many possibilities lie between the two extremes. Say:

    > People often use words to describe their thoughts like *never* or *always*, or *perfect* or *horrible*, or *all* or *nothing*. Can you give me some examples of when someone's self-talk is "It's not perfect, so it's a failure"?

    > *Some examples: You either get an A on a test or you think you are stupid and a failure, you never get to do what you want, and you are either the best player or you are the worst player on the team.*

3. Discuss the importance of challenging all-or-nothing thinking:

    > Although it may be easy to come up with reasons to hold negative beliefs, it is important to think of all the realistic evidence to counter and challenge those beliefs. It's like playing detective and gathering information. You can ask yourself, "Does this *always* happen? Do you *never* get the chance to do what you want"?

4. Have two members volunteer to come up with an example of off the mark, all-or-nothing thinking and on the mark thinking. Give each volunteer a magnetic dart. As they offer the examples, have them place the darts in the appropriate spots on the dartboard.

    > *They might also use a marker to draw lines on the continuum to illustrate several alternative thoughts, placing them closer to "all," closer to "none," or somewhere in between.*

Discuss and Demonstrate Filtering

1. Write the word "Filtering" on the board. Tell the group:

    > Filtering means that you are magnifying the negatives of a situation and minimizing the positives. You think about the bad things that happened and not about the good things. For example, the day in school goes fairly well overall; however, you have one negative interaction. When asked how the school day went, the answer is "Terrible!"

2. Demonstrate filtering: Fill a glass with water and drop in stones, marbles, or coins. Tell the group that the stones, marbles, or coins symbolize negative thoughts and the water

symbolizes positive thoughts. The water-filled glass demonstrates on the mark thinking because it shows that the negative thoughts, or negative self-talk (stones) that might reflect reality, fall to the bottom, and the positive thoughts, or positive self-talk (water), are what dominate.

It is important that the group understands that on the mark thinking does not deny negative thoughts or events, but rather puts them in perspective relative to positive thoughts or possibilities.

3. Then take the glass of water and pour it through the strainer. Ask, "What is left in the strainer *(the negative thoughts)*? This is an example of off the mark filtering.

4. Give a volunteer the glass of water, strainer, and rocks. Ask the volunteer to come up with an example of off the mark filtering and on the mark thinking and to demonstrate with the props. Invite group members to play detective and gather evidence to help challenge the cognitive distortion. For example:

> Suppose you attended a party with a lot of friends and had fun. You had to leave the party earlier than others. When someone asks the next day if you had fun, you keep talking and thinking about the fact that you had to leave early. You can challenge that thought by looking at the "big picture" and thinking about your good feelings about going to the party, even if you had to leave earlier than you wanted.

Ask additional volunteers to demonstrate as time allows.

Discuss and Demonstrate Catastrophizing

1. Write the word "Catastrophizing" on the board. Say, "What does *catastrophe* mean?" Explain that catastrophizing is when you expect the worst to happen and expect that you will not be able to handle it.

2. Convey the idea that this type of thinking is a common cause of anxiety:

> We call these thoughts "What ifs?" For example, you think, "What if I mess up on this writing assignment?" and automatically jump to the conclusion that you will fail and will never be able to write well. One way to think of catastrophic thinking is by blowing up a balloon.

3. Hand each group member a balloon. Say:

> Every time you think "What if?" blow into the balloon. Let's try it. Think of a worry or "What if?" and each time, breathe into the balloon. The more anxious you get, the faster you blow until the balloon is ready to explode. You notice that your breathing is affected, too. You are more likely to breathe through your chest than to use calm breathing, through your belly.

Have group members put their balloons in the trash. Let them know you'll give them a new one at the end of group to take home.

4. Discuss challenging the catastrophizing thinking error:

    > There are some questions we can ask ourselves to challenge catastrophizing and change to more balanced self-talk. You could say to yourself, "What's the worst thing that can happen if it comes true? How likely is it to happen? Can I handle the situation if it happens?"

5. Again, give two volunteers two magnetic darts each and ask them to come up with an example of off the mark catastrophizing and on the mark thinking. As they offer the examples, have them place the darts in appropriate spots on the dartboard.

Free Play/Behavioral Rehearsal

Provide the group with a selection of age-appropriate toys, games, or other activities to choose from that encourage joint play and follow the procedure described in Session 2.1 for choosing play partners and facilitating free play.

Relaxation/Self-Regulation

1. Have group members find a comfortable place to sit or lie down. Read the following script slowly and in a calm and soothing voice:

    ▶ Gently close your eyes and take a deep breath in through your nose. Hold it: 1, 2, 3, 4, and 5. Now slowly breathe out through your mouth.

    ▶ This is your time for relaxation. Clear your mind and let go of any stress or tension that you might be holding onto. Get your body in a comfortable position. Take another deep breath in through your nose. Hold it: 1, 2, 3, 4, and 5. Now very slowly breathe out through your mouth.

    ▶ We are going to tense different muscle groups. I want you to pay attention to the difference in how the muscles feel when they are tight and tense versus when they are loose and relaxed. The muscles might even hurt a little when they are tensed.

    ▶ Start by bending your head down until your chin touches your chest. Hold it and feel the tension. Hold it. Hold it. Now very slowly bring your head up.

    ▶ Now bend your head, trying to touch your right shoulder. Bring it as far down as you can. Feel the tension on the other side of your neck. Hold it. Hold it. Now slowly bring your head back to its normal position.

    ▶ Next, bend your head, trying to touch your left shoulder. Bring it as far down as you can. Feel the tension on the other side of your neck. It might hurt a little. Hold it. Hold it. Now slowly bring your head back to its normal position.

    ▶ Now very slowly bend your head back. Hold that position: 1, 2, 3, 4, and 5. Now slowly bring your head back to its resting position.

▶ Let's move down to your stomach. Pretend someone just punched you in the stomach or that a heavy dog sat on your stomach as you were lying down. Pull it in as much as you can. Hold it. Hold it. Slowly release the tension. Remember be aware of how it feels to have the muscles be tight and tense compared to when you loosen the muscles and release them.

▶ Last we will pretend someone pumped your stomach up with air. Let your stomach blow up as big as you can. Feel the tension. Now slowly let the stomach relax.

▶ I am going to count to five. At five you will open your eyes. Ready . . . one, wiggle your head. Two, lift your shoulders. Three, loosen your arms. Four, wiggle your legs. Five, slowly open your eyes.

2. Ask group members:

How did that feel? What part of your body was the most tense? What were the sensations you had when you relaxed the muscles? *(Acknowledge responses.)* When you do this relaxation exercise, it's always important to be aware of the difference in the way the muscles feel when they are tight, compared to what they feel like when they are loose and relaxed.

Leadership Award

Select a group member to receive the Leadership Award and provide praise for what the child did well.

Generalization: Resilience Builder Assignment

Give each group member a copy of the Resilience Builder Assignment for the next session. Go over the assignment and answer any questions. (See the chart for a sample description of Roger's thinking error and more realistic way of thinking.)

Roger's Thinking Error

All-or-Nothing Thinking because even though he only made one small mistake, he thought since it wasn't perfect, it was a failure. It might also be filtering. He filtered out the mostly positive and thought it was terrible. He might have a belief that he doesn't do well in these situations, so even though he received an A, he may remember times when he stumbled before and think, "I'm not good at this—see I stumbled."

A More Realistic Way of Thinking

He did stumble over a few words, but what percentage of the time did he stumble? Even if it was a lot, he received an A. The teacher evaluated it objectively and thought it was excellent.

Parent Component

Give each participant a copy of the parent letter for the session. Have participants place the letter and Resilience Builder Assignment in the appropriate sections of their notebooks.

OPTIONAL ACTIVITY: CAST OF CHARACTERS

If time permits, or as a session alternative, you may choose to introduce a "cast of characters" that exemplify the thinking distortions.

1. As you write these names on the board, say: "I am going to share with you some friends who personify these types of off-the-mark thinking. They are Abby All-or-Nothing (all-or-nothing thinking), Negative Nelly (filtering), and Captain Catastrophe (catastrophizing)."

2. Explain to the group how each character thinks.

Abby-All-or-Nothing

Our first friend is Abby-All-or-Nothing. Guess how she thinks. She thinks to herself that things are either perfect or terrible! When Abby gets an A on a test, she thinks, "Today is the perfect day!" Then later, if she forgets her lunch money, she begins thinking, "This is the worst day of my life!" She's on a roller coaster; her thinking is EXTREME.

Negative Nelly

Our next character is Negative Nelly. She had fun playing outside for most of the afternoon. Her dad calls her in to start her homework. She thinks "my whole afternoon is ruined." She filtered out the fun she had this afternoon and magnified the fact that she has to go inside and cut short her playtime. Her thinking is focused on the NEGATIVE.

Captain Catastrophe

Finally, we have our friend Captain Catastrophe. When something happens, Captain Catastrophe overreacts. So when Captain Catastrophe trips and stubs his toe, he says, "Oh, no—I am going to need a cast. And maybe I will need my leg amputated! This is a catastrophe!" He sees small events as CATASTROPHIC.

3. Group members may then volunteer to role-play these characters as the activity.

Identifying Thinking Errors: Part 1

Name _____ Date _____

Review the types of thinking errors (self-talk) people often make. Then read the questions below and fill in your answers.

All-or-Nothing Thinking

Thinking in extremes. It's either right or wrong, perfect or a complete failure. For example, you missed a shot in the basketball game, you feel you've failed.

Filtering

Magnifying the negatives of a situation and minimizing the positives; thinking about the bad things that happened and not much about the good things. For example, the day in school goes fairly well overall, but one negative thing happens. When someone asks you how the school day went, your answer is "Terrible!"

Catastrophizing

Expecting the worst to happen and that you won't be able to handle a situation. This type of thinking is a common cause of anxiety. We call these thoughts "What ifs?" For example, your self-talk is "What if I mess up on this writing assignment?" and automatically jump to the conclusion that you will fail and will never be able to write well.

Answer the following questions.

1. Roger gave a presentation in front of his science class. He stumbled over a few words. His teacher told him that he did a good job and gave him an A. He thought he did a terrible job. What is Roger's thinking error here? Explain.

   _____

   _____

   _____

   What might be a more realistic and balanced way to think about the situation? Note: Realistic doesn't mean always positive. It means you gather information and see it from a different perspective or angle.

   _____

   _____

   _____

2. Write about a situation during the week when your thoughts were based on all-or-nothing thinking, filtering, or catastrophizing. Ask your parents to help you with this. Sometimes we don't recognize these kinds of thinking ourselves, but they might!

_____

_____

_____

_____

_____

What might be a more realistic and balanced way to think about the situation? What is the evidence to support the balanced way?

_____

_____

_____

_____

_____

On the Mark/Off the Mark Thinking:
Part 1

Dear Parents:

This week, we will begin the first of two sessions on the cognitive, or thinking, component of cognitive-behavior therapy. We will discuss recognizing and changing distorted assumptions and inaccurate thinking patterns. We can also think of them as habitual patterns of reaction. What we think leads us to how we feel and to how we act or react. Understanding the links among thoughts, feelings, and behavior is critical to change.

Over the next two sessions we will review thinking that is "off the mark"; the group will be asked to identify what thoughts they have in certain situations and what self-talk would actually make more sense. Our list, while not all inclusive, will help your child begin to recognize "thinking errors," also known as cognitive distortions. We will also discuss challenging those unhelpful thoughts by gathering evidence to support alternative and more realistic thoughts, referred to as "on the mark" thinking.

Today we will start with the following thinking errors, or "off the mark" thinking, and some examples that might apply to your child:

All-or-Nothing Thinking

Thinking in extremes. It's either right or wrong, perfect or a complete failure. For example, you missed a shot in the basketball game, and you feel you've failed.

Filtering

Magnifying the negatives of a situation and minimizing the positives; thinking about the bad things that happened and not much about the good things. For example, the day in school goes fairly well overall, but one negative thing happens. When someone asks you how the school day went, your answer is "Terrible!"

Catastrophizing

Expecting the worst to happen and that you won't be able to handle a situation. This type of thinking is a common cause of anxiety. We call these thoughts "What ifs?" For example, your self-talk is "What if I mess up on this writing assignment?" and automatically you jump to the conclusion that you will fail and will never be able to write well.

Please help point out the thinking errors by labeling those that you can identify, and also suggest more on the mark ways of thinking about the situation(s).

Resilience Builder Assignment: Identifying Thinking Errors—Part 1

This assignment asks your child to consider three off the mark thoughts when responding to a given scenario and one situation he or she faces this week. Please assist by pointing out any thinking errors you have noticed, as well as on the mark, balanced thinking you observe in your child. Ask your child to demonstrate a favored relaxation exercise. If time allows, have a family meeting and use the Compliment Basket technique.

Sincerely,

Program Leader

On the Mark/Off the Mark Thinking: Part 2

PURPOSE

This session reinforces how realistic thinking contributes to happiness and positive results and introduces four additional thinking errors that tend to produce negative outcomes. These errors can be corrected through awareness and effort. Additional practice at changing such habitual off the mark patterns of thinking to on the mark self-talk is provided.

GOALS

To reinforce the concept of on the mark and off the mark thinking

To reinforce understanding of the connection between what we think, our self-talk, and how we feel

To teach four off the mark thinking errors: personalization, shoulds, "it's not fair," and blaming others

To identify examples of thinking errors used by group members

To practice a relaxation/self-regulation technique

MATERIALS

Chalkboard or dry erase board and markers

Program Notebooks (brought by group members)

Points Charts

Name Cube

Dartboard and magnetic darts

Hand mirror

Toys and games for free play

Copies of the following:

    Leadership Award (Appendix C)

    Seven Thinking Errors handout

    Resilience Builder Assigment 2.6

    Parent Letter 2.6

PROCEDURE

Individual Greeting

Conduct the individual greetings, as described in Session 2.1.

Review Success Journal and Resilience Builder Assignment

Have each group member discuss his or her individual goal and Success Journal entry and experiences completing the Resilience Builder Assignment. When each member finishes speaking, ask him or her to throw the Name Cube to determine the next speaker.

> *Record points on each group member's Points Chart for this portion of the session. Record the point for participation at the end of the session.*

Review On the Mark and Off the Mark Thinking

Using the dart board, review how thoughts can be completely on target, be a little bit off the mark, or be way off the mark. Provide an example that errors can be along a continuum: small, medium, or large:

> One example might be that you said something to a friend that came across differently than you had wanted. On target, on the mark self-talk might be "I made a

mistake and will apologize and be positive." If you are way off the mark, you might think, "I should have said it the right way the first time, and now I will lose that friend." A little off the mark would be "I should have said it differently and the other person might be upset, but I can repair this."

Discuss and Demonstrate Personalization

1. Write "Personalization" on the board. Say:

> Personalization is thinking, "It's all about me"—that is, immediately assuming that everything people do or say is some kind of reaction to you. When you see your classmates talking or laughing, for example, you automatically jump to the conclusion that they are saying something negative about you.

2. Hold the mirror up close to a group member and ask, "What do you see?" *(Myself.)* Then say, "Now, let's pull the mirror back and get the bigger picture. What else might your classmates be talking about?" *(Someone or something else.)*

3. Give two volunteers two magnetic darts each and ask them to come up with an example of off the mark personalization and on the mark thinking. As they offer the examples, have them place the darts in the appropriate spots on the dartboard.

Discuss and Demonstrate "Shoulds"

1. Write "Shoulds" on the board. Say:

> People who think they or other people *should* behave in just one certain way often get overly upset when their expectations are not met. For example, an off the mark thought would be "I should always know the right thing to say, and since I don't, I won't say anything." An on the mark thought would be "No one is perfect, so I'll do the best I can."
>
> Or suppose you have an expectation that if your friend really likes you, he or she should always call you first to do an activity, rather than understanding that it's normal to get together with a variety of people. When you believe you or your friend should measure up in an unreasonable way, you might feel sad or depressed, your feelings might get hurt, or you might react in a mean way toward your friend.

2. Give one or two volunteers two magnetic darts each and ask them to come up with an example of off the mark shoulds and on the mark thinking. As they offer the examples, have them place the darts in the appropriate spots on the dartboard.

Discuss and Demonstrate "It's Not Fair!"

1. Write "It's Not Fair!" on the board. Say:

This type of thinking assumes things will happen a certain way and, when they don't, you feel like you've been mistreated. For example, your parents say it's time to stop playing video games, clean up, and go visit some relatives. Another example might be that a friend asks you to go the movies, but your family has planned something else. Can you all demonstrate how someone who thinks "It's not fair!" might react?

Some reactions might be whining, yelling, or even stomping away.

2. Contrast with on the mark thinking:

An example of on the mark thinking might be "My family already planned something. I can go to the movies another time."

3. Give one or two volunteers two magnetic darts each and ask them to come up with an example of off the mark and on the mark self-talk. As they offer the examples, have them place the darts in the appropriate spots on the dartboard.

Discuss and Demonstrate Blaming Others

1. Write "Blaming Others" on the board. Say:

When bad things happen, a person who thinks this way automatically assumes that it's someone else's fault and reacts with anger or sadness. For example, when someone says something mean to you and you hit him, you blame him for your action. An on the mark thought would be "He was mean to me, but I could have handled it better."

2. Ask the group members for their own examples of the blaming others thinking error and write these on the board. Choose one of the group's scenarios for a two-person role-play.

   ▶ Hand the mirror to one of the group members. When that person blames the other, he or she is to point the mirror at the other person and make a blaming statement.

   ▶ Instruct the person doing the blaming to then look at himself or herself in the mirror and make a more balanced statement about the situation.

Free Play/Behavioral Rehearsal

Provide the group with a selection of age-appropriate toys, games, or other activities to choose from that encourage joint play and follow the procedure described in Session 2.1 for choosing play partners and facilitating free play.

Relaxation/Self-Regulation

1. This session's relaxation exercise involves a mental imagery exercise aimed to reinforce realistic thinking and help group members visualize on the mark thoughts. Have group

members find a comfortable place to sit or lie down, then read the following script slowly and in a calm and soothing voice:

▶ Gently close your eyes and take a deep breath in through your nose. Hold it: 1, 2, 3, 4, and 5. Now slowly breathe out through your mouth.

▶ Today we will imagine some situations in which you can practice your "on the mark" thinking.

▶ Picture yourself at a bowling alley. You are with a few friends. You see two other kids from school in another lane. They look at you and say something to each other.

▶ Your automatic response is to think they are speaking negatively about you. Then you notice that they smile at you and start bowling.

▶ Change this personalization error, this habitual self-talk, to another thought. Think about what your friends and others like about you. Picture them making positive comments. What would they say?

▶ Take a deep breath in. Hold it: 1, 2, 3, 4, and 5. And now slowly breathe out.

▶ Think of a situation that happened to you when you thought something wasn't fair.

▶ Is there another way to think about this situation? Decide what the "on the mark" thought might be. Hold onto that thought.

▶ Is there another on the mark thought about that situation?

▶ Now bring your shoulders back and hold that position. Hold it: 1, 2, 3, 4, and 5. Slowly bring them back to their normal position.

▶ Now open your eyes.

2. Ask the group, "What situation did you imagine? What were some of your on the mark thoughts?"

Leadership Award

Select a group member to receive the Leadership Award and provide praise for what the child did well.

Generalization: Resilience Builder Assignment

Give each group member a copy of the Resilience Builder Assignment for the next session. Go over the assignment and answer any questions. (See the chart on the next page for sample thinking errors.)

Collin's Thinking Errors

Shoulds: Collin thought that Tyler should only have invited one friend.

Personalization: Collin thought that his friends don't listen to him and think he's stupid (because they didn't listen to him).

Blaming others: Collin thought it was all Tyler's fault that his day was ruined (because he wasn't the only one invited and because the kids wanted to go out for pizza instead of going to his house).

Filtering: *(From Session 2.5)* Collin went to the basketball game and had fun. However, when the other boys didn't want to do what he suggested, he became upset and thought the whole day was ruined. He focused only on the negative and filtered out the positive.

All-or-nothing thinking: *(From Session 2.5)* Collin thought it would be great if they went to his house after the game and that if they went out for pizza it would ruin the day. It was either perfect (they did what he wanted) or he thought the whole day was ruined.

Parent Component

Give each participant a copy of the parent letter for the session. Have participants place the letter, Resilience Builder Assignment, and Seven Thinking Errors handout in the appropriate sections of their notebooks.

OPTIONAL ACTIVITY: CAST OF CHARACTERS

If time permits, or as a lesson alternative, you may choose to introduce a "cast of characters" that exemplify the thinking distortions.

1. As you write these names on the board, introduce the concept with the following: "I am going to share with you some more friends who personify off-the-mark thinking. They are Polly Personal (personalization), Sam Should (shoulds), It's-Not-Fair Claire (it's not fair), and Blamin' Byron (blaming others).

2. Explain to the group how each character thinks.

Polly Personal

Our first friend is Polly Personal. Polly assumes everything is a personal reaction to her. For example, if someone has an irritable tone of voice, she immediately assumes they are angry with her and says, "Why are you upset with me?" She forgets that people may do things or feel things that have nothing to do with her. Polly thinks it's ALL ABOUT HER.

Sam Should

Our next character is Sam Should. Sam has a lot of his own rules about how he and others should be, and believe me, his list is very long! When other people don't conform to those rules, it really shakes Sam up. He gets frustrated, annoyed, and overwhelmed because others do not follow his internal rules. He has clear ideas about how everyone SHOULD BE.

It's-Not-Fair Claire

Then, there's It's-Not-Fair Claire. Whenever things don't go the way she wants, she says, "It's not fair!" She thinks that anyone who can't make what she wants happen is not on her side. When her parents refuse to go to her favorite restaurant, she proceeds to stick her lip out and feels very upset. She is upset so often, you might say that she thinks that life is JUST NOT FAIR.

Blamin' Byron

Finally, we have Blamin' Byron. Byron sees problems everywhere—and it is never because he did something wrong. It's always all someone else's fault! Blamin' Byron is upset with others all the time. When his school group science project failed to work, he was quick to point his finger at his group members, scolding, "Why didn't you glue this right!" and "It's because you didn't mix the compounds correctly." He thinks it's always SOMEONE ELSE'S FAULT.

3. Group members may then volunteer to role-play these characters as the activity.

Seven Thinking Errors

*Here is a list of common **off the mark** thinking errors we have reviewed in group. Use this handout to "catch your self-talk" and examine the evidence to get more realistic, **on the mark** thoughts. You can also use this guide to help you complete your Resilience Builder Assignment.*

1. All-or-Nothing Thinking

Thinking in extremes. It's either right or wrong, perfect or a complete failure. For example, you missed a shot in the basketball game, and you feel you've failed.

2. Filtering

Magnifying the negatives of a situation and minimizing the positives; thinking about the bad things that happened and not much about the good things. For example, the day in school goes fairly well overall, but one negative thing happens. When someone asks you how the school day went, your answer is "Terrible!"

3. Catastrophizing

Expecting the worst to happen and that you won't be able to handle a situation. This type of thinking is a common cause of anxiety. We call these thoughts "What ifs?" For example, you think "What if I mess up on this writing assignment?" and automatically jump to the conclusion that you will fail and never be able to write well.

4. Personalization

Thinking that everything people do or say is some kind of reaction to you. This involves not considering other reasons that could explain why someone is whispering or laughing or looking at you, for example.

5. Shoulds

You have certain beliefs or expectations about how you and other people should act or how the world should work. For example, you think that there is only one way to play a game and believe that someone else should play the same game with the exact same rules. People who break the rules upset and may even anger you.

6. It's Not Fair!

You assume things will happen a certain way and, when they don't, you feel like you've been mistreated. For example, your parents say it's time to clean up and go out with them when you'd rather not. Another example might be that a friend gets to go to the movies, but your family has planned something else.

7. Blaming Others

When bad things happen, you assume it's someone else's fault and react with anger or upset feelings. For example, someone said something mean to you and you hit them. You blame them for what they said and say it's the cause for your hitting them.

From *Resilience Builder Program for Children and Adolescents,* © 2011 by M.K. Alvord, B. Zucker, & J.J. Grados, Champaign, IL: Research Press (800-519-2707, www.researchpress.com).

Identifying Thinking Errors: Part 2

Name _____ Date _____

Our thoughts are linked to our feelings and how we act. Read the passage below and help Collin think and feel better. Identify Collin's thinking errors (there is more than one!) and help him enjoy his next get-together by coming up with a new way of thinking ("on the mark" thinking). Refer to your handout of the errors we learned about in group.

Collin's friend Tyler asked Collin to go to a basketball game. Collin was looking forward to it until he found out that Tyler also invited some other boys. Collin was offended and thought Tyler should only have one friend go with him. Collin went anyway and had a good time. After the game, the boys talked about going out to get pizza. Collin didn't want to do that and suggested going back to his house instead, but the boys still wanted to go for pizza. Collin thought, "My friends never listen to me, and they think I'm stupid." He became upset and angry and went home. Collin was so upset that he decided the whole day was ruined, and it was all Tyler's fault.

1. Describe the thinking errors Collin made:

   _____

   _____

   _____

   _____

2. What would have been more "on the mark" thinking by Collin? What's the evidence that supports the "on the mark" thoughts?

   _____

   _____

   _____

3. Describe one "off the mark" thinking error you had this week and one helpful, "on the mark" thought you could replace it with.

   "Off the mark" thought: _____

   _____

   "On the mark" thought: _____

   _____

On the Mark/Off the Mark Thinking: Part 2

Dear Parents:

This session continues the cognitive component of the program—identifying and replacing thinking patterns that are unrealistic and unhelpful. In today's session, we review the three thinking errors introduced last week: all-or-nothing thinking, filtering, and catastrophizing. We then discuss four additional thinking errors. After we define them, group members will give examples of both "off the mark" and "on the mark" self-talk. Here are the four additional thinking errors, or types of off the mark thinking.

Personalization

Thinking that everything people do or say is some kind of reaction to you. This involves not considering other reasons that could explain why someone is whispering or laughing or looking at you, for example.

Shoulds

You have certain beliefs or expectations about how you and other people should act or how the world should work. For example, you think that there is only one way to play a game and believe that someone else should play the same game with the exact same rules. People who break the rules upset and may even anger you.

It's Not Fair!

You assume things will happen a certain way and, when they don't, you feel like you've been mistreated. For example, your parents say it's time to clean up and go out with them when you'd rather not. Another example might be that a friend gets to go the movies, but your family has planned something else.

Blaming Others

When bad things happen, you assume it's someone else's fault and react with anger or upset feelings. For example, someone said something mean to you and you hit them. You blame them for what they said and say it's the cause for your hitting.

Resilience Builder Assignment: Identifying Thinking Errors—Part 2

Your child received a handout summarizing all seven thinking errors we've discussed over the past two sessions. You can use it to help your child complete the Resilience Builder Assignment and substitute on the mark thinking for thinking errors. Please remind your child to practice a relaxation exercise this week.

Sincerely,

Program Leader

2.7

Being a Good Sport: Team Play

PURPOSE

Being a good sport is essential to being accepted as a teammate and as a potential friend. Whether on a sports team, playing games at recess, or participating in activities in one's neighborhood, the real winners are those who can behave positively and respectfully while maintaining good self-control. This session builds on the skills learned in Session 1.7 and serves to reinforce the skills of being a good sport: playing fair, showing good teamwork, following rules and instructions, encouraging and complimenting others, controlling frustration and disappointment, trying your best, and being a good winner and a good loser.

GOALS

To identify and discuss the elements necessary for successfully playing a sport or other team game

To encourage group members to learn how to respond to and manage common frustrations when playing in a team format

To practice being a good sport while playing a team game

To practice a relaxation/self-regulation technique

MATERIALS

Chalkboard or dry erase board and marker

Program Notebooks (brought by group members)

Individual Points Charts

Name Cube

Items for scavenger hunt (for example, pencil, ball, paper, deck of cards, an orange, packet of sugar, popsicle stick, four paper clips, stapler, paper cup, umbrella, magazine, photograph, leaf, rock, sock, red pen, tissues, shoelace, sticky note)

Toys and games for free play

Copies of the following:

> Leadership Award (Appendix C)
>
> Resilience Builder Assignment 2.7
>
> Parent Letter 2.7

If you are conducting Session 2.8, the optional field trip, be sure you have signed permission forms from parents. Also provide a clear description of the activity and directions for getting to the site along with the usual parent letter.

PROCEDURE

Individual Greeting

Conduct the individual greetings, as described in Session 2.1. Require group members to demonstrate sustained eye contact and a confident greeting to enter the room.

Review Success Journal and Resilience Builder Assignment

Have each group member discuss his or her individual goal and Success Journal entry and experiences completing the Resilience Builder Assignment. When each participant finishes speaking, ask him or her to throw the Name Cube to determine the next speaker.

> *Record points on each group member's Points Chart for this portion of the session. Record the point for participation at the end of the session.*

Discuss Being a Good Sport

1. Write "Being a Good Sport" on the board. Ask the group to review what they have learned about the topic, including what they may have learned in previous sessions.

If applicable, reflect on the time they played Charades in Session 1.7 and what they learned from that experience.

2. Ask, "What does it mean to be a good sport? What are some examples of 'good sport' behavior?" and then write down group members' ideas on the board.

   Suggestions include encouraging your teammates, trying your best, listening to a coach's or teammates' ideas, and continuing to play even when you're frustrated without giving up or losing control.

3. Summarize the idea that being a good sport applies both when you are playing well and when you are playing poorly—whether your team wins or loses. Also try to include specific ways teammates can encourage one another, such as complimenting a teammate's effort with comments like "Nice catch," "Keep it up!" or "Nice try."

4. Emphasize that part of being a good sport is handling frustrations well. Say:

   When you or your teammate is playing poorly—and this happens to everyone—the goal is to be able to manage yourself well and maintain appropriate behavior, show respect, and be encouraging.

5. Reinforce the skills of optimistic thinking, "on-the-mark" thinking and positive self-talk, and resilience. Point out that this frustration is specific to this game, temporary, that you have the power to do better next time, and that you can keep playing and not give up until the game ends.

6. Emphasize that being a good sport helps to further social relationships. Say:

   When you're a good sport, it's easier to make and keep friends. When a person gets mad or loses control, others are turned off and become less interested in playing with that person again. Also, others get annoyed and frustrated when a teammate continually makes negative statements. Negativity can rub off on others, and this makes them less interested in being around you. On the other hand, when you stay calm and act in a positive and encouraging way, other people like to play with you and be on your team. The focus should be on doing your best and having fun.

Free Play/Behavioral Rehearsal

The point of free play is to practice negotiating and interacting in a flexible, prosocial manner as the leader observes and intervenes when necessary. Demonstrating being a good sport in a team play situation is the goal of today's free play/behavioral rehearsal.

One game that works well to practice good teamwork is a scavenger hunt because it emphasizes the skills of cooperation and problem solving. The challenge is to help participants work collaboratively, as opposed to having one or two group members take the lead and do all the hunting themselves. Ensure that participants don't argue over strategy or decision making and work through frustrations effectively.

Before beginning the game, hide the different items you have chosen around the room or rooms in which the hunt will take place.

Scavenger Hunt

1. Divide the group into two teams. Provide each team with a list of 15 to 20 items to search for and clarify the searching grounds (the room or rooms the search is limited to). Instruct each team to make sure that each player gets to search for items and encourage team members to work collaboratively. Explain that the team that collects the most items on the list wins.

2. Let the teams know that it is likely that they will need to make trades and negotiate with each other during the hunt. For example, one team may find two paper clips and a red pen, while the other finds two other two paper clips and a sheet of paper; the teams then trade with each other to make an item on the list complete. Assist in this process and encourage participants to trade and negotiate as good sports.

3. Say, "Before you begin, it is wise to read through the list and decide on an approach, or a strategy, to use. Remember that this is an opportunity to practice being a good sport."

If a scavenger hunt is not feasible (due to limited space, for example), then you can use the game Twenty Questions. This game also can be played after the scavenger hunt if time permits. The group can play several times, until time runs out.

Twenty Questions

1. Divide the group into two teams. One participant can be elected to select the "answer."

2. The person elected comes up with an object (a noun), and then the other participants get to ask up to 20 questions about it to figure out what the object is. The object is an animal, a mineral, or a vegetable, and this category is shared with the group at the beginning (for example, "I'm thinking of an object. It is a vegetable"). Every question that is asked must be answerable with either a yes or a no.

3. The teams take turns asking questions, and the team that figures out the item first is the winner. If the group needs assistance in selecting an item/answer, some suggestions include a book, a mouse, an apple, an airplane, or a football.

If participants have not played before or are confused about what questions to ask, offer examples of common questions—for example, "Is it bigger than a breadbox?" "Can you eat it?" and "Can I see it in this room?" Remind them that the best way to ask questions is to try to identify which category the item is in or to eliminate categories in which it is not.

Relaxation/Self-Regulation

First have the group find a comfortable place to sit or lie down and close their eyes for a guided imagery exercise. Read the following script slowly and in a calm voice.

▶ Take a deep breath in through your nose and slowly breathe out through your mouth.

▶ This is your time for relaxation. Clear your mind and let go of any stress or tension that you might be holding onto. Take another deep breath in through your nose and out through your mouth.

▶ Imagine that you are standing tall on the top of a mountain. You can breathe easily, and you feel calm but also strong. Look around and notice all of the beautiful things around you. Do you see green trees or trees covered with glistening white snow? Are there other mountains around you and valleys in between?

▶ You are surrounded by nature and are fully aware of this moment. Your breath is calm, and you feel clear in your mind and good energy in your body. You can feel the energy around you, and this makes you feel uplifted.

▶ While on this mountain, you notice how good you feel about yourself and your body. You are aware of how special you are and how able you are to do whatever you set your mind to. You feel strong and confident.

▶ If there is something you want to do or need to do, you feel confident about your ability to do it and handle yourself well. You think of several good things about your-self . . . and you love who you are.

▶ Take another deep breath. Spend a minute or two feeling what it feels like when you think well of yourself and when you are in touch with how special you are.

Allow 1–2 minutes for silent meditation.

▶ When you are ready, gently open your eyes and notice how calm your body feels. Remember that you can be this relaxed and feel confident about yourself anytime you want.

Leadership Award

Select a group member to receive the Leadership Award and provide praise for what the person did well.

Generalization: Resilience Builder Assignment

Give each group member a copy of the Resilience Builder Assignment for the next session. Go over the assignment and answer any questions.

Parent Component

Give each participant a copy of the parent letter for the session. Have participants place the letter and Resilience Builder Assignment in the appropriate sections of their notebooks.

Being a Good Sport: Team Play

Name _____ **Date** _____

Answer the following questions about being a good sport, keeping in mind the game you played in group.

What are three ways to show you are being a good sport?

1. _____

2. _____

3. _____

How do you feel when others act like good sports when you are playing a game? What do you think about people who are good sports?

_____

_____

_____

_____

Give an example of a time when you were playing with others and showed you were being a good sport.

_____

_____

_____

_____

List three healthy ways to handle your team's losing or a time you have played poorly.

1. _____

2. _____

3. _____

Being a Good Sport: Team Play

Dear Parents:

Today's group is about being a good sport and team play. Being a good sport goes beyond playing fair and not cheating. It also encompasses showing respect for others, taking pride in accomplishments, using self-control, making good decisions, and dealing well with winning and losing. Being a good sport includes supporting and encouraging others both when things are going well and when they are not.

This session reviews what it means to be a good sport when you are a member of a team: listening to a coach and cooperating with the coach's instructions, working with and encouraging teammates (rather than hogging the ball, for example), and sticking with the game until the end with a positive attitude.

Today, after the discussion of being a good sport, the group will break into two teams and have a scavenger hunt. In addition to practicing being a good sport, they will apply what they have learned about on-the-mark thinking and positive self-talk.

Being a good sport is demonstrated through both words and actions. When your child is playing well and his or her team is winning, he or she should smile, compliment others on the team, and express encouragement to members of the losing team. If playing poorly and losing, your child should stay calm, continue to try his or her best until the game ends, say something positive to the winning person or team, and continue to be cooperative.

Resilience Builder Assignment: Being a Good Sport—Team Play

Please assist your child in answering the questions about being a good sport, including how to handle losing or not playing one's best. Please also encourage your child to continue to practice relaxation exercises.

Sincerely,

Program Leader

SESSION

2.8

Being a Good Sport: Field Trip

PURPOSE

When children and teens learn how to be good sports and respect others, whether they are teammates or on an opposing team, they develop an essential skill of social competence. This greatly influences how others respond to them. Central to the program is the opportunity to practice acquired skills correctly in real-life settings. This field trip provides that opportunity and promotes generalization of skills. The experience allows members to demonstrate many skills, including teamwork, being a good winner and loser, self-regulation, empathy, establishing deeper connections with others, and respectfully interacting with adults in a public setting.

The example described is for a mini-golf field trip. Other outings may of course be appropriate for your circumstances. Reservations at a mini-golf course or another suitable recreational setting are often necessary. Depending on the size and needs of the group, consider asking parents to act as scorekeepers.

GOALS

To apply meeting and greeting skills and appropriately interact with adults in a community setting

To practice being a good sport for successful participation

To manage following the rules of the game, turn taking, and using public property appropriately

To negotiate challenges and manage typical frustrations that arise from team play through positive self-talk

MATERIALS

Group members do not generally bring their notebooks and assignments to this session. Rather, the assignments are reviewed the following session.

Individual Points Charts

Copies of the following:

Leadership Award (Appendix C)

Good Sport Certificate (Appendix C)

Resilience Builder Assignment 2.8

Parent Letter 2.8

PROCEDURE

Individual Greeting

1. As group members arrive at the mini-golf park, greet them and instruct them to wait until all members arrive. Encourage them to greet one another as each arrives. After all are present, explain the procedures of the facility: where they pick up equipment, how they pay, and where they go once they have their equipment.

    Payment is made by the participant either before or after the game, as directed by the facility.

2. Next, go to the front desk and have each group member make eye contact with the attendant and ask for a golf club or other equipment, as appropriate. This provides direct practice of waiting until the attendant is available to talk and then asking politely and in a friendly tone for what is needed.

3. Throughout this process, guide and prompt the participants as necessary. Compliment them in turn with specific feedback on what they did well. For example, say, "I like the way Monica waited patiently while others were getting their equipment."

Discuss Being a Good Sport in the Setting

1. Before dividing up into groups, review basic points around being a good sport and team play. Review what being a good sport will "look like" in this setting:

    > I am so glad we are all here today. We want to focus on following the rules at this facility and showing respect for the equipment and workers. And, of course, we want to be good sports while having fun. First, let's briefly go over the kinds of behaviors we will expect to see today. What do you think we need to do?

2. Solicit answers from the group encouraging them to speak one at a time.

    > *Examples include standing quietly and watching as each player putts; giving full attention, both out of respect for others and so each person knows when to take a turn (we don't want to keep others waiting unnecessarily); and making positive comments after another person has putted ("Good shot" or "Nice try").*

3. Discuss handling frustration and disappointment. Explain:

    > Remember that being a good sport applies both when you're doing well and your team wins, and when you play poorly or your team loses. You will all probably get frustrated or disappointed at some time when you play today. What are some helpful ways of handling yourself?

    > How can you help encourage each other? What self-talk can you use to make it possible to keep playing with a good attitude? Just as we talked about in the last session, the goal today is to do your best and have fun.

    > *Review constructive ways to handle the frustrations of not getting a lower score than someone else or getting a stroke handicap for hitting the ball off the green.*

    Strategies for Dealing with Frustration

    Saying what you are frustrated about to see what, if anything, can be done about it

    Reminding yourself that you are here to have fun and can keep trying to do your best

    Telling yourself that no one can have a perfect score or do well all the time

    Taking a few deep breaths

4. Remind the group that it is not appropriate to cheer if someone misses a shot, even though it may improve your chances of winning. Tell participants that being a good sport is not only about what we say but also what we communicate nonverbally (facial expressions, body posture). Watching and smiling will communicate interest, whereas eye rolling, walking away, yawning, and other negative behaviors communicate a lack of interest.

Review Points Earning

Explain:

> Today you can earn five points on your Points Charts, but it's for slightly different behavior. You can earn one point for following the rules, one point for showing good manners with the facility staff, one point for encouraging others and maintaining a positive attitude, one point for good self-control and persistence with the activity, and one point for complimenting others throughout the game and at the end.

Free Play/Behavioral Rehearsal

> *As play proceeds, the challenge is to help group members sustain their attention while watching others play and to control their disappointment when they don't do as well as they would like. Watch for opportunities to praise appropriate behavior and correct less desirable actions.*

1. Ask the group to divide into two teams and have them decide which team will go first. Provide assistance as needed in being fair during this process. It is beneficial to have just one group member putt at a time, alternating teams, so that it's easier to focus on each player.

2. Provide the structure for the activity: Review the rules of the game, emphasizing where participants should stand when they are watching (and cheering or encouraging). After a player putts, he or she should wait at the other end of the green and should not proceed to the next hole until everyone on their team has taken a turn.

> *There is no formal relaxation exercise for this activity. However, a reminder to take a few deep breaths before making shots and visualizing a successful shot may be useful. Remind the group to also use positive self-talk to help deal with frustrations and to persevere with the activity.*

Leadership Award and Good Sport Certificates

Select a group member to receive the Leadership Award and provide praise for what the child did well. In addition, before leaving the setting, give each group member a Good Sport Certificate. As you do, ask each group member to identify at least two things that he or she did well and check these off on the certificate, along with anything else you think is appropriate.

Generalization: Resilience Builder Assignment

Show the group a copy of the Resilience Builder Assignment and answer any questions. Explain that you will be giving a copy to their parents when they arrive.

Parent Component

Give parents a copy of the Resilience Builder Assignment and parent letter when they pick up their child. Encourage them to help their child complete the assignment if necessary. Use this opportunity to thank parents personally for supporting their children in learning the program skills.

Being a Good Sport: Field Trip

Name _____ **Date** _____

Please state three ways in which you were a good sport during our field trip.

1. _____

2. _____

3. _____

What was some of your positive "self-talk" during the activity?

_____

_____

_____

_____

_____

We all get frustrated or feel disappointed sometimes. Describe any negative emotions you felt during our field trip. How did you handle them?

_____

_____

_____

_____

_____

What did you do today to encourage your teammates?

_____

_____

_____

_____

_____

Being a Good Sport: Field Trip

Dear Parents:

While on our field trip, we focus on being a good sport and team play. We emphasize respect for others, taking pride in accomplishments, using self-control, sticking with the game until the end with a positive attitude, making good decisions, and dealing graciously with winning and losing.

Resilience Builder Assignment: Being a Good Sport—Field Trip

This session's assignment asks your child to evaluate his or her thoughts, feelings, and behavior during the field trip. Please discuss your child's experience, focusing on what your child found positive in his or her own behavior and the behavior of others. Ask your child to lead the family in a relaxation exercise this week.

Sincerely,

Program Leader

2.9

Self-Regulation: Anxiety Management

PURPOSE

Anxiety disorders are the most common form of psychopathology in children and teens. Whether or not a child's anxiety is significant enough to meet the criteria for an anxiety disorder, many children experience anxiety symptoms at some point, including worries and physiological tension, and can benefit from understanding these symptoms and learning ways to cope. Research shows that anxiety is treatable and that the cognitive-behavioral approach is the most effective. This session provides children with an explanation of anxiety and its three parts, according to a cognitive-behavioral model.

GOALS

To explain the concept of anxiety and how it affects the body and the mind (the thought-feeling connection)

To discuss the three parts of anxiety (body, thoughts, behavior)

To identify body signals, or physiological symptoms, associated with anxiety

To encourage reducing anxiety through self-talk, calming the body to calm the mind, and coping thoughts and coping actions

To learn the "facing your fears" mindset (that gradual exposure helps reduce anxiety)

To practice a relaxation/self-regulation technique

MATERIALS

Chalkboard or dry erase board and marker

Program Notebooks (brought by group members)

Individual Points Charts

Name Cube

Toys and games for free play

Copies of the following:

> Leadership Award (Appendix C)
>
> Resilience Builder Assignment 2.9
>
> Parent Letter 2.9

PROCEDURE

Individual Greeting

Conduct the individual greetings, as described in Session 2.1. Require participants to demonstrate sustained eye contact and a confident greeting to enter the room.

Review Success Journal and Resilience Builder Assignment

> *If you went on the optional field trip (Session 2.8), review the Resilience Builder Assignments for it and Session 2.7.*

Have each group member discuss his or her individual goal and Success Journal entry and experiences completing the Resilience Builder Assignment. When each member finishes speaking, ask him or her to throw the Name Cube to determine the next speaker.

> *Record points on each group member's Points Chart for this portion of the session. Record the point for participation at the end of the session.*

Discuss Anxiety

1. To introduce the concept, ask participants if they know what *anxiety* means and help them define it. Say:

Everyone feels anxious at one time or another. In fact, anxiety is a biological process that warns us that there is trouble ahead or that we are being threatened. For example, if a lion is chasing you, your body prepares itself for "fight or flight" because you will either need to fight the lion—if it catches you—or you will need to run really, really fast.

Your body feels anxiety as a means of survival, to help you survive. But most of us never encounter a lion, right? Instead, our body ends up feeling anxious when we see a situation as threatening, even though there isn't a real threat like a lion.

2. Explain that things like having to perform in a game or in school, having a lot of school work, or being in certain situations that we don't like can cause anxiety. We can also feel anxious when we *think* of scary things, such as something bad happening to us or someone we love. We can *think* about making mistakes, getting bad grades, being teased by others, and just from *thinking* it, we can feel anxious.

3. Highlight this connection between thoughts and feelings by saying, "So if thinking about something can cause you to feel something, then changing the way you think can change the way you feel."

4. Ask participants to describe situations and thoughts that they find anxiety provoking and list these on the board. The goal is to make this discussion relevant to the particular issues group members experience.

Explain the Components of Anxiety

1. Explain that anxiety has three parts: body, thoughts, and behavior. Draw three separate circles on the board and write "Body" in one, "Thoughts" in one, and "Behavior" in one. Label the drawing "Three Parts of Anxiety."

2. Ask, "When you feel nervous or scared, how does your body feel?" Record ideas in the appropriate circle.

   Many children and teens experience physiological symptoms of anxiety, including but not limited to muscle tension, shallow breathing, rapid heart rate, stomachaches, headaches, sweating, feeling dizzy or light-headed, and hot flushes.

3. Point out that our bodies are related to our minds, so if we think anxious thoughts, we will likely feel the anxiety in our bodies. Ask, "When you are in a scary situation, what do you think?" Record ideas in the appropriate circle.

   You may want to reference a personal story, such as a time you gave a presentation and thought about messing up or a time you felt embarrassed and had negative self-talk such as "I can't do it."

4. Finally, have the group generate a list of anxious behaviors. Ask, "When you are nervous or anxious, what do you do?" Record ideas in the appropriate circle.

   Most responses will be versions of avoidance (for example, if you are scared of dogs, you will try to avoid them), reassurance seeking, checking behaviors (for example, that doors are locked), fidgeting, and restlessness.

Discuss Self-Talk and Anxiety

1. Review the idea that self-talk refers to the things that we say to ourselves in our own minds—the private conversation we have with ourselves. Say:

   When people feel anxious, they often have negative self-talk and say things like "I can't handle this" and "I'm going to mess up, make a mistake, or fail." Self-talk is a part of the "thoughts" part of anxiety. Self-talk affects our feelings and our behavior. We want to be able to change our self-talk to challenge anxiety just like we want to change our other negative thoughts.

2. Ask the group to share examples of their own self-talk, both negative and positive. Ask, "What are things you say to yourself?" Have participants practice replacing their negative self-talk with positive self-talk, interacting with one another in the process. Record their ideas on the board. For example: "Before soccer games, John tells himself that he will mess up and that he is not good at playing soccer. What could he tell himself instead?" *(I enjoy soccer and will try my best in today's game. Even if I mess up, it will be OK—everyone messes up from time to time, even the best players.)*

3. Briefly review on the mark and off the mark thinking (cognitive distortions) from Sessions 2.5 and 2.6 in the context of anxiety, focusing on the idea that everyone makes thinking errors that need to be challenged. Say:

   Remember that everyone makes thinking mistakes and that when you feel anxious, you are likely having off the mark thinking. For example, when you worry about the worst case scenario, you are doing "What if" thinking, also known as catastrophizing. So if you do this, you need to change these thoughts to on the mark thoughts.

4. Using one or two of the sample anxiety-provoking situations already described, point out the off the mark thinking and encourage the group to make suggestions of on the mark thoughts instead.

Discuss Coping with Anxiety

1. Explain that the body cannot be anxious and relaxed at the same time; therefore, if you learn how to relax your body, you will be less anxious. Point out that learning how to calm your body will help you calm your mind and that all of the relaxation techniques the group has learned so far can help them deal with anxiety.

2. Have the group list the different forms of relaxation that they have learned and practiced in group so far. Among the forms practiced in this unit are calm breathing, progressive muscle relaxation, guided imagery, and yoga poses.

3. Demonstrate and have the group practice a new type of calm breathing:

   ▶ Now we are going to learn a type of calm breathing called "one-nostril breathing."

   ▶ I'd like you to close your mouth and close one nostril by holding the nostril down with your finger.

   ▶ Very, very slowly breathe in and out through *only* one nostril. The goal is to breathe in slowly, for 8 to 10 seconds, then breathe out slowly, for 8 to 10 seconds. *(Model and have participants practice.)*

   ▶ You can breathe in and out through the same nostril or switch nostrils, but at any one time, the breath is going in only one nostril and going out only one nostril.

   ▶ OK, let's practice again. Close your mouth and hold one nostril closed. Slowly, slowly breathe in through only one nostril and breathe out through only one nostril. Notice how calm your body feels the more you do this.

   ▶ The more you practice, the easier it will be to get to 8 to 10 seconds in and 8 to 10 seconds out. Also, it is important that you do this for at least 3 minutes and up to 5 minutes. As you breathe this way for a full 3 to 5 minutes, you will notice how calm and relaxed you feel.

4. Briefly review coping thoughts and coping actions, as discussed in Session 1.11, "Stress Management":

   ▶ Have the group come up with *coping thoughts:* Ask, "What could you say to yourself or what might you think about in order to help handle the stressful feelings or the stressful situation?"

   ▶ Also have them develop *coping actions:* Say, "What can you do in response to the anxiety? What is your coping plan?"

   For example, sample coping thoughts and actions for stress and anxiety related to schoolwork include "I will take one step at a time. I will make a list of all the work I have to do and do each item, one by one, only focusing on the one thing that I'm working on. And I will take breaks in between which will make it easier."

Additional Coping Thoughts and Actions

I will be OK. Everything will work out.

I can get through this. I can handle it.

Stay calm.

Get an adult.

Be assertive.

Find something else to do.

Exercise.

Face Your Fears Through Exposure

1. Finally, explain the concept of challenging your anxiety by using the "face your fears" mindset and gradually exposing yourself to feared situations. Say:

> The third part of anxiety is behavior, and the most common behavior is avoidance. But if you face your fears, you will overcome them. In fact, it is almost impossible to get rid of your fears *without* facing them. For example, if someone is afraid of dogs and usually avoids them, he or she will need to practice being near dogs, and this can be done gradually, in steps.

2. Emphasize that once you do something difficult over and over, it generally becomes easier to deal with and you begin to get used to it. It's the same thing with anxiety: When you face your fears repetitively and frequently, you become unafraid.

Free Play/Behavioral Rehearsal

Provide the group with a selection of age-appropriate toys, games, or other activities to choose from that encourage joint play and follow the procedure described in Session 2.1 for choosing play partners and facilitating free play.

Relaxation/Self-Regulation

1. The relaxation exercise for the session involves guided imagery in which each participant creates a mental image of "My Relaxing Place." If you wish, you may play some calming music (without lyrics, as they can be distracting) in the background to set the atmosphere. Have group members find a comfortable place to sit or lie down, then read the following script.

   ▶ Begin to relax your body by slowing your breathing. Focus on your lower abdomen—around your belly button—and feel your stomach rise and fall as you slowly breathe in and out.

▶ Calm your mind and let your thoughts settle down. If thoughts come up, just allow them to float on by—no need to focus on them. This is your time for relaxation. You have nowhere to go and nothing to do.

▶ Now I want you to imagine a special place that is very relaxing and calming to you. This place can be real or made up, and it can be anywhere you would like. Maybe it is a place you have been or would like to go.

▶ Imagine this place and think about what you see. What colors are there? *(Pause.)* What does it smell like? *(Pause.)* How does you body feel when you are there? *(Pause.)* What do you hear? *(Pause.)* What is the temperature? *(Pause.)* How is the light—is it light or dark or in between? *(Pause.)* Imagine the details of this place and what it looks like.

▶ What are you doing? Are you lying down, looking up at something, or are you sitting or standing? Are you alone, or are you with others? Imagine this place and now take a few minutes to be there. *(Remain quiet for 2–3 minutes.)*

▶ Conclude by saying, "OK, in just a moment, you will open your eyes and come back into the room. I will count: 5, 4, 3, 2, and 1. Gently open your eyes, stretch your body, and return to this room.

2. Encourage the group to remember this relaxing place and let them know that they can go there anytime they like.

   To help them remember, the Resilience Builder Assignment for this session includes a section for them to write about their relaxing place.

Leadership Award

Select a group member to receive the Leadership Award and provide praise for what the person did well.

Generalization: Resilience Builder Assignment

Give each group member a copy of the Resilience Builder homework assignment for the next session and answer any questions.

Parent Component

Give participant a copy of the parent letter for the session. Have participants place the letter and Resilience Builder Assignment in the appropriate sections of their notebooks.

Self-Regulation: Anxiety Management

Name _____ Date _____

Three Parts of Anxiety

Think about a situation that makes you feel anxious, nervous, or afraid. It can be a current situation or one from the past. Then write about how your body felt, what you thought, and how you handled the situation (how you behaved).

Body

_____

_____

_____

Thoughts

_____

_____

_____

Behavior

_____

_____

_____

Now write new thoughts, positive self-talk statements, that would help you overcome the anxious feelings. You may also note how you could have behaved differently.

1. _____

   _____

2. _____

   _____

My Relaxing Place

Write about a relaxing place that you imagine. Try to include as much detail as possible: what it looks like, what it feels like to be there, and what it sounds like and smells like.

_____

_____

_____

_____

_____

_____

_____

_____

_____

_____

_____

Self-Regulation: Anxiety Management

Dear Parents:

Today's group focuses on anxiety management, a skill of self-regulation. The term *self-regulation* describes the ability to manage one's behavior and emotional reactions. Part of healthy self-regulation is the ability to think rationally and therefore respond appropriately to situations. Regulating behavior is an essential social skill because it directly impacts how your child responds in social situations and with peers. Learning how to manage anxiety, and one's response in anxiety-provoking situations, is a key component of self-regulation.

In the session, we discuss the mind-body connection. The group learns about the three parts of anxiety—body, thoughts, and behavior. They provide examples of anxiety-provoking situations, including how they feel, think, and behave in response to these situations. We also discuss physiological changes that occur in the body in response to anxiety, including rapid heartbeat, muscle tension, shallow breathing, and stomachaches, among others.

We review different relaxation strategies the group has learned and practice a new type of calm breathing. Each group member also creates his or her own image of a relaxing place. We discuss self-talk, or what we say to ourselves, in anxiety-provoking situations and review "on the mark/off the mark" thinking in relation to anxiety. Finally, we discuss avoidance behavior and what they can do differently to improve coping, including the "face your fears" mindset.

Resilience Builder Assignment: Self-Regulation—Anxiety Management

This session's assignment asks your child to describe reactions to anxiety-provoking situations and ways to improve his or her reactions by changing thoughts and behavior. Please provide assistance in writing the section on "My Relaxing Place" if necessary, and encourage your child to practice the relaxation strategies learned in group, particularly calm breathing techniques and the relaxing place guided imagery, at times of stress or before going to bed at night. Family meetings and the Compliment Basket are always good ideas.

Sincerely,

Program Leader

2.10

Self-Regulation:
Anger Management

PURPOSE

Self-regulation skills represent an essential component of healthy social interaction. In particular, learning how to manage the emotions of anger and frustration allows children and teens to engage appropriately with others. This session provides an explanation of anger signals, including physiological reactions and self-talk, and covers how to handle anger effectively. By learning to identify their triggers to anger and physiological reactions, or "body signals," group members become aware of their individual experience of anger and are better able to prevent inappropriate expression through aggressive behavior. They also continue to explore the mind-body connection.

GOALS

To explain the concept of anger and how it affects the body and the mind (the thought-feeling connection)

To encourage understanding of body signals (physiological symptoms) and thought signals (including self-talk) associated with anger

---

To review methods of calming the body

To practice replacing negative self-talk with positive self-talk

To review challenging thinking errors (cognitive distortions) and to come up with new thoughts to be more flexible and overcome anger

To practice a relaxation/self-regulation technique

MATERIALS

Chalkboard or dry erase board and marker

Program Notebooks (brought by group members)

Individual Points Charts

Name Cube

Toys and games for free play

Copies of the following:

> My Anger Body Signals handout
>
> Anger Warning Signs: Body Signals and Negative Self-Talk handout
>
> Leadership Award (Appendix C)
>
> Resilience Builder Assignment 2.10
>
> Parent Letter 2.10

PROCEDURE

Individual Greeting

Conduct the individual greetings, as described in Session 2.1. The components of a good first impression—a smile and a courteous hello, and sustained eye contact—by now should be fairly automatic.

Review Success Journal and Resilience Builder Assignment

Have each group member discuss his or her individual goal and Success Journal entry and experiences completing the Resilience Builder Assignment. When each member finishes speaking, ask him or her to throw the Name Cube to determine the next speaker.

> *Record points on each group member's Points Chart for this portion of the session. Record the point for participation at the end of the session.*

1. Ask participants what *anger* means and help them define it. For example:

   > Anger is a feeling we have when we are upset, irritated, or annoyed (a low level of anger) or when we are mad and frustrated (a medium level of anger), or when we are really upset, enraged, and screaming angry (high level of anger).

2. Introduce the concept that anger is normal:

   > Everyone is capable of feeling angry. We often feel angry when something doesn't go our way, when we feel someone has done something wrong to us, or when we get in trouble. Anger is often an appropriate feeling, such as when someone teases or insults you. Your response to anger, however, can be appropriate or inappropriate. The goal is to handle situations that make you feel angry well and to express yourself appropriately.

Discuss Body Signals of Anger

1. Let the group know that the first step is to identify how it feels when you are angry, specifically how your body feels. Say:

   > Your body feels a certain way when you are angry. You all have body signals that are cues that you are feeling angry. You may feel muscle tension, have a fast heartbeat, clench your fists or jaw, feel a stiff body posture, or use a loud, mean voice.

2. Ask the group to describe body signals of anger, highlighting those areas by coloring them in or circling them in red marker on a blank My Anger Body Signals handout. For example, color the hands if a participant says "clenched fists."

3. Give group members their own copies of the My Anger Body Signals handout and red crayons or markers and have them mark their own personal signals in the same way.

Discuss Thought Signals of Anger

1. Remind the group of the mind-body connection and the link between thinking angry thoughts and feeling angry.

   > When you are angry, you have certain ways of thinking. Sometimes the angry feelings come from the thoughts you have. When you think this way, it is a sign that you are feeling angry, so these are your thought signals.

2. Ask the group to list situations that they find anger inducing. Ask, "What are situations, events, or things that make you feel angry and irritated? When you are in these situations, how do you feel? When you are tired and haven't had enough sleep, you might get angry more easily."

   Again, the goal is to make this discussion relevant to the particular issues experienced by the group. Using specific examples is ideal.

3. Review the concept of self-talk. Say, "Remember that your self-talk, or what you say to yourself, in these situations matters a lot. When people feel angry, they often have negative self-talk and think things like "I hate this" and "It's not fair." Ask the group to share examples of their own self-talk, both negative and positive. Ask, "What are things you say to yourself when you are angry or upset?"

4. Give each group member a copy of the Anger Warning Signs: Body Signals and Negative Self-Talk handout. Have participants check off common body signals and negative self-talk and discuss.

5. Briefly review on the mark/off the mark thinking (cognitive distortions) and the idea that everyone makes thinking errors that need to be challenged. Say:

    > Remember that everyone makes thinking mistakes and that when you feel angry, you are likely having "off the mark" thinking. For example, when you get upset because someone doesn't do what you want them to do, you may be using "shoulds." Or if you get angry because you think that a situation is unfair, you may be using "all-or-nothing" thinking instead of thinking flexibly about the situation.

Discuss Coping with Anger

1. Discuss the importance of coping with anger by calming the body and changing thinking. Explain that it is hard to feel angry when the body is calm and relaxed; thus, if we learn how to relax our bodies, we will likely feel less angry. Say, "Just as when you're dealing with anxiety, learning how to calm your body will help you calm your mind and help you feel less angry."

    > *Briefly review the different forms of relaxation the group has learned and practiced in group so far: two types of calm breathing, progressive muscle relaxation, guided imagery, and yoga.*

2. Review the connection between thoughts and feelings by saying, "Remember that you can change the way you *think* to change the way you *feel*." Have the group practice replacing their negative self-talk with positive self-talk, interacting with one another in the process. For example: "Marie's problem is that while playing soccer, she often gets mad at other players for stealing the ball. Her self-talk might be 'It's not fair, they are mean to me' or 'They can't do that to me.' What could she tell herself instead?" (*This is part of playing the game. I just need to keep trying my best.*)

    > *Refer to the chart of sample negative self-talk with replacement positive self-talk statements for guidance in teaching this part of the session.*

Negative and Positive Self-Talk

Negative Self-Talk	Positive Self-Talk
It's so unfair that we lost!	I tried my best. You can't win all the time.
I'm so stupid. I'm an idiot.	I'm a good person in many ways.
Today was horrible! Everyone is mean!	Tomorrow will be a better day.
Nobody understands.	It might feel like no one understands, but let me try to explain my feelings to someone who is good at listening.
He is a jerk!	Sometimes others do things that upset me, but name-calling won't help.
Life stinks.	There are a lot of good things in my life.
I want to quit.	I can keep trying until I get close enough or until I get there. Success is about putting in the effort.
I want to hit him.	I can calm myself down by clenching my fists and then relaxing them and by using calm breathing.

Let the group know that everything they learned about managing anxiety will help with anger, too, especially on-the-mark/off-the mark thinking. You may also summarize or review the information about coping thoughts and coping actions, as discussed in Session 2.9.

Free Play/Behavioral Rehearsal

Provide the group with a selection of age-appropriate toys, games, or other activities to choose from that encourage joint play and follow the procedure described in Session 2.1 for choosing play partners and facilitating free play.

Relaxation/Self-Regulation

1. Have group members stand and tell them that they will all do a yoga position called downward-facing dog. Read the following to guide them into the position.

   ▶ Lie down on the floor on your stomach, bend your elbows, and put your hands down on the floor next to your armpits or chest.

▶ Now get up on all fours, on hands and knees, and spread your fingers apart, but keep your palms on the floor.

▶ Now lift up onto your feet, standing mainly on your toes, lifting your hips up and keeping your hands on the floor. Your hands should be shoulder-width apart.

▶ Continue to lift your hips up and stretch your back. Continue to spread your fingers apart and push your hands against the floor, to encourage more lengthening in your spine and more lift in your hips. Hips up, hips up. Feel the stretch.

▶ Very good! Now gently come back down onto all fours and lie back down on your stomach and relax.

2. Ask the group how it felt to do the position and encourage them to practice it and the other yoga positions they have learned on their own.

Leadership Award

Select a group member to receive the Leadership Award and provide praise for what the person did well.

Generalization: Resilience Builder Assignment

Give each group member a copy of the Resilience Builder Assignment for the next session. Go over the assignment and answer any questions.

Parent Component

Give each participant a copy of the Parent Letter for the session. Have participants place the letter, Resilience Builder Assignment, and other handouts in the appropriate sections of their notebooks.

My Anger Body Signals

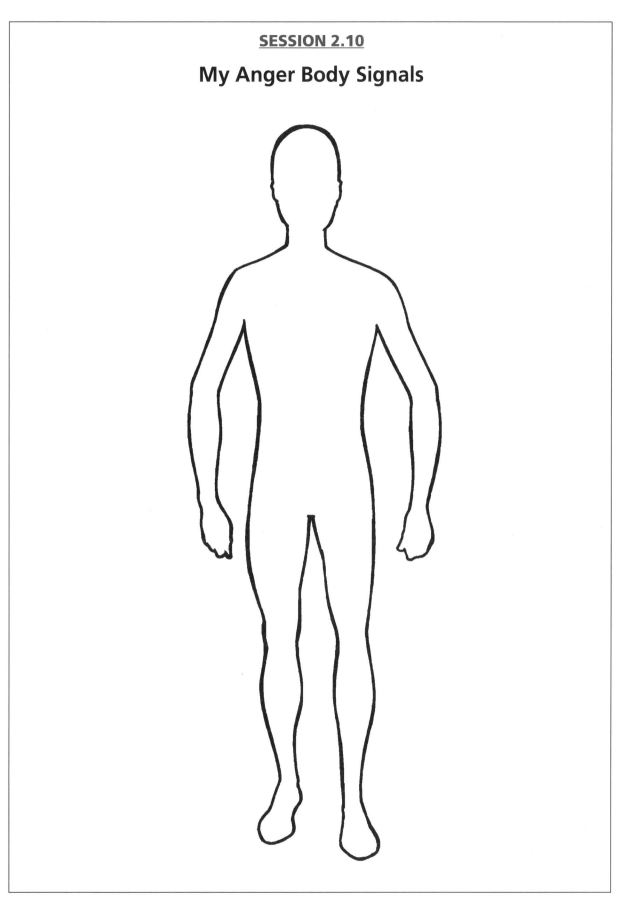

Anger Warning Signs: Body Signals and Negative Self-Talk

Name_____**Date**_____

Check the warning signs that apply to you when you are angry.

Anger Warning Signs: **Body Signals Checklist**	**Anger Warning Signs** **Negative Self-Talk Checklist**
☐ Tense muscles	☐ Everybody is against me.
☐ Tight fists	☐ Nobody understands.
☐ Racing heartbeat	☐ I know that I'm going to lose.
☐ Crossed arms	☐ Life stinks.
☐ Clenched jaw	☐ I want to quit.
☐ Sweaty palms	☐ I can't stand him.
☐ Fast breathing	☐ I want to hit him.
☐ Red, hot face	☐ I want to break something.
☐ Loud voice	☐ I hate doing this work.
☐ Trembling or shaky feeling	☐ I hate myself.
Other: _____	Other: _____
Other: _____	Other: _____
Other: _____	Other: _____

Self-Regulation: Anger Management

Name_____Date_____

Describe a time you felt angry.

1. What happened that made you feel angry, annoyed, frustrated, or upset?

   _____

   _____

2. How did your body feel? What were your body signals?

   ☐ tense muscles   ☐ fast breathing

   ☐ tight fists   ☐ red, hot face

   ☐ racing heartbeat   ☐ loud voice

   ☐ crossed arms   ☐ trembling or shaky feeling

   ☐ clenched jaw   ☐ lowered eyebrows

   ☐ sweaty palms   ☐ other _____

3. What were you thinking? What self-talk or thought signals did you have?

   _____

   _____

   _____

4. What did you do or could you have done to calm your body?

   _____

   _____

   _____

5. How did you change your thinking or what could you have thought instead? List a few positive self-talk statements.

   _____

   _____

   _____

Self-Regulation: Anger Management

Dear Parents:

This session is on anger management, another skill of self-regulation. To review, healthy self-regulation includes the ability to think rationally and therefore respond appropriately to situations. Learning how to manage anger and control one's response in frustrating or challenging situations is a key component of self-regulation.

The group will learn about body signals, or physiological cues, that they are feeling angry or upset. For example, muscle tension, tight fists, rapid heartbeat, and a loud voice are all possible signs of anger. They will also learn about thought signals, which include negative self-talk associated with feeling angry or annoyed (for example, "It's not fair," "I hate him," "Nobody understands"). What we say to ourselves in our minds affects how we feel and react; negative self-talk often triggers bad feelings and inappropriate responses. We review ways to calm the body and ways to change thoughts, including the use of positive self-talk.

Whenever possible, parents are encouraged to model healthy coping skills. It is important to give your child the message that feelings are neither good nor bad—they just *are*. However, our reactions and behaviors can be healthy and effective or unhealthy and ineffective. Modeling appropriate reactions and openly talking through situations with your child, including how he or she *felt, thought,* and *behaved* (reacted), will be beneficial.

Resilience Builder Assignment: Self-Regulation—Anger Management

This session's assignment asks your child to describe a situation in which he or she got angry, upset, or frustrated and then to describe body signals and thought signals (including self-talk) during the situation and how he or she could have calmed down and thought differently. It is recommended that you encourage your child to practice a relaxation exercise and positive self-talk for improved self-regulation. If time allows, please continue with the family meetings and Compliment Basket.

Sincerely,

Program Leader

SESSION

2.11

Self-Esteem

PURPOSE

Self-esteem is one of the best predictors of success in life. Self-esteem, or our assessment of our self-worth, has a profound impact on most aspects of our lives, including how we select and participate in relationships. Self-esteem comes from the ability to have competence in life, particularly being able to accomplish difficult and challenging tasks. Fostering positive feelings of self-worth is largely accomplished by addressing how we think about ourselves and the interpretations we make of what happens to us.

GOALS

To discuss self-esteem and teach the three parts of self-esteem (self, others, and events)

To help participants identify their own strengths and own them even when they experience failure

To develop positive self-talk statements affirming self-worth

To learn the connection between how they think about the events that occur and the way they feel about themselves

To understand the importance of handling failures and disappointments effectively

To practice a relaxation/self-regulation exercise

MATERIALS

Chalkboard or dry erase board and marker

Program Notebook (brought by group members)

Individual Points Charts

Name Cube

Toys and games for free play

Copies of the following:

Leadership Award (Appendix C)

Resilience Builder Assignment 2.11

Parent Letter 2.11

PROCEDURE

Individual Greeting

Conduct the individual greetings, as described in Session 2.1. The components of a good first impression—a smile and a courteous hello, and sustained eye contact—by now should be fairly automatic.

Review Success Journal and Resilience Builder Assignment

Have each group member discuss his or her individual goal and Success Journal entry and experiences completing the Resilience Builder Assignment. When each member finishes speaking, ask him or her to throw the Name Cube to determine the next speaker.

> *Record points on each group member's Points Chart for this portion of the session. Record the point for participation at the end of the session.*

Discuss the Three Parts of Self-Esteem

1. Ask the group if they know what *self-esteem* means and help them define it. Record their ideas, then summarize that self-esteem is what you believe and how you feel about yourself and your abilities.

2. Explain that self-esteem develops from three different sources. Write "Three Parts of Self-Esteem" on the board. To demonstrate, draw a big triangle and label the three points as "Self," "Others," and "Events" (with "Self" at the top point). Say:

Self-esteem is made up of three parts: the self, others, and events, meaning that self-esteem comes from yourself, from others, and from positive events that happen. The way you think about what happens to you will play a role in how you feel about what happens. For example, someone with good self-esteem about school can get a failing grade on one test and still feel smart. Someone with poor self-esteem about his or her academic ability might get an A and believe it's a fluke.

3. Discuss the three sources of self-esteem in detail. Review and record examples of each of the three parts, including the following ideas.

Self

▶ Knowing and owning your strengths and positive qualities

▶ Complimenting yourself

▶ Being flexible with yourself even when you fail or fall short of perfect

▶ Nurturing yourself

Clarify that owning your strengths means that even if you fail at something that you are generally good at, you do not relabel yourself as a failure in that area; rather, you own the quality and accept that you just had a bad day in this one area. Say:

> Knowing your strengths is one part, but owning them is also very important because that means that even if you don't do well or fail at something, you still know that it is your strength. For example, if you believe that you are an excellent soccer player and you have a bad game, you do not question your ability in soccer and reevaluate whether you are a good player; rather, you understand that occasional poor performance is normal—we all have bad days. Likewise, if you are strong at math but have trouble with one part of it (fractions, for instance), you do not allow that one piece to interfere with your knowledge of your strong math ability.

> In other words, the goal is not to be "all or nothing" but to be flexible in the way you think about yourself and your performance. It's not that you are either perfect or a failure; you can be good and skilled at something and simply have a bad day. Be kind to yourself and compliment yourself through positive self-talk.

Others

▶ Receiving a compliment

▶ Being invited for a play date or sleepover

▶ Being listened to by others, such as your parents

Discuss the importance of giving and receiving compliments. Point out that many people dismiss compliments by making excuses. Say:

Part of feeling good about who you are is being able to accept compliments and appreciate it when someone points out something great about you or something you accomplished. We need to be able to accept compliments well, as opposed to either dismissing them or downplaying them with comments such as "It was just luck." Also, it can feel great to give someone a compliment when they do a good job on a class project, when they win a game, or when they handle it well when they lose a game.

Summarize the idea that when others pay attention to you, listen to your ideas, do nice things for you, invite you to do things, and so on, they help you to feel good about yourself.

Events

▶ Receiving an award

▶ Getting a good grade

▶ Being invited to a party

▶ Competing in a piano competition

Explain that when good things happen to you, when you learn something new, or gain mastery over it, it helps you feel good about yourself. When you put in good effort and get a good grade, for example, you feel good because you have accomplished a goal. When we earn awards or are asked to join a team, others are letting us know that they recognize our accomplishments.

> *Explain that there is some overlap between "Others" and "Events." For instance, getting invited to a party involves both.*

4. Personalize the three parts of self-esteem by having group members provide examples of one or more of the three parts from their own lives. Use the Name Cube to proceed. Say, "When your name comes up, you can describe a personal strength, something someone else did or said that made you feel good about yourself, or a personal achievement that you are proud of."

> *Encourage the group to come up with meaningful examples. For example, if a group member shares that someone complimented something they possess (such as a video game system or clothing), redirect that person to provide a compliment more rich in meaning (for example, about being a good friend).*

5. Summarize that the way we think about what happens in our lives will directly impact how we feel about what happens. Say:

> Like downplaying compliments, many people make excuses for or minimize their achievements. For instance, if you earn a good grade on a group project, it is key

that you recognize how you contributed to the good grade, rather than minimizing your part.

Discuss Effort Versus Outcome

1. Point out that there are two ways to define success: by the effort you put forth or by the outcome.* Say:

> Success is not necessarily based on *outcomes*. For example, if you try out for a team and do your best at all the practices but don't make the team, the effort still counts, and this should be thought of as an achievement. Trying out counts as positive effort. Most people who try out are able to see the benefit from all the practice, even if they won't end up playing as part of the team.

2. Explain the idea that effort = success (versus talent = success), then discuss strengths in this light. Paraphrase:

> When you face a challenge or a problem you're not sure how to solve and then struggle with it until you find a solution, you can feel good about yourself for doing it on your own. Self-esteem doesn't just come from compliments or praise from others, it also comes from your effort and hard work. It is the effort that you put into something that counts the most. Success is sticking with a task and trying your best.

3. Have each member of the group share about a time when he or she put forth excellent effort and worked hard at something that did not come easy. Discuss the value of this type of experience, asking, "What did you learn from this experience?"

Dealing with Failures and Setbacks

1. Explain that everyone has failures and setbacks—these are a part of life. The goal is to manage these difficult times well and not let failures interfere with your sense of self-confidence.

2. Explain that the messages you give yourself at these times help shape self-esteem and how we think of ourselves. Say:

> When failures and disappointments happen, we have to be very careful not to make negative judgments about ourselves. Remember that thinking in a certain way can cause you to feel a certain way, and so by changing the way you *think*, you can change the way you *feel*. When things are not going well, you want to make sure that your thinking and self-talk are positive and realistic.

3. Have the group share examples of times when they had realistic and positive thinking, emphasizing what group members can say to themselves when they are feeling down—

---

*This topic overlaps with Carol Dweck's research on success (Dweck, 2006), which shows that rising to a challenge and approaching it with persistence and a desire to learn is a strong indicator of ability to succeed.

for example, "I know I will feel better tomorrow," "Everybody has a bad day from time to time," "I believe in myself and my ability to handle this." Summarize that it is important to celebrate your strengths, enjoy your own company, and appreciate yourself!

Free Play/Behavioral Rehearsal

Provide the group with a selection of age-appropriate toys, games, or other activities to choose from that encourage joint play and follow the procedure described in Session 2.1 for choosing play partners and facilitating free play.

Relaxation/Self-Regulation

1. Today's relaxation combines a guided imagery exercise focusing on creating a sense of empowerment and confidence in the group participants and a variation of the yoga mountain pose (see Session 1.12). Read the following aloud:

   ▶ Find a comfortable place to sit or lie down. Gently close your eyes and take a deep breath in through your nose and slowly breathe out through your mouth.

   ▶ This is your time for relaxation. Clear your mind and let go of any stress or tension that you might be holding onto. Take another deep breath in through your nose and out through your mouth.

   ▶ Imagine that you are standing tall on the top of a mountain. You can breathe easily, and you feel calm but also strong. Look around and notice all of the beautiful things around you. Do you see green trees or trees covered with glistening white snow? Are there other mountains around you and valleys in between?

   ▶ You are surrounded by nature and are fully aware of this moment. Your breath is calm. You feel clear in your mind and good energy in your body. You can feel the energy around you, and this makes you feel uplifted.

   ▶ While on this mountain, you notice how good you feel about yourself and your body. You are aware of how special you are and how capable you are to do whatever you set your mind to. You feel strong and confident. If there is something you want to do or need to do, you feel confident about your ability to do it and handle yourself well. You think of several good things about yourself . . . and you love who you are.

   ▶ Take another deep breath. Spend a minute or two feeling what it feels like when you think well of yourself and when you are in touch with how special you are.

   Allow 1 to 2 minutes for silent meditation.

   ▶ When you are ready, gently open your eyes and notice how calm your body feels. Remember that you can be this relaxed and feel confident about yourself anytime you want.

2. Once the script is finished, have the participants stand. Read and model the following to guide them into a standing mountain pose.

   ▶ Stand with your feet together (big toes touching) and your arms down by your sides.

   ▶ Stand up tall and straight, with your shoulders back and your chest lifting up, as if someone has a string attached to the top of your chest and is pulling it up.

   ▶ Now face your palms out and slowly lift your arms straight up to the ceiling, with your palms facing together. Keep your elbows straight and lift up high.

   ▶ I want you to imagine that your feet are like roots of a tree, pushing down into the earth and rooting you firmly to the ground. Push your feet into the floor and tighten your leg muscles.

   ▶ Now, I want you to lift the upper part of your body and arms all the way up to the sky, as much as you can lift, so your feet and legs are stretching down and your chest and arms are stretching up high. Feel the stretch and feel how strong you are.

3. Following the pose, say, "Great job, everyone! See, when we stand strong with good posture, we can breathe easily and feel good about ourselves. This helps us handle any problems that may come up."

Leadership Award

Select a group member to receive the Leadership Award and provide praise for what the person did well.

Generalization: Resilience Builder Assignment

Give each group member a copy of the Resilience Builder Assignment for the next session. Go over the assignment and answer any questions.

Parent Component

Give each participant a copy of the parent letter for the session. Have participants place the letter and Resilience Builder Assignment in the appropriate sections of their notebooks.

Self-Esteem

Name _____ **Date** _____

Self-Esteem: Three Parts

Self

```
          Self
           /\
          /  \
         /    \
        /      \
       /        \
Events /_____\ Others
```

Write three examples of times when you felt really great about yourself when (1) you felt this on your own because you were proud of yourself, (2) someone else helped you feel this way, and (3) something happened (an event) that helped you feel this way.

Self

_____

_____

Others

_____

_____

Events

_____

_____

List five positive things about yourself.

1. _____

2. _____

3. _____

4. _____

5. _____

Self-Esteem

Dear Parents:

Establishing a strong sense of self-esteem is possibly the most important development in childhood. Self-esteem, or our assessment of our self-worth, has a profound impact on most aspects of our lives. This session deals with the three ways that self-esteem develops: from ourselves (for example, knowing and owning our strengths, believing in ourselves, and positive self-talk), from others (for example, positive feedback from parents, teachers, and peers), and from events (for example, scoring a goal or getting invited to a party). We review examples of each and discuss the importance of "owning" our strengths, even on a bad day or when things are not going well.

Parents play a primary role in the development of self-esteem. Providing approving comments to your child and to others about your child in your child's presence is one way to teach your child about his or her strengths, though it is essential that this praise be authentic, genuine, and specific. In addition, helping your child gain mastery in certain areas by providing your child with opportunities to do so is imperative to developing self-confidence.

How you model interpreting certain events for your child helps establish the framework for how your child will interpret events. For example, if your son earns a poor grade on a project but tried his best on it, highlight that he is capable and that sometimes projects are very difficult. Be truthful and let him know that no one is great at everything and that we all have good and not-so-good subjects. Remind him that the goal is to persist on challenging tasks and emphasize the idea that effort, not outcome, equals success. If your daughter does well on a test, make sure she knows it's because she put forth excellent effort and rose to the challenge. Comments like "You really worked hard—great job!" are better than "You are so smart." Do not let your child minimize success by saying the test was easy or that the high grade was a fluke.

Resilience Builder Assignment: Self-Esteem

Please assist your child in writing about times he or she felt great that illustrate the three parts of self-esteem and in recording positive statements. For the positive statements, encourage your child to list characteristics and traits that are meaningful, such as "I am honest and trustworthy," rather than superficial comments like "I have a nice house." Ask your child to lead the family in a relaxation exercise and have members of the family practice positive self-statements. Please continue with family meetings and the Compliment Basket as you can.

Sincerely,

Program Leader

Teasing and Bullying

PURPOSE

Children and teens who are the recipients of teasing and bullying often consider this aspect of their lives extremely distressing and disempowering. Because external support from peers is an important factor in resilience relating to connections and attachments, children derive great benefit from learning how to address teasing. With guidance and support, they can learn effective ways to be less affected. Often, by sharing their examples and becoming aware of the universality of this experience, group members feel better and more empowered to be proactive.

GOALS

To define teasing and bullying and its impact

To identify behaviors that put one at-risk for being teased or bullied and learn how to be less of a target for bullying

To learn how to respond to being teased or bullied by being proactive, assertive, and setting appropriate boundaries

To review assertiveness skills and "I-statements"

To learn how to be and act less affected by teasing and bullying

To practice relaxation/self-regulation techniques

MATERIALS

Chalkboard or dry erase board and marker

Program Notebooks (brought by group members)

Individual Points Charts

Name Cube

Toys and games for free play

Copies of the following:

    Leadership Award (Appendix C)

    Resilience Builder Assignment 2.12

    Parent Letter 2.12

PROCEDURE

Individual Greeting

Conduct the individual greetings, as described in Session 2.1. The components of a good first impression—a smile and a courteous hello, and sustained eye contact—by now should be fairly automatic.

Review Success Journal and Resilience Builder Assignment

Have each group member discuss his or her individual goal and Success Journal entry and experiences completing the Resilience Builder Assignment. When each member finishes speaking, ask him or her to throw the Name Cube to determine the next speaker.

> *Record points on each group member's Points Chart for this portion of the session. Record the point for participation at the end of the session.*

Discuss Teasing and Bullying: Definition and Impact

1.   Ask participants to raise their hands if they have ever been teased or bullied by a peer. Most likely, all the hands will be raised; if not, prompt further and say, "Are you sure there hasn't been at least one time when you were teased by someone else?" Explain that most people, unfortunately, are teased or bullied at some point in their lives.

2. Generate a discussion of what constitutes teasing and bullying. Ask, "How do you know when you are being teased or bullied by other kids?" Have group members generate examples of times they were teased or bullied.

   Sample Responses

   When friends say something to you in a mean but joking way

   When someone calls you a name

   When someone gets in your physical space and makes a threatening move

   When someone makes faces at you, such as a disgusted look

   When people gossip about you

   When you are excluded from an activity

   When you are threatened in any way

   When someone puts you down either through words, facial expressions, or other actions

3. Explain that teasing is generally thought of as less severe than bullying, which tends to have more of an aggressive, threatening component to it. Bullying also often involves more than the person doing the bullying; it also includes kids called bystanders, who either encourage or do nothing to stop the bullying.

4. Discuss that teasing and bullying are generally done by certain kids at school, on a sports team, or in the neighborhood. However, it also can happen in the context of friendships. Say:

   > Sometimes, our friends might tease us, and even though this isn't the same as being teased by bullies, it can be hurtful. It might be when a friend is joking around and ends up making fun of you. When this happens, the intention is probably not to hurt your feelings, but your feelings might get hurt anyway. So you need to talk to your friend about the teasing and tell the person that you'd like him or her to stop saying those things. Any good friend will stop.

5. Discuss the impact of teasing and bullying—for example, hurt feelings, feelings of anger, feeling bad about yourself, disliking school, and feeling powerless. Point out that being teased is a serious matter and that it is important to know good ways to deal with it.

Discuss Boundaries and Assertiveness

1. Discuss behaviors or mindsets that may make some children and teens the targets of bullying. Say:

While the bully is responsible for his or her behavior, there are some things that might put someone at risk of being teased or bullied. For example, when someone is very passive and doesn't stick up for herself, a bully might see that person as a good target for bullying. Also, someone who shows he is really affected by the bullying—maybe by crying or getting really mad in response—might be a good target for a bully. Finally, it is possible for people to be "too nice"—always willing to do things for others, even when it isn't what they want or when it doesn't work for them. People who let others boss them around and do not set appropriate boundaries may be at greater risk of being bullied.

It is important not to give the wrong message: Identifying factors that put someone at risk does not mean that a person is responsible for the bullying, that there is something wrong with them, or that they caused the bullying in any way.

2. Explain the importance of setting boundaries. Say:

    Good boundary setting is a part of managing your friendships and relationships. When someone is teasing or bullying you, you need to let them know that it is not acceptable to treat you that way. Remember, being resilient and proactive is about bouncing back when challenges come your way, like being teased or bullied. You need to come up with a plan to handle it well.

    Point out that one way to prevent being bullied is to be assertive and stick up for yourself even when you are not being teased or bullied.

3. Let the group know that if their rights are violated, they can speak up and politely but assertively tell the other person that it is not OK to treat them that way. Also, if they are too nice, too agreeable, too accommodating to others, others may get the message that they can be pushed around. If they see themselves acting this way, they can act in a more confident manner by being assertive and using "I-statements."

    For group members who have already participated in Unit 1, the following will be a review of material in Session 1.12.

Assertiveness

▶ Posture: Body should be tall and straight, with shoulders back.

▶ Eye contact: Maintain eye contact when talking.

▶ Tone of voice: Speak in a firm but friendly way.

I-Statements

"I feel _____ when you_____."

Let group members know that they also may add a request after the "I-statement," if appropriate. For example: "I feel *uncomfortable* when *you stand so close to me. Please step back a bit.*"

Discuss Effective Responses to Teasing and Bullying

Explain the concept of social power. Help group members understand that there are things they can do to make the bully less powerful. Summarize the following ideas:

Be Assertive but Don't Overreact

There are a few things to keep in mind when dealing with bullies. Bullies don't like it when you seem like you don't care about what they are saying to you. So, acting like you are not affected by what they are saying or doing is very important and makes the bully less likely to keep bullying you. You want to act like you don't care, but this doesn't mean being passive. Acting like a passive victim lets bullies know that they can bully you. You want to show bullies that it's not OK, and you need to respond assertively.

Minimize Contact with Bullies

The goal is to minimize the impact of bullying by minimizing the amount of time you are near bullies, if possible. Try to be with friends when bullies are around because this will make it harder for them to give you a hard time.

Avoid Responding Aggressively

Responding aggressively is not the right way to handle being teased or bullied; in fact, if you do this, it makes it harder to tell which one is the bully and which one is the victim. Someone might see you behaving aggressively and not understand that you were bullied first.

Go to an Adult for Help

If you try these ideas and find that the bully continues to give you a hard time, then you need to get an adult involved. Sometimes this will be a teacher or a coach; other times it might be your parents. The school can have a meeting with you, your parents, the bully and his or her parents, and they can come up with a plan to stop the bully from treating you this way. This is a last resort, but it is another way of being proactive and handling the situation well.

Role-Play Teasing/Bullying Situations

1. Ask group members to offer real-life examples of times that they have been teased or bullied and role-play a situation in which two group members model poor handling of a bullying situation. The participant playing the bully might call the other a name,

pretend to push him or her, and so forth. The participant being bullied might become very upset, cry, or act passively and "just take it."

The group member role-playing the bully can call names and make fun of the other group member, but limit the role-plays to make sure there is no real physical contact like pushing or hitting.

2. Role-play the same situation but with effective handling of bullying. The participant playing the bully should do the same thing, but the person being bullied should respond by being assertive (in posture, eye contact, and tone of voice), setting boundaries by using an "I-statement," and showing that he or she is unaffected by what the bully is saying or doing.

3. Following the role-plays, briefly discuss what group members thought about it.

If time permits, they can do another role-play of effective handling of bullying, but the situation should be varied, with the bully saying or doing something different.

Free Play/Behavioral Rehearsal

Provide the group with a selection of age-appropriate toys, games, or other activities to choose from that encourage joint play and follow the procedure described in Session 2.1 for choosing play partners and facilitating free play.

Relaxation/Self-Regulation

1. This session's relaxation is a specific form of calm breathing: diaphragmatic breathing. Have group members find a comfortable place to lie down or sit. Read the following and model calm breathing:

   ▶ Now we are going to practice a special kind of calm breathing. The goal is to breathe in through your nose and out through your mouth, with the air going all the way down to your lower belly.

   ▶ Tense or anxious breathing causes your upper chest to rise and fall, and the air only goes into your upper chest, while relaxed or calm breathing causes your lower stomach—around your belly button—to go up and down, and the air goes into your lower abdomen.

   ▶ Slowly breathe in through your nose for a count of five: 1, 2, 3, 4, and 5. Hold the breath for five: 1, 2, 3, 4, and 5. Now slowly breathe out through your mouth for five: 1, 2, 3, 4, and 5.

▶ Again, breathe in through your nose: 1, 2, 3, 4, and 5. Hold it: 1, 2, 3, 4, and 5. And out through your mouth: 1, 2, 3, 4, and 5. Remember to let the air go all the way down to your lower abdomen.

If participants are having difficulty getting the air to go down into the lower abdomen, then have them lie down on the floor and put a lightweight object (ideally a foam yoga block) on their upper chest. Have them use the block as a way of measuring if their breathing is in their upper chest or lower abdomen. If they are doing calm breathing, the block should not move while their lower belly should move up and down. If you have one group member do this, it is recommended that they all be asked to do it so no one is singled out.

2. Once the script is finished, have the participants stand and tell them that they will all do the yoga tree pose, originally introduced in Session 1.3. Read the following to guide them into the position.

   ▶ Take a deep breath. Hold it in.

   ▶ As you breathe out, bend your right leg and bring your right foot to your left knee. If you feel that you might lose your balance, then bring the leg as low to the ground as you need or stand against the wall for support.

   ▶ As you breathe in, stretch your arms out to make a "T" or put your hands on your hips.

   ▶ Hold this position to a count of five or as long as you can: 1, 2, 3, 4, and 5.

   ▶ If you need to, bring your legs together but keep your arms outstretched. Notice the tension in your muscles as you hold the position.

   ▶ Bring your hands together so that the palms touch.

   ▶ Slowly bring your arms to your sides.

   ▶ Slowly bring your right leg down.

   Repeat the preceding steps with the left leg, then continue.

   ▶ Take a deep breath in: 5, 4, 3, 2, and 1.

   ▶ Slowly breathe out. Let your muscles loosen and your body relax.

   ▶ Now take a seat.

3. Say, "Very good! Great job!" Remember that it's easy to take two or three minutes each day to practice breathing or a yoga pose.

Leadership Award

Select a group member to receive the Leadership Award and provide praise for what the person did well.

Generalization: Resilience Builder Assignment

Give each group member a copy of the Resilience Builder Assignment for the next session. Go over the assignment and answer any questions.

Parent Component

Give each participant a copy of the parent letter for the session. Have participants place the letter and Resilience Builder Assignment in the appropriate sections of their notebooks.

Teasing and Bullying

Name _____ **Date** _____

Assertive Ways to Handle Being Teased

Circle the reactions that are assertive ways to handle being teased.

1. Crying and running away from the bully.

2. Telling the bully to stop talking to you that way.

3. Kicking the bully in the leg and calling the bully a name.

4. Getting a teacher.

5. Speaking in a firm voice while making eye contact.

6. Standing up straight with confidence.

7. Softly telling the bully to leave you alone.

8. Doing nothing.

9. Using "I-statements" to express how you feel.

10. Acting like you don't care what the bully is saying.

   List three ways you can be assertive with bullies or prevent being bullied.

1. _____

   _____

   _____

2. _____

   _____

   _____

3. _____

   _____

   _____

From *Resilience Builder Program for Children and Adolescents,* © 2011 by M. K. Alvord, B. Zucker, & J. J. Grados, Champaign, IL: Research Press (800-519-2707, www.researchpress.com).

Teasing and Bullying

Dear Parents:

This session is on teasing and bullying, an important and powerful topic for group members. Discussing the impact of teasing and understanding that most children have been teased to some extent creates a framework for establishing, or reestablishing, personal power. Group members will learn to identify behaviors that put them at risk for being teased, and, more important, will learn how to respond confidently to being teased and bullied.

In particular, we review the importance of being proactive and resilient and focus on being assertive and using "I-statements" to deliver direct communication to bullies. The group learns how being passive victims or showing how affected they are by the bullying behavior can maintain the dynamic of being bullied. They then learn how to shift this dynamic by being proactive and establishing healthy boundaries.

It is very easy and understandable for children to want to respond to aggression with aggression; however, they will learn that responding with aggression not only shows the bully how affected they are, thus maintaining the dynamic, but also makes it less clear who is the aggressor and who is the victim.

In efforts to gain mastery of this "talking back" approach, group members will role-play and practice how to deal with being teased. They will also practice what it looks like to show that they are not affected by the bullying and how to respond proactively and assertively.

Resilience Builder Assignment: Teasing and Bullying

Please assist your child in completing the assignment. Remind your child of what was learned in group—ways to be proactive and deal effectively with the bullying situation, including not showing that he or she is affected by the bully. Please also encourage your child to continue to practice relaxation and positive self-talk for self-calming.

If you become aware of frequent bullying in school or another setting, intervention may require the involvement of multiple adults—on a systematic level—to correct the problem. Please notify those adults.

Sincerely,

Program Leader

SESSION

2.13

Choices for Handling Challenges

PURPOSE

When we face a challenging situation, such as having disagreements with others, simply knowing that we have a choice regarding how to respond leads to a sense of empowerment. This allows us to cope more effectively. Solving problems by generating alternatives provides a means by which we may better influence how we react. This session focuses on helping group members make proactive choices. Generating choices requires flexibility in thinking. This, in turn, helps participants have more control over outcomes.

GOALS

To recognize that we have choices about what we think, say, or do

To learn nine different choices we always have

To discuss the importance of making proactive, responsible decisions

To learn that we always have choices, even in situations we cannot control

To practice a relaxation/self-regulation exercise

MATERIALS

Chalkboard or dry erase board and marker

Program Notebooks (brought by group members)

Individual Points Charts

Name Cube

Game Spinner (made from heavy stock)

Toys and games for free play

Copies of the following:

Leadership Award (Appendix C)

Nine Choices handout

Choices Scenarios (cut into slips and folded in half)

Resilience Builder Assignment 2.13

Parent Letter 2.13

Before the session, prepare the **Choices for Handling Challenges** *poster and Game Spinner.*

PROCEDURE

Individual Greeting

Conduct the individual greetings, as described in Session 2.1. The components of a good first impression—a smile and a courteous hello, and sustained eye contact—by now should be fairly automatic.

Review Success Journal and Resilience Builder Assignment

Have each group member discuss his or her individual goal and Success Journal entry and experiences completing the Resilience Builder Assignment. When each member finishes speaking, ask him or her to throw the Name Cube to determine the next speaker.

> *Record points on each group member's Points Chart for this portion of the session. Record the point for participation at the end of the session.*

Discuss Advantages of Making Good Choices

1. Write "Choices" on the board. Say:

Being a good friend or a responsible person requires that you think about the situation you're in and recognize that you have choices about what you think, say, or do. For example, suppose a friend is upset with you because you don't want to do the activity that he or she planned. You can think to yourself, "OK, let me give it a chance and find out more about it." Or you could tell your friend that you understand that he or she is upset, but that you've tried the activity before and prefer not to do it. Maybe you can discuss a few other activities that you both might enjoy. You can agree on which one you would like to do on another day.

2. Facilitate discussion by asking group members to suggest situations they have faced, state what choices they had, and what choices they made. Continue with the following:

   Another example might be that you have a test tomorrow. You can choose how much time you want to put into studying. If you don't put in enough time studying, what do you think will happen on the test? *(If you make a choice not to study for the test, you are likely to get a low grade.)* Now, let's talk about when you make a reactive choice. If someone in school says something mean, and you get angry and push the person, what do you think will happen? Or what would happen if you are playing soccer, and you miss a goal and then blame another player? *(Accept responses.)*

3. Explain that we can't always control how others react to us or how situations turn out. But we can consider what choices we have—and we can make good decisions about what to think, say, and do. Making positive, responsible choices helps us get better results.

Discuss Available Choices

Give each group member a Nine Choices handout. Refer to the Choices for Handling Challenges poster and discuss the ways we make many choices about what we think, what we say, and what we do.

Choices for Handling Challenges

	Think	Say	Do
Positive (proactive/optimistic)	Choice 1	Choice 4	Choice 7
Negative (reactive/pessimistic)	Choice 2	Choice 5	Choice 8
Do nothing (avoid/passive)	Choice 3	Choice 6	Choice 9

I Can Choose What I Think

I can think (self-talk) something positive (proactive and optimistic).

I can think (self-talk) something negative (reactive and pessimistic).

I can avoid thinking about the situation (be passive).

I Can Choose What I Say

I can say something positive (proactive and optimistic).

I can say something negative (reactive and pessimistic).

I can say nothing (be passive).

I Can Choose What I Do

I can take a positive action (proactive and optimistic).

I can take a negative action (reactive and pessimistic).

I can do nothing (be passive).

Choices Activity

1. Let group members know you will be playing a game using these various choices.

2. Give each group member a Choices Scenario. Ask each member to read the scenario aloud, then discuss three possible choices out of the nine available for each scenario. Have each group member use the game spinner to determine the three choices.

3. After each group member has taken a turn, ask if others agree or disagree with the choices.

Free Play/Behavioral Rehearsal

Provide the group with a selection of age-appropriate toys, games, or other activities to choose from that encourage joint play and follow the procedure described in Session 2.1 for choosing play partners and facilitating free play.

Relaxation/Self-Regulation

1. Ask group members to sit in a comfortable position on the floor or in a chair, then read the following guided imagery procedures:

   ▶ Today you will use your imagination to relax.

   ▶ Close your eyes and sit quietly with your arms at your sides.

▶ Take a deep breath in, and hold it until the count of five: 1, 2, 3, 4, and 5. Slowly breathe out.

▶ Today we are making a choice to go on a timeless journey. Picture a glow-in-the-dark watch that sparkles as you wave your arm in a darkened room.

▶ Notice the glow of the sparkles in the room. You can choose the colors of the sparkles. Enjoy the colors as they twirl around the room.

▶ Now decide if you want to stay in this room or choose to open a door and to go another place. *(Pause for about 5 seconds.)* If you choose to open the door, slowly turn the door handle and open it wide. Walk to the other side. There you find yourself in a special, relaxing, safe place.

▶ You choose the place to go. It might be a cozy spot on a sunny day at the park, or it might be in a special place you like by a campfire, or it might be a white sand beach on a perfect summer day. It can be any place you choose that is relaxing and calm. Imagine yourself there now.

▶ I want you to notice all of the sights and sounds you might experience. Notice what you see and hear. Choose to hear and see other things that you find pleasant.

▶ Feel the sun or the breeze or the heat on your face. Notice the smells that bring you comfort and peace.

▶ Enjoy this time in your special place. Just relax for a few moments. *(Pause about 15 seconds.)*

▶ Now you hear a clock chime in the background. *(Pause 5 seconds.)* With each chime, you feel a little more relaxed and calm.

▶ Good. Enjoy this calm state that you have chosen, knowing that you can make a choice to take this feeling with you. You can use it at any time during the day that you may need to feel quiet and relaxed.

▶ Now, with each chime I will count from 1 to 5. With each number, you will feel a little more awake and alert. Let's begin now. One, take a deep, quiet breath in. *(Wait 5 seconds.)* Two, slowly blow the breath out through your mouth. *(Wait 5 seconds.)* Three, gently shake your head. Four, slowly open your eyes. And 5, you are ready for the rest of the day. *(Wait 15–20 seconds before continuing.)*

2. Ask the group, "How did that feel? What did the glow-in-the-dark watch look like? If you chose to open the door, where did you go? If you chose to stay in the room, what was comfortable and relaxing about being there?

Leadership Award

Select a group member to receive the Leadership Award and provide praise for what the person did well.

Generalization: Resilience Builder Assignment

Give each group member a copy of the Resilience Builder Assignment for the next session. Go over the assignment and answer any questions.

Parent Component

Give each participant a copy of the parent letter for the session. Have participants place the letter, Resilience Builder Assignment, and Nine Choices handout in the appropriate sections of their notebooks.

FOR YOUNGER CHILDREN

Instead of nine choices, you can simplify and put six choices on a cube (like the Name Cube):

1. Think + (think something positive)

2. Think – (think something negative)

3. Say + (say something positive)

4. Say – (say something negative)

5. Do + (do something positive)

6. Do – (do something negative)

Read scenarios one at a time. Have participants roll the cube and give responses to the scenarios corresponding to the suggestion (for example, "Do +") facing up.

OPTIONAL ACTIVITY

Distribute white typing paper and markers. Explain to the participants that they will be making and illustrating a book about friendship choices. Have group members fold several sheets of paper in half. Next have them title their book. Tell them the title should include the word "Choice" or "Choices" and the word "Friend" or "Friendship." Once they have titled their book, they can write and illustrate a brief story.

Nine Choices

	Think	Say	Do
Positive (proactive/optimistic)	Choice 1	Choice 4	Choice 7
Negative (reactive/pessimistic)	Choice 2	Choice 5	Choice 8
Do nothing (avoid/passive)	Choice 3	Choice 6	Choice 9

I can choose what I think.

1. I can think (self-talk) something positive (proactive and optimistic).

2. I can think (self-talk) something negative (reactive and pessimistic).

3. I can avoid thinking about the situation (be passive).

I can choose what I say.

4. I can say something positive (proactive and optimistic).

5. I can say something negative (reactive and pessimistic).

6. I can say nothing (be passive).

I can choose what I do.

7. I can take a positive action (proactive and optimistic).

8. I can take a negative action (reactive and pessimistic).

9. I can do nothing (be passive).

Game Spinner

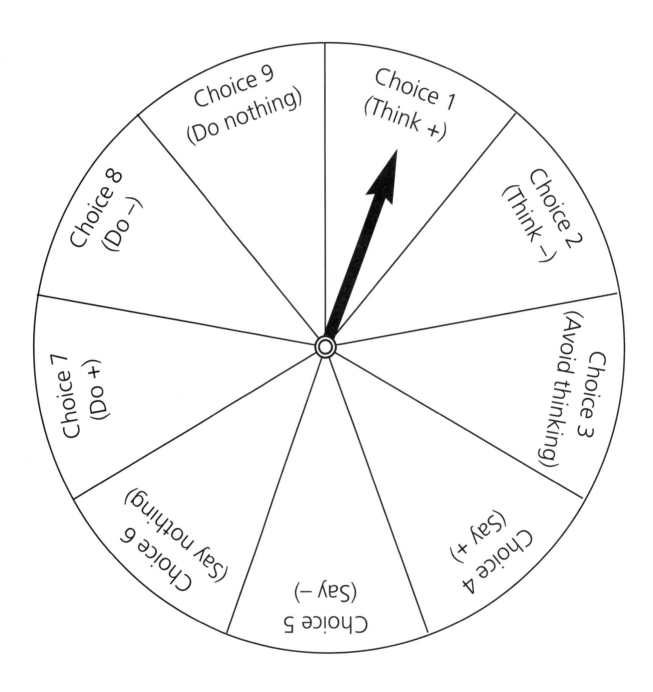

Choices Scenarios

1. You have just learned that an acquaintance has been spreading a vicious rumor about you to everyone in the school. You have no idea why he is doing this, and he denies spreading these rumors. What are your choices?

2. There is a party this Saturday at a friend's house. One of your best friends has organized it. You have just found out about it, and no one has invited you. What are your choices?

3. Your classmate tried to cheat off your paper during a test. When you noticed, you tried to tell the person to stop. The teacher looked over at the wrong time, and now you are the one given detention! What are your choices?

4. Your best friend since first grade has always sat next to you at lunch. Recently, a new girl started at your school and your friend has been spending a lot of time with her. Now, for the third day in a row, she is not sitting with you at lunch. You find yourself sitting alone at the lunch table. What choices do you have?

5. A movie you want to see is being released. Several of your friends are going this Friday night. Your parents have just informed you that you need to go out of town this weekend to visit your grandparents. What choices do you have?

6. A new friend is really fun to be with but is sometimes mean to you. Recently, she has also begun putting you down and hanging the phone up on you when she gets angry. Today, when you told her that you didn't want to do what she wanted, she became angry with you and hung up the phone. What are your choices?

7. Your friend down the street gets together with you on most weekends. Recently at school, your friend has stopped saying hello to you when he is with other friends. You even think your friend and his other friends were making fun of you today when you walked by them (but you did not hear or see what was actually said). What are your choices?

8. Classroom assignments are out for the new school year. None of your good friends is in your classes. You are really bummed. What are your choices?

Choices for Handling Challenges

Name _____ Date _____

We make choices every day. Remember, you always have at least nine choices:

► You can think something positive, think something negative, or avoid thinking about the situation.

► You can do something positive, do something negative, or do nothing.

► You can say something positive, say something negative, or say nothing.

Describe two situations you experienced this week and state how you handled them. Circle the choice you made. Then write down other choices you could have made in each situation.

Situation 1 and How I Handled It

_____

_____

_____

_____

Another Choice = Think something positive or negative (What could I have thought?)

_____

Another Choice = Avoid thinking (How would that help?)

_____

Another Choice = Do something positive or negative (What could I have done?)

_____

Another Choice = Do nothing (How would that help?)

_____

Another Choice = Say something positive or negative (What else could I have said?)

_____

Another Choice = Say nothing (How would that help?)

_____

Situation 2 and How I Handled It

_____

_____

_____

_____

Another Choice = Think something positive or negative (What could I have thought?)

_____

Another Choice = Avoid thinking (How would that help?)

_____

Another Choice = Do something positive or negative (What could I have done?)

_____

Another Choice = Do nothing (How would that help?)

_____

Another Choice = Say something positive or negative (What else could I have said?)

_____

Another Choice = Say nothing (How would that help?)

_____

Choices for Handling Challenges

Dear Parents:

This session teaches your child that he or she can make choices. When children and teens are aware that they have choices, they can make good, responsible decisions that lead to better outcomes. For example, if your child calls a friend who declines an invitation to go to the movies, help him or her explore what choices are available. Your child could think positively ("That's OK—I can invite someone else") or take an action (call another friend or ask to go with the family member) or speak with the friend about other possible plans. You can remind your child that while we can't control what our friends do, we have choices about how to react.

When your child completes this week's assignment, please keep the following choices in mind:

I can choose what I __think.__

1. I can think (self-talk) something positive (proactive and optimistic).

2. I can think (self-talk) something negative (reactive and pessimistic).

3. I can avoid thinking about the situation (be passive).

I can choose what I __say.__

4. I can say something positive (proactive and optimistic).

5. I can say something negative (reactive and pessimistic).

6. I can say nothing (be passive).

I can choose what I __do.__

7. I can take a positive action (proactive and optimistic).

8. I can take a negative action (reactive and pessimistic).

9. I can do nothing (be passive).

As parents, we can help our children understand how choices are generated by solving some of our own challenges out loud. We can let them in on our thought processes. In this way, we can model healthy decision making for our children.

Resilience Builder Assignment: Choices for Handling Challenges

This assignment asks that your child recall situations faced this week, choices made, and possible alternative choices. Please discuss choices available in specific situations to assist transfer of this skill and continue to practice relaxation. As time allows, continue with family meetings and the Compliment Basket.

Sincerely,

Program Leader

Being a Good Sport:
Game Etiquette at Home

PURPOSE

While electronic media from computers to cell phones provide increased opportunity for virtual relationships, one danger of their pervasiveness is that children and teenagers often neglect to initiate and enjoy face-to-face interactions. Using an electronic game system or board games, group members learn how to host and show good "game etiquette." Skills highlighted include inviting a peer over and being a good host.

GOALS

To discuss the advantages of inviting someone over to play an electronic game rather than playing alone

To discuss and practice initiating a social gathering

To identify elements necessary for success while playing electronic or other games with others

To discuss common frustrations and obstacles in the way of a successful and enjoyable interaction and coping strategies such as positive self-talk

To encourage understanding that their actions help determine the outcome of getting together with others

To play a game while applying the skills of good game etiquette

To practice a relaxation/self-regulation technique

MATERIALS

Chalkboard or dry erase board and marker

Program Notebooks (brought by group members)

Individual Points Charts

Name Cube

Markers (for role-play)

Toys and games for free play

An electronic gaming system (if unavailable, use board games instead)

Copies of the following:

> Leadership Award (Appendix C)
>
> Game Etiquette Award (Appendix C)
>
> Showcase Time form
>
> Resilience Builder Assignment 2.14
>
> Parent Letter 2.14

In addition to the usual parent letter, you will want to provide parents with an invitation to attend the last 15 minutes of Session 2.15, the final session in the series. In the invitation, you can explain that parents will have a chance to see what the group has learned and describe any special arrangements your group has decided on.

*Before beginning, prepare the **Invitation Steps** poster.*

PROCEDURE

Individual Greeting

Conduct the individual greetings, as described in Session 2.1. The components of a good first impression—a smile and a courteous hello, and sustained eye contact—by now should be fairly automatic.

Review Success Journal and Resilience Builder Assignment

Have each group member discuss his or her individual goal and Success Journal entry and experiences completing the Resilience Builder Assignment. When each member finishes speaking, ask him or her to throw the Name Cube to determine the next speaker.

Record points on each group member's Points Chart for this portion of the session. Record the point for participation at the end of the session.

Discuss Game Etiquette at Home

1. Begin by facilitating a conversation about how often group members invite their peers over to play electronic games and how those gatherings go. Ask, "What are the advantages of playing an electronic game face-to-face? Of initiating contact and having a guest in your home?"

2. Refer the group to the Invitation Steps poster and discuss the steps necessary to invite someone to your home to play a game.

Invitation Steps

1. Decide whom you would like to invite over to get to know better.

2. Think about what you need to do to invite the person over.

3. If the person says no, think about what it might mean and how you'll react.

4. Think about what you have to do to be a good host.

5. Show good game etiquette.

---

3. Write "Being a Good Sport at Your Home" on the board. Under that heading, make three columns. Write "Inviting Someone," "Being a Good Host," and "Game Etiquette," as column headings. Facilitate discussion of these aspects of inviting a guest to play a game.

The chart on the next page illustrates possible responses.

Free Play/Behavioral Rehearsal

The challenge in this session is helping the group members negotiate what they will play and in which group. Ideally, they will play a multiplayer computer or video game. If these are not available, you may substitute board games. The practice should include making compromises, taking turns, and sustaining attention while watching those who are actively playing.

Being a Good Sport at Your Home

Inviting Someone	Being a Good Host	Game Etiquette
Call the person—ask politely if they would like to come over.	Greet your guest.	Teach your guest the rules if necessary or at least make sure you are playing by the same rules.
Or ask your parent to make arrangements.	If you have a pet, make sure the person is comfortable with it, or put the pet in another room.	Be generous and give your guest tips on how to advance in the game.
Text an invite.	Ask your guest if he or she needs something (food, bathroom).	Control your anger and frustration.
E-mail an invite.	Let your guest choose the first game or activity.	Stay focused on your guest as well as the game.
Use other social media to invite.	Engage in a conversation.	Deal well with disappointment.
Be aware of time limitations the person may have.	Ask if your guest is enjoying this activity and switch if not.	Deal well with failure or loss and use self-control.
If the person is unable to accept this time, see if he or she would like to come over another time.	At the end, tell the person you had a good time.	Compliment your guest and make positive statements.
If the person says no or is busy even for an alternative date, invite someone else.	Escort your guest to the door when it's time to leave.	Don't quit.
Be courteous and direct!	Be flexible and agreeable!	Be flexible and agreeable!

1. Provide several choices of video or computer games.

2. Let participants know how many controllers there are or how many may play at a time. Inform them that they will have to divide up into pairs or groups of three and decide which pair or group of players will go first. One can take the role of host and the others the role of guests.

There are many opportunities for negotiation here! You can also have group members draw straws or flip a coin to determine order of play.

3. Encourage those who are waiting their turn to play to watch and, ideally, cheer the players on.

4. Have group members observe and take turns until all groups or pairs have had a chance to play.

5. Give all members who played fairly and maintained good self-control a Game Etiquette Award.

Relaxation/Self-Regulation

1. This week's relaxation will be brief due to time spent on the game exercise. Have participants stand, then read and model the following to guide them into the crescent moon yoga pose:

> Today we will learn a yoga pose called crescent moon. Stand up straight and bring your arms out to the sides to shoulder height, with your palms facing the sky.

> Inhale as you lift your arms above your head toward the ceiling: 1, 2, 3, 4, 5. Interlace your fingers. Keep your shoulders relaxed. Hold your breath: 1, 2, 3, 4, 5.

> Exhale while you press the right hip out to the side, leaning to the left. Reach to the right with your arms. Keep your feet firmly on the floor.

> Inhale as you bring yourself to a standing position, reaching your arms above your head toward the ceiling.

> Exhale while you press the left hip out to the side, leaning to the right. Reach to the right with your arms, keeping your feet firmly grounded.

> Inhale as you bring yourself to a standing position: 1, 2, 3, 4, 5. Exhale as you relax your arms to your sides.

2. Ask the group how it felt to do the pose and encourage them to continue practicing the yoga poses and other relaxation exercises on their own.

Leadership Award

Select a group member to receive the Leadership Award and provide praise for what the person did well.

Generalization: Resilience Builder Assignment

1. Give each group member a copy of the Resilience Builder Assignment for the next session. Go over the assignment and answer any questions.

2. Explain that the next session will be the final one and that the group will "showcase" all members. Hand out copies of the Showcase Time form and discuss. Ask group members to fill it out at the beginning of the week so they may have a chance to think about and practice their presentation before next week's session. Let them know they will also have an opportunity to present a topic from one of the sessions.

Parent Component

Give each participant a copy of the parent letter for the session. Have participants place the letter, Resilience Builder Assignment, and Showcase Time form in the appropriate sections of their notebooks.

> *Let the group know that the next session will be the final session in the series and that they will have an opportunity to redeem final points for prizes and show parents what they have learned over the course of the group. Discuss any special arrangements. Refreshments are optional for the final session and provide another opportunity to work on manners and cooperation.*

Showcase Time

Name _____ **Date** _____

Fill in each blank with information about yourself. Next, choose an activity, talent, project, or anything else that you feel you have put effort into and are proud of, that you would like to share with other group members and parents. Bring in any equipment (for example, a baseball, books, uniform, CD, trophies, something you've built, etc.) that you would like to show everyone. Prepare to talk or perform for about three minutes. Please practice what you will say at home in front of your parents.

Hello my name is _____.

I would like to share some things about myself.

I want to be a _____ after I graduate from school.

My favorite activity is _____.

I am happiest when _____.

It makes me laugh when _____.

I like to _____ with friends.

Some people who love me are _____.

Something I've learned about myself is _____.

What I like most about myself is _____.

I would like to share _____ with everyone.

Being a Good Sport: Game Etiquette at Home

Name _____ Date _____

Your assignment this week is to invite someone over to your home. If you are unable to invite someone over, think about a time you hosted someone at your home.

Answer the following questions:

1. Who did you invite over? How do you know this person?

_____

2. How did you invite him or her (call, text, ask during lunch at school)?

_____

3. Review the following list and check off those "good host" behaviors you exhibited:

   ☐ I greeted my guest.

   ☐ I made sure the person was comfortable with my pet (if you have one).

   ☐ I asked my guest if he or she needed something (food, bathroom).

   ☐ I let my guest choose the first game or activity.

   ☐ I engaged in a reciprocal conversation.

   ☐ I asked if my guest was enjoying the activity and switched to another, if not.

   ☐ At the end, I said that I had a good time.

   ☐ I escorted my guest to the door when it was time to leave.

   ☐ I was flexible and agreeable! How? _____

4. What part of being a good host was hard?

_____

_____

5. What did you do to cope with the difficulty?

_____

_____

_____

Being a Good Sport: Game Etiquette at Home

Dear Parents:

Electronic media, from game systems to cell phones, provide increased opportunity for relationships, but they also have the potential to isolate children and teenagers and limit face-to-face interactions. We encourage using electronic games and gaming as a means to increase and improve peer contact. The group will discuss the importance of playing games with peers, learning how to host, and showing good "game etiquette." Good game etiquette applies to both electronic and nonelectronic games.

During today's session, group members will learn five steps involved in inviting a guest to their home:

1. Decide whom you would like to invite over and get to know better.

2. Think about what you need to do to invite the person over.

3. If the person declines, think about what it might mean and how you'll react.

4. Think about what you have to do to be a good host.

5. Show good game etiquette.

You can help reinforce these skills by encouraging your child to invite someone over specifically to play an electronic or other game. Most children do best when there is structure and a time limit set on the activity. Prior to hosting, review desirable behaviors with your child and discuss a plan if the activity does not go well. You might have to intervene and guide your child and guest toward a better course. Please praise flexibility, reciprocity, and handling any upset.

Resilience Builder Assignment

Group members have two assignments this week: The Resilience Builder Assignment asks your child to invite a peer over this week to practice being a good host at home. Practice hosting and good game etiquette skills. Also, please help identify challenging situations when having someone over (sharing, dealing with frustration, staying interested while the other person plays, etc.). Encourage problem solving and positive self-talk during challenging times.

The next session will be our final session of this unit. Please plan on joining the final half of group. We will have a quick review of some topics we have learned during the sessions. Each group member will also talk about his or her accomplishments and may bring any "props" to support the discussion. Please help your child fill out the Showcase Time form and rehearse what he or she will say. Please also continue to practice relaxation and encourage positive self-talk.

Sincerely,

Program Leader

2.15

Review and Showcase

PURPOSE

The first part of this session is devoted to review of the Resilience Builder Assignment, individual goal, and Success Journal. The majority of the session is spent with group members briefly reviewing session topics and "showcasing" themselves by bringing in and discussing tokens of achievement (trophies, book reports, projects, etc.). While there is no free play for this session, the session does provide the opportunity for behavioral rehearsal of speaking assertively to adults (parents) in a public setting.

GOALS

To briefly review what has been taught and discussed during the past sessions

To have each group member discuss personal achievements in front of the parent group

To review a relaxation/self-regulation technique with parents in the session, as time allows

To provide each group member with a Certificate of Program Completion and celebrate work done in the group

MATERIALS

Chalkboard or dry erase board and marker

Program Notebooks (brought by group members)

Individual Points Charts

Prizes

Refreshments (optional)

Copies of the following:

Leadership Award (Appendix C)

Certificate of Program Completion (Appendix C)

Resilience Builder Assignment 2.15

Parent Letter 2.15

Resilience Builder Program Parent Evaluation (Appendix A)

Before the session, prepare the topic cards and assemble the props.

Suggested Props and Illustrations

2.1 Introduction to Group: Declaration of Group Rights

2.2 Flexibility: Dry spaghetti

2.3 Maintaining Conversations: Ball of yarn

2.4 Intent Versus Impact: Intent→Behavior→Impact poster

2.5 and 2.6 On the Mark/Off the Mark Thinking: Dartboard

2.7 Being a Good Sport—Team Play: Scavenger hunt items

2.8 Being a Good Sport—Field Trip: Good Sport Certificate

2.9 Self-Regulation—Anxiety Management: Three parts of anxiety (three circles)

2.10 Self-Regulation—Anger Management: Body and thought signals of anger

2.11 Self-Esteem: Three parts of self-esteem

2.12 Teasing and Bullying: Demonstration of "I-statements"

2.13 Choices for Solving Challenges: Nine Choices poster

2.14 Being a Good Sport—Game Etiquette at Home: Game controller or board game

Post the topic cards naming all session topics and display the props so group members can select one they would like to present. In addition, you can make topic cards with key concepts taught throughout all sessions: flexibility, effort, reciprocity, being proactive, and self-regulation (self-talk and relaxation).

PROCEDURE

Individual Greeting

Conduct the individual greetings, as described in Session 2.1. The components of a good first impression—a smile and a courteous hello, and sustained eye contact—by now should be automatic.

Review Success Journal and Resilience Builder Assignment

Have each group member discuss his or her individual goal and Success Journal entry and experiences completing the Resilience Builder Assignment. When each member finishes speaking, ask him or her to throw the Name Cube to determine the next speaker.

All points are tabulated. Those who have completed all Resilience Builder Assignments receive a bonus of 20 points; those who have completed at least half get 5 extra points. Have the group select prizes before the parents join the session.

Review of Sessions

1. Ask each group member to choose a session topic to present to the parent group. Hand out the corresponding props.

2. Have one of the group members invite parents into the room, then say: "Today the group will review some of the topics we have discussed over the course of the sessions. After we've finished, I'll ask each group member to present his or her Showcase."

3. Ask for a volunteer to start: The group member stands and faces the parents, making eye contact, and says: "Hello, my name is _____ , and I'll tell you what I've learned about _____ *(topic)*." The group member explains the topic, using the prop to illustrate.

Showcase Time

1. Ask for a volunteer to begin the Showcase presentation. Make sure that he or she is standing and makes eye contact with the audience before beginning to speak. The speaker may either read the responses from the Showcase Time form or simply speak about the points covered. The speaker then discusses what he or she is proud of, sharing whatever award or other materials chosen.

2. After all have had a turn, present each group member with a Certificate of Program Competion.

3. If time allows, ask each parent to give his or her child one compliment about effort demonstrated during group sessions.

    This is a festive session; model and encourage the audience to applaud and cheer for each member.

Relaxation/Self-Regulation

Typically, time does not allow for a relaxation exercise, but if one is possible, ask group members if they have a favorite one that you can lead for group members and parents.

Leadership Award and Certificate of Program Completion

Give everyone a Leadership Award for being brave and speaking in front of all the parents. Have each group member come up and receive a Certificate of Program Completion.

Generalization/Parent Component

1. Have group members place their Certificate of Program Completion in the appropriate section of their notebooks.

2. Give parents the parent letter and Resilience Builder Assignment, along with a copy of the Resilience Builder Program Parent Evaluation. If time allows, have parents complete the evaluations and return them to you before leaving. (The review of key topics will be helpful for parent reference as parents fill out the evaluations.)

    If you are unable to have parents fill out their evaluations at the end of the session, arrange another time for them to do so.

Unit 2 Review of Key Concepts

Keep up the good work with everything we learned in group! Remember to continue to use your positive self-talk and relaxation techniques whenever you need them.

Session 2.1—Introduction to Group

Introductions and review of group format

Leadership Award and leader of the week

Joining a group

Session 2.2—Flexibility

Doing things others' way, adapting and trying something new

"Snap and stretch" concept

Demonstration of flexible thinking with dry spaghetti

Session 2.3—Maintaining Conversations

Review conversations, rhythm and flow

Say Three and See Rule, verbal exchange and reciprocity

Giving opinions using steps

Session 2.4—Intent Versus Impact

Intent ⟶ Behavior ⟶ Impact

Steps to match what you want with what you get

Tone of voice, facial expressions, and body language convey intent

Session 2.5—On the Mark/Off the Mark Thinking: Part 1

Thinking errors on a continuum—small, medium or large—dartboard

All-or-nothing, filtering, and catastrophizing thinking errors

Balanced thinking, realistic and examines the evidence

Session 2.6—On the Mark/Off the Mark Thinking: Part 2

Thinking errors cause anxiety, sadness

Personalization, shoulds, "it's not fair," and blaming others thinking errors

Examples of on the mark thinking

Session 2.7—Being a Good Sport: Team Play

Definition of being a good sport

How to manage frustrations and mistakes, using self-control and positive self-talk

How to negotiate and be flexible during team play

Session 2.8—Being a Good Sport: Field Trip

Optional mini-golf or other field trip

Generalize skills of meeting and greeting and interacting with public, as well as problem solving and frustration tolerance

Review and reinforce behaviors in being a good sport and following rules of fair play

Session 2.9—Self-Regulation: Anxiety Management

Mind-body connection (how anxiety manifests in body and in mind)

Three parts of anxiety

Facing your fears

Session 2.10—Self-Regulation: Anger Management

Mind-body connection (body signals, thought signals)

Positive self-talk for anger management

Knowing how to calm your body when angry

Session 2.11—Self-Esteem

Three parts of self-esteem

Identifying and owning your strengths

Handling failures and disappointments effectively while preserving self-esteem

Session 2.12—Teasing and Bullying

Identifying behaviors that put someone at risk for being teased

Learning how to act and be unaffected by bullying

Setting boundaries with others

Session 2.13—Choices for Handling Challenges

Recognizing that we have choices about what we think, say, and do

Discussing nine different choices that we have

Importance of making proactive, responsible decisions

Session 2.14—Being a Good Sport: Game Etiquette at Home

Initiating a social gathering for games

Being a good host

Game etiquette—verbal statements and actions

Session 2.15—Review and Showcase

Review key concepts

Showcase each group member's accomplishments

Parent compliments *(optional)*

Review and Showcase

Dear Parents:

We will use today's session to briefly review the skills learned in this unit, talk about individual goals and accomplishments, and turn points in for prizes. You are invited to join us as each group member is showcased and receives a certificate for his or her hard work. This is a time to praise the parents as well, as it takes great effort and consistency to reinforce the resilience skills and concepts that are taught. Thank you!

The Resilience Builder Assignment for this session is a summary of key concepts learned in this unit. Please refer to it to catch your child exhibiting the behaviors you want to encourage. Remember that specific praise works much better than general praise. Saying, "I like the way that you did _____ . That showed real effort" is more powerful and rewarding than saying, "That's great."

After the session today, please engage your child in a discussion of what he or she learned during the group and what was most helpful. Encourage your child to continue to take small steps toward change and practice what they have learned. As always, I recommend that you continue to practice relaxation together, conduct family meetings, and use the Compliment Basket.

Thank you for allowing me to work with your child, and feel free to contact me in the future.

Sincerely,

Program Leader

APPENDIX A

Program Intake and Evaluation Forms

Telephone Contact, Screening, and Disposition Form

Today's date: _____

☐ Boys' group   ☐ Girls' group   ☐ Co-ed group   Office location _____

Name of caller _____ Relationship to client: parent/other _____

Referred to _____ Referred by _____

Child's name _____ Home phone _____

Age _____ Grade in school _____ School _____

Address _____   Work phone _____

_____   Cell phone _____

_____   E-mail _____

Description of Need and Background Information

Continue on back of page if needed.

_____

_____

_____

_____

_____

_____

Contact Log

Date, summary (left message, spoke with parent, agreed to speak again, etc.), and your initials

_____

_____

_____

_____

☐ Reviewed procedures   ☐ Reviewed fees, including intake

Disposition

☐ Intake scheduled for _____ Group leader: _____

Registered for group: Fall   Spring   Summer

☐ Found another provider   ☐ Will call back after checks insurance

☐ No longer interested   ☐ Will call back if interested

☐ Our groups not appropriate, or   ☐ Referred to _____
    we do not have the services needed

☐ <u>WAITLIST</u> for ☐ Fall ☐ Spring ☐ Summer

Return to _____ after disposition determined. Thank you.

Social Interactions and Self-Regulation

These supplemental questions are asked of parent and child during the clinical interview.

Child's Name _____ **Date** _____

Does the child have a best friend now?

_____

Have there been best friends in the past? What has changed?

_____

_____

Does the child sit with and interact with other children during lunch?

_____

What does the child do during recess?

_____

Does he or she avoid other children or play alone?

_____

Does he or she play with one or more other children?

_____

Typically, is the child drawn into structured activity during recess/free time, or is he or she able to initiate spontaneous play?

_____

Is the child invited for play dates? If yes, how frequently?

_____

How long does a play date typically last?

_____

Is there reciprocity during activities, or does one child dominate?

_____

How flexible is the child in deciding what to play?

_____

Is the child invited to birthday or other parties? Is the child invited for sleepovers?

_____

Does the child want to invite other children to play?

_____

If there is a desire, does the child extend the invitation or do you make the call?

_____

What are the child's play interests, alone or with others?

_____

How does the child handle compromise when playing?

_____

Does it have to be your child's way, or does he or she negotiate or problem-solve?

_____

How does the child interact in a dyad, a triad, and in small and large groups?

_____

How well can he or she collaborate on a group project?

_____

Has the child been teased or bullied? Are you aware of any cyberbullying?

_____

Does the child tease or bully other children?

_____

How does the child handle frustration?

_____

How does the child handle the frustration of losing and the satisfaction of winning?

_____

Does the child tend to be bossy, assertive, or passive? Please cite an example.

_____

Is the child socially anxious or shy?

_____

Intake Interview (p. 2 of 2)

RESILIENCE AND SOCIAL COMPETENCE MEASURE

Parent Form

Child's name _____ Date _____

Parent(s) or significant adult _____

*Circle the number that best describes your child's behavior over the **past three weeks**.*

BEING PROACTIVE	Never	Almost Never	Sometimes	Often	Very Often	Almost Always	Always
1. Demonstrates problem-solving ability and generates alternatives to challenges.	1	2	3	4	5	6	7
2. Accepts responsibility and is able to apologize.	1	2	3	4	5	6	7
3. Demonstrates flexibility in thinking.	1	2	3	4	5	6	7
4. Demonstrates optimistic thinking.	1	2	3	4	5	6	7
5. Appears to feel good about himself/herself.	1	2	3	4	5	6	7
6. Asserts self. Speaks up for self. Holds body posture in assertive stance.	1	2	3	4	5	6	7
7. Adapts well to change and/or transitions.	1	2	3	4	5	6	7
DEMONSTRATES SELF-REGULATION							
8. Is able to stay in own personal space or protect space.	1	2	3	4	5	6	7
9. Speaks with appropriate voice volume.	1	2	3	4	5	6	7
10. Is calm with good activity in the waiting room.	1	2	3	4	5	6	7
11. Calms self when upset.	1	2	3	4	5	6	7
12. Listens to others without interruption.	1	2	3	4	5	6	7
13. Stays on topic in conversation.	1	2	3	4	5	6	7
14. Is able to calm self with group relaxation exercises.	1	2	3	4	5	6	7

From *Resilience Builder Program for Children and Adolescents,* © 2011 by M. K. Alvord, B. Zucker, & J. J. Grados, Champaign, IL: Research Press (800-519-2707, www.researchpress.com).

	Never	Almost Never	Sometimes	Often	Very Often	Almost Always	Always
15. Controls irritability/temper with peers and is able to express negative feelings in appropriate way.	1	2	3	4	5	6	7
16. Thinks before he/she acts.	1	2	3	4	5	6	7

HAS POSITIVE CONNECTIONS AND ATTACHMENTS

	Never	Almost Never	Sometimes	Often	Very Often	Almost Always	Always
17. Shares and takes turns.	1	2	3	4	5	6	7
18. Joins other children appropriately.	1	2	3	4	5	6	7
19. Understands how others might be feeling.	1	2	3	4	5	6	7
20. Uses eye contact when speaking to others.	1	2	3	4	5	6	7
21. Demonstrates reciprocity in relationships (conversations and actions).	1	2	3	4	5	6	7
22. Is aware of how he/she comes across to others.	1	2	3	4	5	6	7
23. Reads nonverbal cues accurately.	1	2	3	4	5	6	7
24. Listens to and accepts others' ideas.	1	2	3	4	5	6	7
25. Shows a connection with peers.	1	2	3	4	5	6	7
26. Offers positive comments or compliments to peers.	1	2	3	4	5	6	7
27. Treats peers with respect.	1	2	3	4	5	6	7
28. Compromises appropriately.	1	2	3	4	5	6	7
29. Starts a conversation with a peer.	1	2	3	4	5	6	7

RECOGNIZES ACHIEVEMENTS

	Never	Almost Never	Sometimes	Often	Very Often	Almost Always	Always
30. Is sensitive to others' feelings.	1	2	3	4	5	6	7
31. Is sought by others to play/interact.	1	2	3	4	5	6	7
32. Is a good loser/winner.	1	2	3	4	5	6	7

Resilience and Social Competence Measure–Parent Form (p. 2 of 3)

	Never	Almost Never	Sometimes	Often	Very Often	Almost Always	Always
33. Completes weekly Resilience Builder Assignments.	1	2	3	4	5	6	7
34. Adds to weekly Success Journal.	1	2	3	4	5	6	7

IS INVOLVED IN COMMUNITY

	Never	Almost Never	Sometimes	Often	Very Often	Almost Always	Always
35. Is involved in after-school activities.	1	2	3	4	5	6	7
36. Initiates getting together with peers.	1	2	3	4	5	6	7
37. Asks for help when needed.	1	2	3	4	5	6	7

BENEFITS FROM PROACTIVE PARENTING

	Never	Almost Never	Sometimes	Often	Very Often	Almost Always	Always
38. Uses Compliment Basket strategy.	1	2	3	4	5	6	7
39. Engages in family meetings.	1	2	3	4	5	6	7
40. Practices relaxation/positive self-talk with family.	1	2	3	4	5	6	7
41. Other: _____	1	2	3	4	5	6	7

_____

Comments and priority goals

_____

_____

_____

_____

_____

_____

Resilience and Social Competence Measure–Parent Form (p. 3 of 3)

RESILIENCE AND SOCIAL COMPETENCE MEASURE

Group Leader Form

Child's name _____ Date _____

Group leader _____

*Circle the number that best describes the group member's behavior over the **past three weeks.***

	Never	Almost Never	Sometimes	Often	Very Often	Almost Always	Always
BEING PROACTIVE							
1. Demonstrates problem-solving ability and generates alternatives to challenges.	1	2	3	4	5	6	7
2. Accepts responsibility and is able to apologize.	1	2	3	4	5	6	7
3. Demonstrates flexibility in thinking.	1	2	3	4	5	6	7
4. Demonstrates optimistic thinking.	1	2	3	4	5	6	7
5. Appears to feel good about himself/herself.	1	2	3	4	5	6	7
6. Asserts self. Speaks up for self. Holds body posture in assertive stance.	1	2	3	4	5	6	7
7. Adapts well to change and/or transitions.	1	2	3	4	5	6	7
DEMONSTRATES SELF-REGULATION							
8. Stays in own personal space or protects space.	1	2	3	4	5	6	7
9. Speaks with appropriate voice volume.	1	2	3	4	5	6	7
10. Behaves appropriately in group.	1	2	3	4	5	6	7
11. Calms self when upset.	1	2	3	4	5	6	7
12. Listens to others without interruption.	1	2	3	4	5	6	7
13. Stays on topic in conversation.	1	2	3	4	5	6	7
14. Calms self with group relaxation exercises.	1	2	3	4	5	6	7

	Never	Almost Never	Sometimes	Often	Very Often	Almost Always	Always
15. Controls irritability/temper with peers and is able to express negative feelings in appropriate way.	1	2	3	4	5	6	7
16. Thinks before he/she acts.	1	2	3	4	5	6	7

HAS POSITIVE CONNECTIONS AND ATTACHMENTS

	Never	Almost Never	Sometimes	Often	Very Often	Almost Always	Always
17. Shares and takes turns.	1	2	3	4	5	6	7
18. Joins other children appropriately.	1	2	3	4	5	6	7
19. Understands how others might be feeling.	1	2	3	4	5	6	7
20. Uses eye contact when speaking to others.	1	2	3	4	5	6	7
21. Demonstrates reciprocity in relationships (conversations and actions).	1	2	3	4	5	6	7
22. Shows awareness of how he/she comes across to others.	1	2	3	4	5	6	7
23. Reads nonverbal cues accurately.	1	2	3	4	5	6	7
24. Listens to and accepts others' ideas.	1	2	3	4	5	6	7
25. Shows a connection with group members.	1	2	3	4	5	6	7
26. Offers positive comments or compliments to peers.	1	2	3	4	5	6	7
27. Treats peers with respect.	1	2	3	4	5	6	7
28. Compromises appropriately.	1	2	3	4	5	6	7
29. Starts a conversation with a peer.	1	2	3	4	5	6	7

RECOGNIZES ACHIEVEMENTS

	Never	Almost Never	Sometimes	Often	Very Often	Almost Always	Always
30. Shows sensitivity to others' feelings. Shows empathy toward others.	1	2	3	4	5	6	7
31. Sought by others to play/interact.	1	2	3	4	5	6	7
32. Responds appropriately to losing and winning. Is a good sport.	1	2	3	4	5	6	7

Resilience and Social Competence Measure–Group Leader Form (p. 2 of 3)

	Never	Almost Never	Sometimes	Often	Very Often	Almost Always	Always
33. Completes weekly Resilience Builder Assignments.	1	2	3	4	5	6	7
34. Adds to weekly Success Journal.	1	2	3	4	5	6	7

IS INVOLVED IN COMMUNITY

	Never	Almost Never	Sometimes	Often	Very Often	Almost Always	Always
35. Engages in after-school activities.	1	2	3	4	5	6	7
36. Initiates getting together with peers.	1	2	3	4	5	6	7
37. Asks for help when needed.	1	2	3	4	5	6	7

BENEFITS FROM PROACTIVE PARENTING

	Never	Almost Never	Sometimes	Often	Very Often	Almost Always	Always
38. Uses Compliment Basket strategy.	1	2	3	4	5	6	7
39. Engages in family meetings.	1	2	3	4	5	6	7
40. Practices relaxation/positive self-talk outside the group setting.	1	2	3	4	5	6	7

Parent conference held _____

In attendance

_____

_____

_____

Comments and priority goals

_____

_____

_____

_____

_____

_____

_____

Resilience and Social Competence Measure–Group Leader Form (p. 3 of 3)

How Am I Doing?

Name _____ **Date** _____

*Circle the number that best shows how you feel about yourself **today**.*

	Never	Almost Never	Sometimes	Often	Very Often	Almost Always	Always
1. I feel good about myself.	1	2	3	4	5	6	7
2. I can make new friends.	1	2	3	4	5	6	7
3. I am a good friend to others.	1	2	3	4	5	6	7
4. I can calm myself down when upset.	1	2	3	4	5	6	7
5. I stay in my personal space.	1	2	3	4	5	6	7
6. I think positively.	1	2	3	4	5	6	7
7. I can come up with a plan when I have a problem.	1	2	3	4	5	6	7
8. I feel good about myself.	1	2	3	4	5	6	7

From *Resilience Builder Program for Children and Adolescents,* © 2011 by M. K. Alvord, B. Zucker, & J. J. Grados, Champaign, IL: Research Press (800-519-2707, www.researchpress.com).

RESILIENCE BUILDER PROGRAM

Parent Evaluation

We are eager to receive your feedback regarding your child's group experience. This information will help us to improve our services for future group sessions. We greatly appreciate your comments and welcome your candid feedback. (Identifying yourself is optional.)

Group Leader _____ **Group** _____ **Day/time** _____

Please check the best response.

How satisfied were you with:	Poor	Acceptable	Good	Very Good	Excellent
The initial phone contact	☐	☐	☐	☐	☐
The initial session	☐	☐	☐	☐	☐
Group topics	☐	☐	☐	☐	☐
Convenience of time/day of week group held	☐	☐	☐	☐	☐
Management of group logistics (on time, organization, materials, etc.)	☐	☐	☐	☐	☐
Behavior management of group	☐	☐	☐	☐	☐
Parent letters	☐	☐	☐	☐	☐
Individual parent meeting(s)	☐	☐	☐	☐	☐
Billing and fee payment	☐	☐	☐	☐	☐

Please check the best response.

	Not at All	Good	Very Good	Excellent
My child learned useful skills.	☐	☐	☐	☐
My child uses newly acquired skills.	☐	☐	☐	☐
The handouts and Resilience Builder Assignments were helpful.	☐	☐	☐	☐

From *Resilience Builder Program for Children and Adolescents,* © 2011 by M. K. Alvord, B. Zucker, & J. J. Grados, Champaign, IL: Research Press (800-519-2707, www.researchpress.com).

Would you enroll your child in another group at our practice?   ☐ Yes   ☐ No

Would you recommend this group to others?   ☐ Yes   ☐ No

Would you recommend this group leader to others?   ☐ Yes   ☐ No

The most useful things my child learned from group were:

_____

_____

_____

What did you like best about this experience?

_____

_____

_____

What did you like least?

_____

_____

_____

How could your child's group experience be improved?

_____

_____

_____

Thank you for taking the time to complete this. We read every evaluation and consider your comments as we continually strive to improve our groups to better help your children.

APPENDIX B

Parent Materials

Family Meetings

Having weekly family meetings allows family members to spend time with one another in a more relaxed situation, discuss things that concern each member, give compliments, problem-solve together, plan fun activities, and provide leadership opportunities for the children.

Meetings have also been shown to help build family resilience. Time together in activities and conversation fosters improved communication and reciprocity in children. In addition, the National Center on Addiction and Substance Abuse at Columbia University, which has surveyed teens over the past two decades, found a relationship between frequent family dinners and reduced risk that a teen will smoke, drink, or engage in other substance abuse. It also found that frequent family dinners strengthened family ties.

We would like to combine the idea of family meetings, dinners, and the Compliment Basket, which we also recommend. Family meetings can be over a dinner, part of a game or movie night at home, or during any other family activity.

Some Guidelines

1. Generate a "Declaration of Rights" for the family.

2. Make sure that fun and compliments are part of the time, in addition to talk about more difficult subjects or complaints.

3. Leadership can begin with parents but then can rotate among members.

4. This is a great opportunity to demonstrate problem solving. Everyone should be part of brainstorming and, when appropriate, part of making the decisions.

Source

National Center on Addiction and Substance Abuse:
www.casacolumbia.org/upload/2010/20100922familydinners6.pdf

Compliment Basket

We ask that you start a strategy at home that we call the "Compliment Basket." Any container will do (shoebox, plastic container, etc). We ask that every few days you have each member of your family give each other member a compliment. Please write these down, date them, and then add to the basket. At least once a week, revisit previously given compliments and create new ones. It's a great positive conversation starter at dinnertime or at any other time your family gathers together.

From *Resilience Builder Program for Children and Adolescents*, © 2011 by M. K. Alvord, B. Zucker, & J. J. Grados, Champaign, IL: Research Press (800-519-2707, www.researchpress.com).

Relaxation Tips for Parents and Group Members

Relaxation strategies are an integral component of the group sessions. These strategies include a wide range of techniques, such as calm breathing, progressive muscle relaxation, guided imagery, and yoga. Learning how to calm one's body, and often as a result calm one's mind, is an essential part of self-regulation. We encourage you, as proactive parents, to help your child gain mastery over these techniques through regular practice. Parents tend to enjoy learning these strategies as well.

Following are several relaxation techniques and the scripts used during the group sessions to teach them to your child. It is strongly recommended that you go through the scripts repeatedly with your child at home. Read the following scripts slowly and in a calm voice and model the steps for your child.

Calm Breathing

▶ We are going to practice diaphragmatic breathing, which we call *calm breathing*. The goal is to breathe in through your nose and out through your mouth, with the air going all the way down to your lower belly. Tense or anxious breathing causes your upper chest to rise and fall, and the air only goes into your upper chest.

▶ Relaxed or calm breathing, on the other hand, causes your lower stomach—around your belly button—to go up and down and the air to go into your lower abdomen.

▶ Get into a comfortable seated position. Let your shoulders, head, neck, and arms relax. Place one hand on your chest and the other on the belly button area of your stomach. This exercise takes practice because most of us breathe mostly through our chests.

▶ Slowly breathe in through your nose for a count of five: 1, 2, 3, 4, 5. Hold the breath. As you breathe in, your stomach area will extend. The air should naturally push out your stomach as you breathe in: 1, 2, 3, 4, 5. Keep your chest still. Hold it: 2, 3.

▶ Now tighten your stomach muscles and notice your breath as you slowly breathe out through your mouth for five: 1, 2, 3, 4, 5. Again, breathe in through your nose: 1, 2, 3, 4, 5, with your stomach extending out. Hold it: 2, 3. Pay attention to your breath as you breathe out through your mouth—1, 2, 3, 4, 5—pulling your stomach muscles in. Remember to let the air go all the way down to your lower abdomen.

▶ If you have difficulty getting the air to go down into your lower abdomen, lie down on the floor and put a lightweight object (maybe a light book or foam yoga block) on your upper chest. Use the object as a way of measuring whether your breathing is in the upper chest or lower abdomen.

 If your child is doing calm breathing, the object should not move but the lower belly should.

▶ After the exercise, ask your child, "What did you notice about your breath?" "How did that feel in your chest and lower belly?"

From *Resilience Builder Program for Children and Adolescents,* © 2011 by M. K. Alvord, B. Zucker, & J. J. Grados, Champaign, IL: Research Press (800-519-2707, www.researchpress.com).

Progressive Muscle Relaxation

► We are going to do a relaxation exercise called *progressive muscle relaxation.* Find a comfortable place to sit or lie down. We are going to tighten and hold and then release different muscle groups. Pay close attention to the difference in how the muscles feel when they are tight and tense versus when they are loose and relaxed.

► First, I'd like you to make a very tight fist—tighten up and hold the fist. Imagine that you are squeezing out a lemon: 1, 2, 3, 4, 5. Really notice what it feels like when your muscles are tight and tense. Now slowly let go: 1, 2, 3, 4, 5. Notice how it feels when the muscles in your hands are loose and relaxed.

► Now, I'd like you to tighten your arms—forearms, biceps, and triceps, by squeezing your arms into your body and ribs. Be careful not to clench your fists—keep your hands relaxed while you squeeze in your arms. Now hold it: 1, 2, 3, 4, 5. Then let go and release. Again, notice the difference between tight and loose muscles.

► Moving up the arms, pull your shoulders all the way up to your ears and hold it. You will notice the back of your neck will also feel tight—that's good. Hold it: 1, 2, 3, 4, 5. Now drop your shoulders down toward your hips. Again, notice the difference—how your shoulder muscles feel when they are tight and tense versus when they are loose and relaxed.

► Pull your shoulders back and tighten your whole back. Hold it. Hold it. Really tighten. Now relax and bring your shoulders slightly forward. Remember to breathe. Breathe in and breathe out.

► Tighten your stomach muscles—your abs—squeeze them in toward your spine and hold it. Real tight. Now release. Notice how it feels when you release it.

► Squeeze your buttocks muscles in. Hold them tight: 1, 2, 3, 4, 5. Then release.

► I'd like you to straighten out your legs and point your toes away from you. Tighten the muscles in your legs—your thighs should feel very tight. Now, I'd like you to point your toes in toward your chest. Hold it and notice how your calves are tightening up. Now relax. Again, notice the difference when your muscles are tight and when they are relaxed.

► Curl up your toes and your feet, almost like you are cramping them. Hold it. Then release and let go.

► Now clench your jaw and tighten up all the muscles in your face, including around your eyes. Hold it tight . . . then release and relax. Make a few relaxing circles with your jaw to loosen it up.

► Finally, I want you to tighten all the muscle groups in your body. Hold them all very tight: 1, 2, 3, 4, 5. Now relax and let go. Go from being a robot to a rag doll. Now relax and notice how your muscles feel.

Guided Imagery 1

► Find a comfortable place to sit or lie down. Begin to relax your body by slowing your breathing. Focus on your lower abdomen—around your belly button—and feel your stomach rise and fall as you slowly breathe in and out.

▶ Begin to calm your mind and let your thoughts settle down. If thoughts come up, just allow them to float on by—no need to focus on them. This is your time for relaxation. You have no where to go and nothing to do.

▶ Now I want to you imagine a special place that is very relaxing and calming to you. This place can be real or made up, it can be anywhere you would like. Maybe it is a place you have been or would like to go.

▶ Imagine this place and think about what you see—what colors are there? *(Pause.)* What does it smell like? *(Pause.)* How does your body feel when you are there? *(Pause.)* What do you hear? *(Pause.)* What is the temperature? *(Pause.)* How is the lighting—is it light or dark or in between? *(Pause.)*

▶ Imagine the details of this place and what it looks like. What are you doing when you are here? Are you lying down, looking up at something, or are you sitting or standing? Are you alone or are you with others? Imagine this place and now take a few minutes to be there. *(Pause 2–3 minutes.)*

▶ OK, in just a moment, you will open your eyes and come back into the room. I will count: 5, 4, 3, 2, and 1. Gently open your eyes, stretch your body, and be back in this room. Great job! Remember this relaxing place, and remind yourself that you can go there anytime you'd like.

Guided Imagery 2

▶ Find a comfortable place to sit or lie down. Gently close your eyes and take a deep breath in through your nose and slowly breathe out through your mouth.

▶ This is your time for relaxation. Clear your mind and let go of any stress or tension that you might be holding on to. Take another deep breath in through your nose and out to through your mouth.

▶ Imagine that you are standing tall on the top of a mountain. You can breathe easily, and you feel calm but also strong. Look around and notice all of the beautiful things around you—do you see green trees or trees covered with glistening white snow? Are there other mountains around you and valleys in between?

▶ You are surrounded by nature and are fully aware of this moment. Your breath is calm. You feel clear in your mind with good energy in your body. You can feel the energy around you, and this makes you feel uplifted.

▶ While on this mountain, you notice how good you feel about yourself and your body. You are aware of how special you are and how able you are to do whatever you set your mind to.

▶ You feel strong and confident. If there is something you want to do or need to do, you feel confident about your ability to do it and handle yourself well. You think of several good things about yourself . . . and you love who you are.

▶ Take another deep breath. Spend a minute or two feeling what it feels like when you think well of yourself and when you are in touch with how special you are. *(Allow 1–2 minutes for silent meditation.)*

Relaxation Tips (p. 3 of 4)

▶ When you are ready, gently open your eyes and notice how calm your body feels. Remember that you can be this relaxed and feel confident about yourself anytime you want.

Yoga

Downward-Facing Dog Pose

▶ Lie down on the floor on your stomach, bend your elbows, and put your hands down on the floor next to your armpits or chest.

▶ Now get up on all fours, on hands and knees, and spread your fingers apart, but keep your palms on the floor.

▶ Now lift up onto your feet, standing mainly on your toes, lifting your hips up, and keeping your hands on the floor. Your hands should be shoulder-width apart.

▶ Continue to lift your hips up and stretch your back. Continue to spread your fingers apart and push your hands against the floor to encourage more lengthening in your spine and more lift in your hips. Hips up, hips up. Feel the stretch.

▶ Very good! Now gently come back down onto all fours and lie back down on your stomach and relax.

Standing Mountain Pose

▶ Stand with your feet together (big toes touching) and your arms down by your sides.

▶ Stand up tall and straight with your shoulders back and your chest lifting up, as if someone has a string attached to the top of your chest and they are pulling it up.

▶ Now face your palms out and slowly lift your arms straight up to the ceiling with your palms facing together. Keep your elbows straight, and lift up high.

▶ I want you to imagine that your feet are like roots of a tree, pushing down into the earth and rooting you firmly to the ground. Push your feet into the floor and tighten your leg muscles.

▶ Now, I want you to lift the upper part of your body and arms all the way up to the sky, as much as you can lift, so your feet and legs are stretching down and your chest and arms are stretching up high. Feel the stretch and feel how strong you are.

Relaxation Tips (p. 4 of 4)

Resources for Parents and Group Members

Parents

Antony, M.M., & Swinson, R.P. (2008). *The shyness and social anxiety workbook: Proven techniques for overcoming your fears* (2nd ed.). Oakland, CA: New Harbinger.

Barkley, R.A. (2005). *Taking charge of ADHD: The complete, authoritative guide for parents* (3rd ed.). New York: Guilford.

Brooks, R., & Goldstein, S. (2001). *Raising resilient children.* Chicago: Contemporary Books.

Chansky, T.E. (2008). *Free your child from negative thinking.* Cambridge, MA: Da Capo Press.

Cooper-Khan, J., & Dietzel, L. (2008). *Late, lost, and unprepared: A parent's guide to helping children with executive functioning.* Bethesda, MD: Woodbine House.

Duke, M.P., Nowicki, S., & Martin, E.A. (1996). *Teaching your child the language of social success.* Atlanta: Peachtree Publishers.

Dweck, C. (2006). *Mindset: The new psychology of success.* New York: Ballantine Books.

Frankel, F. (1996). *Good friends are hard to find: Help your child find, make and keep friends.* Glendale, CA: Perspective Publishing.

Goleman, D. (2006). *Social intelligence: The new science of human relationships.* New York: Bantam Books.

Hallowell, E.M. (2002). *The childhood roots of adult happiness: Five steps to help kids create and sustain life-long joy.* New York: Ballantine Books.

Kaufman, G., Raphael, L., & Espeland, P. (1999). *Stick up for yourself: Every kid's guide to personal power and positive self-esteem* (2nd ed.). Minneapolis: Free Spirit.

Rapee, R.M., Wignall, A., Spence, S.H., Cobham, V., & Lyneham, H. (2008). *Helping your anxious child: A step-by-step guide for parents* (2nd ed.). Oakland, CA: New Harbinger.

Seligman, M.E.P. (with Reivich, K., Jaycox, L., & Gillham, J.). (1995). *The optimistic child.* New York: Houghton Mifflin.

Zucker, B. (2009). *Anxiety-free kids: An interactive guide for parents and children.* Waco, TX: Prufrock Press.

Children and Teens

Charlesworth, E.A. (2002). *Scanning relaxation* (Audio CD). Champaign, IL: Research Press.

Covey, S.R. (2008). *The leader in me.* New York: Free Press.

DePino, C. (2004). *Blue cheese breath and stinky feet: How to deal with bullies.* Washington, DC: Magination Press.

DeVillers, J. (2002). *GirlWise: How to be confident, capable, cool, and in control.* New York: Three Rivers Press.

Huebner, D. (2007). *What to do when you grumble too much: A kid's guide to overcoming negativity.* Washington, DC: Magination Press.

Lite, L. (2006). *Indigo dreams: Relaxation and stress management bedtime stories for children* (Audio CD). Marietta, GA: Lite Books.

Nadeau, K.G., & Dixon, E.B. (2005). *Learning to slow down and pay attention: A book for kids about ADHD* (3rd ed.). Washington, DC: Magination Press.

Websites

American Psychological Association (Consumer Website): *www.apa.org/helpcenter*

Association for Behavioral and Cognitive Therapies: *www.abct.org*

Children and Adults with Attention Deficit/Hyperactivity Disorder: *www.chadd.org*

Olweus Bullying Prevention Program: *www.olweus.org/public/index.page*

U.S. Department of Heath and Human Services (Stop Bullying Now!): *http://stopbullyingnow.hrsa.gov/kids/*

APPENDIX C

Supplementary Session Materials

Name Cube Template

Resilience Builder
Program

_____

Name

_____

Group

_____

Leader

My individual goal is:

_____

_____

_____

_____

_____

_____

_____

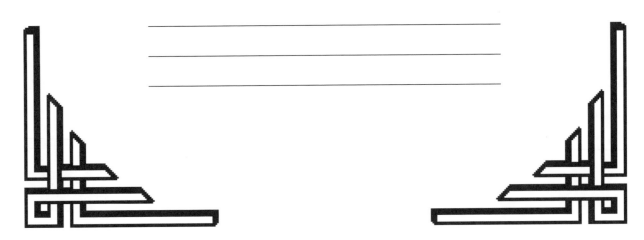

Success Journal

Name _____ **Date** _____

Every week, write about one time when you worked toward your personal goal or had some positive interaction with a peer. Remember, positive attempts count too!

Session 1: Welcome to Group!

Session 2

_____

_____

_____

_____

_____

Session 3

_____

_____

_____

_____

_____

Session 4

_____

_____

_____

_____

_____

Session 5

_____

_____

_____

_____

_____

Session 6

_____
_____
_____
_____
_____

Session 7

_____
_____
_____
_____
_____

Session 8

_____
_____
_____
_____
_____

Session 9

_____
_____
_____
_____
_____

Session 10

_____
_____
_____
_____
_____

Success Journal (p. 2 of 3)

Session 11

_____

_____

_____

_____

Session 12

_____

_____

_____

_____

Session 13

_____

_____

_____

_____

Session 14

_____

_____

_____

_____

Session 15

_____

_____

_____

_____

_____

Success Journal (p. 3 of 3)

Points Chart

Name _____ Group _____ Leader _____

Session	Participant Goal/Leader Notes	Brought notebook to group	Completed Resilience Builder Assignment (RB)	Discussed assignment	Made entry in Success Journal (SJ)	Participated in cooperative manner	Points tally
1							
2							
3							
4							
5							
6							
7							
8							
9							
10							
11							
12							
13							
14							
15							

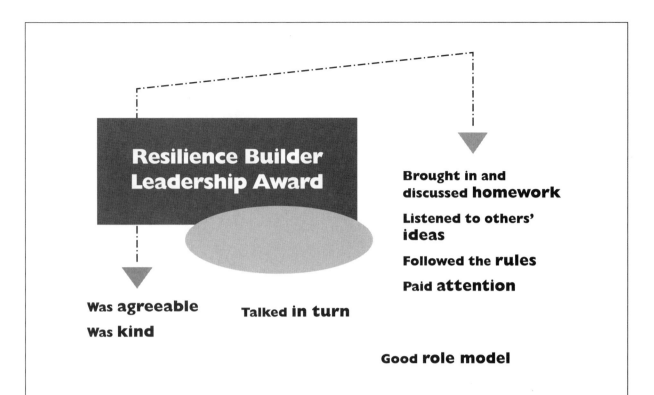

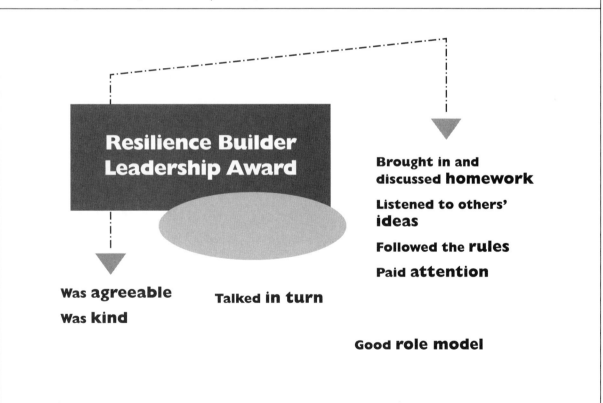

Good Sport Certificate

This certificate is awarded to

_____

_____
Program Leader

Good Sport Certificate

This certificate is awarded to

_____

_____
Program Leader

This certificate is awarded to

_____

Game Etiquette Award

► I negotiated and compromised about which game(s) to play.

► I took turns.

► I handled my frustrations well.

► I had a positive attitude toward the other player(s).

► I was a good winner or a good loser.

► I encouraged the other player(s).

► I helped explain rules or how to beat a level when asked.

_____
Program Leader

_____
Date

This certificate is awarded to

_____

Game Etiquette Award

► I negotiated and compromised about which game(s) to play.

► I took turns.

► I handled my frustrations well.

► I had a positive attitude toward the other player(s).

► I was a good winner or a good loser.

► I encouraged the other player(s).

► I helped explain rules or how to beat a level when asked.

_____
Program Leader

_____
Date

Certificate of Program Completion

presented to

_____

for

Outstanding Performance in
the Resilience Builder Program

on this _____ day of _____

by

_____

Program Leader

From *Resilience Builder Program for Children and Adolescents*, © 2011 by M. K. Alvord, B. Zucker, & J. J. Grados, Champaign, IL: Research Press (800-519-2707, www.researchpress.com).

References

Achenbach, T.M., & Rescorla, L.A. (2001). *Manual for ASEBA School-Aged Forms and Profiles.* Burlington: University of Vermont, Research Center for Children, Youth and Families.

Alvord, M.K., & Grados, J.J. (2005). Enhancing resilience in children: A proactive approach. *Professional Psychology: Research and Practice, 36*(3), 238–245.

Alvord, M.K., & O'Leary, K.D. (1985). Teaching children to share through stories. *Psychology in the Schools 22,* 323–330.

American Psychological Association, Task Force on Resilience and Strength in Black Children and Adolescents. (2008). *Resilience in African American children and adolescents: A vision for optimal development.* Washington, DC: Author.

Atkinson, P.A., Martin, C.R., & Rankin, J. (2009). Resilience revisited. *Journal of Psychiatric and Mental Health Nursing, 16*(2), 137–145.

Bandura, A. (1997). *Self-efficacy: The exercise of control.* New York: Freeman.

Baumrind, D. (1991). Effective parenting during the early adolescent transition. In P.A. Cowan & M. Hetherington (Eds.), *Family transitions* (pp. 111–163). Hillsdale, NJ: Erlbaum.

Bierman, K.L. (2004). Peer rejection: Developmental processes and intervention strategies. New York: Guilford.

Brooks, R.B. (1994). Children at risk: Fostering resilience and hope. *American Journal of Orthopsychiatry 64,* 545–553.

Burt, K.B., Obradovic, J., Long, J.D., & Masten, A.S. (2008). The interplay of social competence and psychopathology over 20 years: Testing transactional and cascade models. *Child Development, 79*(2), 359–374.

Calkins, S.D., & Marcovitch, S. (2010). Emotion regulation and executive functioning in early development: Integrated mechanisms of control supporting adaptive functioning. In S.D. Calkins & M.A. Bell (Eds.), *Child development at the intersection of emotion and cognition* (pp. 37–57). Washington, DC: American Psychological Association.

Cicchetti, D., & Rogosch, F.A. (1997). The role of self-organization in the promotion of resilience in maltreated children. *Development and Psychopathology, 9*(4), 797–815.

Clarke, G.N., & DeBar, L.L. (2010). Group cognitive-behavioral treatment for adolescent depression. In J.R. Weisz & A.E. Kazdin (Eds.), *Evidence-based psychotherapies for children and adolescents* (2nd ed., pp. 110–125). New York: Guilford.

Cohn, M.A., Fredrickson, B.L., Brown, S.L., Mikels, J.A., & Conway, A.M. (2009). Happiness unpacked: Positive emotions increase life satisfaction by building resilience. *Emotion, 9*(3), 361–368.

Conners, K. (2000). *Conners Rating Scales–Revised technical manual.* North Tonawanda, New York: Multi Health Systems.

Denson, T.F., Spanovic, M., & Miller, N. (2009). Cognitive appraisals and emotions predict cortisol and immune responses: A meta-analysis of acute laboratory social stressors and emotion inductions. *Psychological Bulletin, 135*(6), 823–853.

Department of Health and Human Services. (2001). *Youth violence: A report of the Surgeon General.* Washington, DC: Author.

Dishion, T.J., McCord, J., & Poulin, F. (1999). When interventions harm: Peer groups and problem behaviors. *American Psychologist, 54,* 755–764.

Dweck, C. (2006). *Mindset: The new psychology of success.* New York: Ballantine Books.

Elias, M.J., & Haynes, N.M. (2008). Social competence, social support, and academic achievement in minority, low-income, urban elementary school children. *School Psychology Quarterly, 23*(4), 474–495.

Garmezy, N., Masten, A.S., & Tellegen, A. (1984). The study of stress and competence in children: A building block for developmental psychopathology. *Child Development, 55,* 97–111.

Goldstein, A.P., & Martens, B.K. (2000). *Lasting change: Methods for enhancing generalization of gain.* Champaign, IL: Research Press.

Gottman, T., Notarius, C., Gonso, J., & Markman, H. (1976). *A couple's guide to communication.* Champaign, IL: Research Press.

Gresham, F.M., & Elliott, S.N. (2008). Social Skills Improvement System—Rating Scales manual. Minneapolis: Pearson Assessments.

Grotberg, E. (1995). A guide to promoting resilience in children: Strengthening the human spirit (Early Childhood Development: Practice and Reflections Series). Retrieved December 14, 2010 from http://resilnet.uiuc.edu/library/grotb95b.html

La Greca, A.M., Silverman, W.K., & Lochman, J.E. (2009). Moving beyond efficacy and effectiveness in child and adolescent intervention research. *Journal of Consulting and Clinical Psychology, 77*(3), 373–382.

Luthar, S.S., & Cicchetti, D. (2000). The construct of resilience: Implications for intervention and social policy. *Development and Psychopathology, 12,* 555–598.

Masten, A.S., Best, K.M., & Garmezy, N. (1990). Resilience and development: Contributions from the study of children who overcome adversity. *Development and Psychopathology, 2,* 425–444.

Masten, A.S., & Obradovic, J. (2006). Competence and resilience in development. *Annals of the New York Academy of Sciences, 1094,* 13–27.

Masten, A.S., & Wright, M.O.D. (2009). Resilience over the lifespan: Developmental perspectives on resistance, recovery, and transformation. In J.W. Reich, A.J. Zautra, & J.S. Hall (Eds.), *Handbook of adult resilience* (pp. 213–237). New York: Guilford.

The National Center on Addiction and Substance Abuse (CASA) at Columbia University. (2010, September). *The importance of family dinners VI.* New York: Author. (http://www.casacolumbia.org/upload/2010/20100922familydinners6.pdf)

Neeman, J., & Masten, A.S. (2009). Dynamic processes in the promotion of resilience. *The Maryland Psychologist, 54*(3), 2.

Neenan, M. (2009). Developing resilience: A cognitive-behavioural approach. London: Routledge.

O'Brien, F., Olden, N., Migone, M., Dooley, B., Atkins, L., Ganter, K. et al. (2007). Group cognitive behavioural therapy for children with anxiety disorder: An evaluation of the "Friends for Youth" programme. *Irish Journal of Psychological Medicine, 24*(1), 5–12.

Pahl, K.M., & Barrett, P.M. (2010). Interventions for anxiety disorders in children using group cognitive-behavior therapy with family involvement. In J.R. Weisz & A.E. Kazdin (Eds.), *Evidence-based psychotherapies for children and adolescents* (2nd ed., pp. 61–79). New York: Guilford.

Pressman, S.D., & Cohen, S.M. (2005). Does positive affect influence health? *Psychological Bulletin, 131,* 925–971.

Reynolds, C.R., & Kamphaus, R.W. (2004). *Behavior Assessment System for Children: Second edition.* Circle Pines, MN: American Guidance Service.

Rutter, M. (1985). Resilience in the face of adversity: Protective factors and resistance to psychiatric disorder. *British Journal of Psychiatry, 147,* 598–611.

Rutter, M. (2003). Genetic influences on risk and protection. In S. Luthar (Ed.), *Resilience and vulnerability* (pp. 489–509). Cambridge, United Kingdom: Cambridge University Press.

Rutter, M., Tizard, J., Yule, M., Graham, P.J., & Whitmore, K. (1976). Research report: Isle of Wight studies, 1964–1974. *Psychological Medicine, 6,* 313–332.

Seligman, M.E.P. (with Reivich, K., Jaycox, L., & Gillham, J.). (1995). *The optimistic child.* New York: Houghton Mifflin.

Silverman, W.K., Pina, A.A., & Viswesvaran, C. (2008). Evidence-based psychosocial treatment for phobic and anxiety disorders in children and adolescents. *Journal of Clinical Child and Adolescent Psychology, 37*(1), 105–130.

Substance Abuse and Mental Health Services Administration, Center for Mental Health Services. (2007). *Promotion and prevention in mental health: Strengthening parenting and enhancing child resilience* (DHHS Publication No. CMHS-SVP-0175). Rockville, MD: Author.

Werner, E.E., & Smith, R.S. (1982). Vulnerable but invincible: A longitudinal study of resilient children and youth. New York: McGraw-Hill.

Werner, E.E., & Smith, R.S. (1992). *Overcoming the odds: High risk children from birth to adulthood.* Ithaca, NY: Cornell University Press.

Werner, E.E., & Smith, R.S. (2001). *Journeys from childhood to midlife: Risk, resilience, and recovery.* Ithaca, NY: Cornell University Press.

Wiener, J. (2003). Resilience and multiple risks: A response to Bernice Wong. *Learning Disabilities Research and Practice, 18*(2), 77–81.

Weisz, J.R., & Kazdin, A.E. (2010). The present and future of evidence-based psychotherapies for children and adolescents. In J.R. Weisz & A.E. Kazdin (Eds.), *Evidence-based psychotherapies for children and adolescents* (2nd ed., pp. 557–572). New York: Guilford.

Wolin, S.J., & Wolin, S. (1993). *The resilient self.* New York: Villard Books.

About the Authors

MARY KARAPETIAN ALVORD, PHD, is a psychologist and Director of Alvord, Baker & Associates, LLC, located in Rockville and Silver Spring, Maryland. She specializes in the treatment of anxiety disorders in children and adults, and AD/HD and problems of emotional and behavioral regulation in children and teens. With more than 30 years of experience, Dr. Alvord has focused on and coauthored articles on resilience and strengths-based approaches. Frequently interviewed by the national media on topics ranging from stress, anxiety, and social competence to coping with adversity, Dr. Alvord has been honored as the first recipient of the American Psychological Association's Presidential Innovative Practice Citation (2009).

BONNIE ZUCKER, PSYD, is a licensed psychologist in private practice at Alvord, Baker, & Associates, LLC, and at the National Center for the Treatment of Phobias, Anxiety, and Depression. Author of *Anxiety-Free Kids* and *Take Control of OCD,* she was named in 2009 as one of *Washingtonian* magazine's top therapists in the categories of cognitive-behavioral therapy, troubled child, troubled adolescent, OCD, and phobias. In addition to treating children and their families, Dr. Zucker is active in conducting training on cognitive-behavioral therapy for other mental health professionals.

JUDY JOHNSON GRADOS, PSYD, is a licensed psychologist in private practice in Baltimore, Maryland. With over a decade of experience facilitating groups, including several years working with Alvord, Baker & Associates, LLC, Dr. Grados specializes in social skills training and the treatment of anxiety disorders in children and adolescents. Dr. Grados earned her doctoral degree in clinical psychology from Indiana State University and has completed post-doctoral work in children's mental health services in the School of Public Health at Johns Hopkins University.